KEITH JOSEPH

Keith Joseph

A Single Mind

Morrison Halcrow

MACMILLAN
LONDON

First published 1989 by
MACMILLAN LONDON LIMITED
4 Little Essex Street, London WC2R 3LF
and Basingstoke

Associated companies in Auckland, Delhi, Dublin, Gaborone,
Hamburg, Harare, Hong Kong, Johannesburg, Kuala Lumpur,
Lagos, Manzini, Melbourne, Mexico City, Nairobi, New York,
Singapore and Tokyo

British Library Cataloguing in Publication Data

A CIP catalogue record for this book is available
from the British Library.

ISBN 0-333-49016-9

Typeset by Rowland Phototypesetting Limited
Bury St Edmunds, Suffolk.
Printed in Great Britain by
Billings Bookplan Ltd, Worcester.

CONTENTS

PREFACE

The idea for this book emerged (like a great many initiatives in British political journalism over the past forty years) during a conversation with the late Peter Utley. Peter, who helped to persuade Lord Joseph to co-operate, was to have provided constructive criticism as the book was drafted. Alas, he had seen only a few pages of the draft when he was stricken with the illness which rapidly led to his untimely death.

Lord Joseph, before we approached him, had turned down requests from publishers to write his own memoirs; but to me he has been more generous than I could have hoped, with time and patience and memory and political analysis, always characteristically and properly meticulous, almost to a fault, in trying to be fair to all the actors in the political drama, and equally properly meticulous in protecting the privacy of his home life.

It has to be emphasised, though, that the bulk of the information in the book came from sources other than Lord Joseph. And all judgements, and misjudgements, are mine.

After Peter Utley, two other distinguished colleagues must be mentioned as having provided great support during the period when the book was evolving: Lord Bruce-Gardyne and Julian Critchley, MP. A fourth, Sir Alfred Sherman – leading participant in, as well as observer of, the Keith Joseph story – was outstandingly helpful with information and with his robust and stimulating interpretations; his research assistant, Sarah King, helped with documents.

Another ex-colleague, Jane Morton, provided authoritative advice on policy at the Ministry of Housing when Sir Keith Joseph was Minister. Ian Ellison, private secretary to Sir Keith at the Department of Industry, helped me through the complexities of the period 1979–81.

I am grateful to all of these, and to many others who provided help ranging from incidental comments or reminiscences to lengthy interviews. The following is a partial list, which excludes, for instance, serving civil servants:

Sir Roger Bannister; Robert Bessell; the Rt Hon. John Biffen; Sir Richard Body, MP; Colette Bowe; Sir Rhodes Boyson, MP; the Rt Hon. Sir Leon Brittan, QC; Samuel Brittan; Sir Peter Carey; the Rt Hon. Lord Deedes; Gerald Frost; Ian Gow, MP; Lord Harris of High Cross; Nicky Harrison; Sir John Hoskyns; the Rt Hon. Lord Jenkin; Sir Denys Lasdun;

Oliver Letwin; Mr and Mrs William Letwin; David Mitchell, MP; the Rt Hon. Sir John Nott; Chris Patten, MP; the Rt Hon. Lord Pym; Giles Radice, MP; Stuart Sexton; Zuzanna Shonfield; the Rt Hon. Margaret Thatcher; Lord Vinson; Sir Alan Walters; the Rt Hon. Viscount Whitelaw; the Rt Hon. Lord Young.

MH
London, 1989

PROLOGUE

In the early hours of Friday, 12 October 1984 an Irish terrorist bomb exploded in the Grand Hotel, Brighton, where Margaret Thatcher and her senior colleagues were staying for the Conservative Party Conference. The only member of the Cabinet with the presence of mind, and sense of security, to bring his 'box' out with him when the building was evacuated, so it was said, was Sir Keith Joseph. He installed himself, according to *The Times*, on the sea-front, 'wearing an immaculately tied dressing gown from which protruded rather chic, cream pyjama legs – the whole effect resembling Sir Noël Coward at his most characteristic. Sir Keith sat on an upturned red despatch box on the promenade. . . . A bright moon hung in a dark blue sky. . . .'

It was a classic cameo of how Englishmen show their contempt for inconveniences like terrorists. A different, and more interesting, image came from one Conservative, who knew Keith Joseph quite well, and happened to be beside him as they came down the fire-escape after the explosion. At that point he was considerably agitated, although not on his own account; he was muttering: 'How is she? How is she?' His sang-froid returned only when the police assured him that she was safe.

The protective rôle that Keith Joseph has felt for Margaret Thatcher has been at the heart of the politics of his later career. With it goes vicarious pride in her – like the schoolmaster who finds his greatest fulfilment in watching his favourite pupil go on to heights that he was never able to scale himself.

Without him, the phenomenon known as Thatcherism would not have happened, in the way it happened. The decade of his political career from 1974 to 1984 saw him, unlikely revolutionary that he is, enable the emergence of what was no less than a revolution in British politics.

If Keith Joseph's career had ended in 1974, he would have gone down as a well-above-average British politician – a politician, moreover, who contributed impressively to the quality of British public life by what he was, and what he stood for, as much as by what he achieved. In the days of Harold Macmillan he was a successful Macmillanite minister; in the days of Edward Heath he was a successful Heathite minister. It was always agreed that there is a first-class mind here, but possibly a one-track mind. He is all too conscious of having laid himself open to the charge of being a Vicar of Bray. He set new standards for appalling political frankness when he announced, in his late fifties, that he had only just been 'converted to Conservatism. . . . I had thought I was a Conservative but I now see that I was not one at all.'

What moved him into an altogether more important slot in the history of Conservatism was the path on which he then set out. It involved an intellectual crusade which Mrs Thatcher, for the purposes of this book, described in these terms: 'It was Keith who really began to turn the intellectual tide back against socialism. . . . If Keith hadn't been doing all that work with the intellectuals, all the rest of our work would probably never have resulted in success.' She owes a great debt to him for that and for much more. He played a crucial part, although the least scheming of politicians, in the strange sequence of events that led to her unexpected election as party leader in 1975. The takeover of the Conservative Party, for that is what it was, which took place in the late 1970s was often a close-run thing. It depended on argument, organisation, imagination, sheer determination and hard work, and on the all-important ability to seize the opportunity to work with the grain of history. In all these areas, Keith Joseph had a formidable rôle.

The courage of Margaret Thatcher, recognised alike by Thatcherites and non-Thatcherites, has been bolstered at various crucial times by the special kind of courage that Keith Joseph has had to offer. Both have had the courage of their convictions; but in a sense it was he who originally provided the convictions to match her courage.

The protective instinct has shown itself in a variety of ways. Physically, he accepted the abuse, and the eggs and the tomatoes, that were flung at him when they were really aimed at her and what she represented. He helped, rather surprisingly, to smooth her entry into what was still in the 1970s the male-clubland atmosphere of Conservative cabinets. Because Keith Joseph has never quite fitted into the atmosphere of the male club himself – or, more accurately, because he fitted into it easily enough but was somehow never quite *of* it – he was more astute than some of his more worldly-wise colleagues in grasping the implications of sexual politics when a woman became prime minister. He grasped the fact – before the better-known 'image-makers' who stepped in from the advertising world to advise her – that she had enough problems ahead without arousing sexually based prejudice among men or jealousy among women.

He showed the same shrewdness by presiding over the public relations operation, amateurish perhaps but remarkably effective, which from its base in his Centre for Policy Studies sold the new Conservatism to the intellectuals and the media during the late 1970s.

★

Keith Joseph, son of a Lord Mayor of London, was an instinctive Conservative, before as much as after his 'conversion'. Margaret Thatcher, the grocer's daughter from Grantham, was another instinctive Conservative, but of a different kind. Between them they have pulled in a host of new adherents to the party. Many of those new adherents would certainly not, a generation before, have regarded themselves as Conservatives at all: they saw the old Conservatism as a recipe for privilege and stagnation.

Here we come to one of the paradoxes of Keith Joseph's career. He tends not to enjoy being told that the power of free-market forces (which are the dynamic of the new Conservatism) can have a *radical* effect. As a Thatcherite minister he was involved in a revolution, yet a part of him was wedded to the status quo. It was the honourable conflict between the revolutionary and the traditionalist sides of his nature that made his efforts, as Secretary of State for Education, to reform Britain's schools such an interesting operation.

Keith Joseph's career has important lessons to teach about the way in which Britain changed political direction and could presumably do so again. It provides evidence of how certain political campaigning techniques (like the set-piece platform speech), which were thought to be outmoded, can still be used as a powerful weapon. It has lessons about how the Conservative Party replaced its leader, as it will in due course do again. His story also exposes the ineffectiveness of the so-called 'Wet' Conservatives who, over a period of years, seemed pitifully unaware of what was happening.

Not least important, his career, unfinished at the time of writing, is also proof that in a cynical sophisticated world a politician can reach heights of achievement by the force of sincerity and intellectual integrity.

CHAPTER ONE

THE LORD MAYOR'S SON

Man is a being born to believe.
Benjamin Disraeli

I was told that the Privileged and the People formed Two
Nations.
Benjamin Disraeli, *Sybil*

Throughout his adult life, Keith Joseph always had a handle to his
name. He came home from the war, slightly wounded, and Mentioned in
Dispatches, as Captain Sir Keith Joseph, Bt. The hereditary baronetcy
commemorated the fact that his father, who died in 1944, had been Lord
Mayor of London, in the days when that office was invested with an aura
of success and prestige to a degree hard for later generations to grasp.

Like a clergyman's dog-collar, a title may not change the nature of a
man; but it makes people look twice at him. It was with the advantage, or
disadvantage, of being 'Sir Keith' that Keith Joseph started his working
life. When he left the House of Commons it was with a title that he chose
himself: Lord Joseph of Portsoken. 'Portsoken' said quite a lot about him.
It was a tribute to his father, who was alderman for the ward of Portsoken
in the City of London before becoming Lord Mayor. (As a young man
Keith, briefly, followed him as alderman there, after a gap of a couple of
years.) But the 'Portsoken' part of the title also reflected a sentimental
attachment to a certain kind of Londoner. Portsoken, when he represented
it, was unusual among the City wards in actually having ordinary people
living in it. They lived in the hinterland of the Petticoat Lane market, and
he romanticised them for being 'passionately English as well as passionately
Jewish', as he put it later.

The advantage of being Jewish, he once remarked, is that to be successful
you have to spark on all four cylinders. But the world of the Lane was
rather different from his own background.

Keith Sinjohn Joseph was born, an only child, on 17 January 1918, at 63
Portland Place, in the heart of London's West End. It was a stylish place
to be born. Those who appreciate symbolism – and there is no shortage of
it in Keith Joseph's life – may make what they will of the fact that the
house, which was the home of his maternal grandfather, is now the
headquarters of the Institute of Cost and Management Accountants. During the 1890s, Frances Hodgson Burnett, author of *Little Lord Fauntleroy*
and *The Secret Garden*, had lived at 63 Portland Place. She complained
about the cost of running it:

> I have fires everywhere, of course, but the ceilings are so lofty and
> passages so endless that to go from the library to the drawing-room or
> a bedroom is like going on a voyage to the open Polar Sea. I always
> rather expect to encounter icebergs with bears on them in my blue
> bathroom.

She used the basement at Portland Place as the inspiration for a melodra-
matic scene in one of her later books, *A Lady of Quality*.

In due course the house, with its Adam interior, became the home of
Philip A. Solomon Phillips, whose daughter married Keith Joseph's father.
Solomon Phillips was a silversmith and jeweller with a shop in the West
End and an interest in *objets d'art* that was scholarly as well as commercial.
He wrote for the *Connoisseur* and had been concerned in the founding of
the London Museum. He produced authoritative monographs on two
Huguenot craftsmen, Paul de Lamerie and Jean O'Brisset. One of his
grandson's many regrets was that he never fully appreciated his grand-
father. The boy was a late developer in several ways.

Keith Joseph regarded himself as having been brought up in a family of
'minimally observing, but maximally acknowledging, Jews'. The Phillipses
had arrived in England in the eighteenth century, the Josephs in the
nineteenth, but they were well established in London by the end of the
Victorian era.

They were linked into one of the great business dynasties of the early
twentieth century: the Salmons and the Glucksteins (who ran Joe Lyons,
the teashop chain). Keith's father, the future Sir Samuel George Joseph,
could have joined that business, but decided he wanted to do something
on his own. In 1908 he went into business, at the age of twenty, with
Sidney Gluckstein, of the lesser branch of the dynasty.

At the time of Keith's birth, when the First World War had almost a
year still to run, Samuel Joseph was serving in the 56th (1st London)
Divisional Royal Engineers. He had gone off to the war on the spin of a
coin: he and his partner had agreed that one of them ought to stay and

mind the shop while the other joined up; they tossed for it, and Samuel won – or lost, as the case might be. He came back with two Mentions in Dispatches.

The 'shop' which had to be minded had started on a tiny scale. It was a business which the two young men (later joined by yet another cousin, Vincent Gluckstein) had bought from a man called Bovis. All there was to take over, the family liked to say, was 'a horse and cart, a ladder and a telephonist'. They started doing decorating work, then moved into building.

By the 1920s Bovis was a large-scale building organisation which, between the wars, played a major part in changing the face of London. Their major contracts included one of London's most monumental buildings, Bush House at Aldwych, and they built Liberty's Tudor-style store in Regent Street.

Samuel Joseph became a rich man. He also chose at an early stage (although his wife was sometimes less than enthusiastic) to go into local politics. From 1928 to 1930 he was Mayor of St Marylebone, and then he moved into the hierarchy of the City of London. In 1934 (by which time Keith was at Harrow) he was knighted. He became a 'name' on Lloyd's.

In a family as comfortably off, the London of the twenties was a congenial place to pass childhood. Keith Joseph had indulgent parents. It was a metropolitan life – 'no county element', as he put it. Sir Samuel and Lady Joseph had a full social life. She was described by a friend as one of those handsome Jewish ladies who are more English than the English. Years later, when he read C. P. Snow's *The Conscience of the Rich*, Keith detected a superficial resemblance between his own background and the world described by Snow of a wealthy Jewish family between the wars; but perhaps it was mainly the book's title that attracted him.

His father, educated at the City of London School, was a man of lively charm – like a pied piper with children, his son remembered. His son remembered him also, certainly not in any pejorative way, as not being a well-read man – but, then, Keith Joseph came to have alarmingly exacting standards about what constitutes a well-read person.

Keith's first school was a small establishment in Sloane Street, Gibbs Wagner's; and it was there, he liked to think, that his first political instincts were stirred – not in the school, but in Sloane Square. He told the anecdote at the age of seventy: about the beggar who was in the street every day; how the small boy decided to feed the beggar; how, day after day, he surreptitiously purloined food from the breakfast-table to do so. 'End of anecdote,' he concluded.

His schooling was conventional for his social class and for his time, and seems to have been happy enough. Of prep school (Lockers Park), he recalled that the penalty of being a Jew was 'a certain amount of verbal bullying', but Harrow he remembered as taking a more gentlemanly view of these matters, and he regarded his public school as an interesting, rather than a challenging, place to spend a few years. There were some memorable masters, like the man who, it was said, had been cashiered from the Navy for getting drunk and ramming his destroyer, and who opened every lesson with a reading from a John Donne sermon. Joseph felt no great pressure to excel on the academic side. A side-interest was to go off to do good works at the school's mission in the East End, but not to excess. His only excess at Harrow, apparently, was cricket.

Cricket was his passion; he was rather good at it, and he was coached by Wilfred Rhodes. At two matches he scored sixes off the very first ball, and probably never again in his life achieved the simple pleasure that that gave him. He was a 'forcing' opening bat; and he became captain of the second eleven: two facts which both, perhaps, carried their own symbolism.

He went on playing cricket at Oxford, and was a playing member of MCC. All this he saw in retrospect as part of his immaturity, but he looked back on it as a happy and relaxed immaturity.

His Oxford college was Magdalen. He belonged to the last (1936–9) prewar Oxford vintage, and his relative affluence would have enabled him to indulge in a grand way of life that was never to return. On the other hand, his social conscience would have fitted into university politics, which was going through one of its most exciting periods. He seized neither opportunity. Cricket was still more important.

He was at Oxford during the time when Hitler and Mussolini were on the march, the time of the Austrian *Anschluss*, the seizure of Abyssinia, the Spanish Civil War and the flight of Jews from Germany. His last year began with Munich, the issues of which were paraded at the university that autumn in the celebrated Oxford City by-election. The Tory candidate was a future colleague, the young Quintin Hogg, who had the task of defending Neville Chamberlain's concessions to Hitler at Munich. A substantial number of Conservatives came out for the Labour candidate, who was the Master of Balliol, A. D. Lindsay. Harold Macmillan came to speak for Lindsay, and at the university Edward Heath, a Balliol man about to become President of the Union, was active for Lindsay, too.

All this seems to have passed largely over Joseph's head. He had amiable relations with friends on the left, including Andrew Shonfield, who became one of Britain's best-known economic commentators of the fifties and sixties; but his most constructive reaction to the news from Europe was to join the Territorials, not to take up politics. He took no part in the Union;

nor was he noted as an outstanding scholar, although he ended up with a First (in jurisprudence). He attributed the First to the fact that he caught up with his reading during vacations.

At Oxford his social conscience led him to attach himself to a Quaker group doing work among the unemployed and to go with them to stay with a miner's family in Yorkshire. The glimpse of conditions down a coal mine had something of the same effect as the sight of the Sloane Square beggar.

He was once pressed into service by his leftish friends, because he had a car, joining a day's expedition which involved greeting a party of refugees just arrived from Republican Spain. One of the party recalled later that throughout the trip he seemed to exude benevolence and a desire to participate but simply didn't understand much of what these left-wingers were talking about, and he certainly couldn't join in the songs they sang in the car.

In retrospect he saw the Quaker expedition as one of the two things he did at Oxford that represented growing up. The other was signing on for military service. He gravitated first, as boys of his background sometimes did, to one of the grandest of the reserve forces, the Honourable Artillery Company – the City's military club, as it has been called. Unfortunately this involved horses, and the Josephs were not a horsy family; moreover, he had cartilage trouble after a football injury. There were potentially embarrassing commands like 'Without stirrups, trot!' He found it convenient to switch to the Oxford Territorials.

When war came, he was among the first into it, and September 1939 found him in squad number six at his Officer Cadets Training Unit. It was to be a long war for him.

Meanwhile his father, alderman for the Ward of Portsoken, was ascending the strange archaic ladder of the City's local government, leading, for the most privileged, to spending a year as Lord Mayor of London, which in the 1940s was still one of the world's most prestigious posts. There were two clouds on the horizon – leaving aside the war – when eventually Samuel Joseph's name came up. One was his health. He had had several heart-attacks, and his wife pleaded with him not to take on the job. The other shadow was a recent discreditable episode when another Jewish candidate for the lord mayorship had been passed over for what seemed to the City establishment to be good and sufficient reasons. The story had been picked up by the Nazis, and Lord Haw-Haw had had fun on German radio about anti-Semitism in the City. Samuel Joseph saw a duty to the patriotic spirit of the day, and to Jewry. Nor could it be said, given the record of his career, that he was immune to the ordinary urges of ambition. He was installed as Lord Mayor at the height of the war.

Much of the pomp of the office had been put aside for the duration, but the round of duties was punishing. There were morale-boosting tours to be carried out during the bombing, charities to be sponsored, Allied troops in London to be honoured, voluntary workers to be encouraged, visiting grandees to be welcomed. It was a job that came easily to a man of natural gusto, optimism and laughter. In the words of his obituary in *The Times*, 'he vigorously maintained the Mansion House tradition of hospitality' – even if it meant that strange names like *snoek* appeared on the menu. A high point, for him and for his family, was when he presided at the ceremony conferring the freedom of the City on Winston Churchill. The scene was recorded in a painting by Frank O. Salisbury, which his son presented to the City Corporation.

Sir Samuel completed his year, was elevated to the baronetcy that went with the office, and died. His widow continued to wear mourning for him until her death in 1981.

Joseph's military career was not something he looked back on as an outstandingly fruitful period. He was no military romantic. He certainly knew about the boredom of war. One ploy he used to keep his gunners' minds occupied was to teach them shorthand, keeping one lesson ahead of them. He volunteered to be trained in parachuting – it was a challenge, he explained to a friend, and he felt he ought to meet it – but in fact his colonel vetoed the idea.

The Army took him to the Middle East and to Italy (and briefly to Palestine, when his division 'rested' there). He took part in the protracted and bloody battle of Monte Cassino, where he was wounded, earned his Mention in Dispatches, and was said to have received, because of his use of smokescreens, the nickname 'Smokey Joe'.

He was still in the Army for the 1945 general election, which produced the Labour landslide that got rid of Winston Churchill. Captain Joseph regarded himself as a Conservative, but the idea of a Labour government, and of a welfare state and nationalisation, did not outrage him as it did most people of his background in 1945. Looking back, he decided this was because, although a Conservative, he had been – this was to become a favourite word – a 'statist'.

CHAPTER TWO

THE LATE DEVELOPER

If you can fill the unforgiving minute
  With sixty seconds' worth of distance run . . .

Rudyard Kipling, *If*

Keith Joseph belonged to the honourable tradition of politicians whose starting-point was improving the social conditions of the poor. It was how Clement Attlee started, and so did Shaftesbury, but by Joseph's time may have been an anachronism. It was a tradition that was perhaps bound to die along with the world's pre-Freudian innocence; post-Freud, the fashion was to look suspiciously at anyone doing good – what was their real motive? what were they trying to sublimate? Even leaving Freudian concepts aside, it was becoming unfashionable by the 1950s to think in terms of the rich helping the poor.

Joseph saw a perfectly logical pattern to his political development: the vague ambition as a schoolboy and an undergraduate to do something about the underprivileged. After the war, social work in East London; next, the realisation that there is no point in treating the symptoms of poverty unless you get at the roots, and that this involves politics; then the recognition that in Britain the power of local politics is minimal because the important levers are at Westminster. No doubt there was more to it than that – Keith Joseph may have been unworldly in some ways but he was an ambitious young man – but it was in terms of the abolition of poverty that he rationalised his path to Parliament. Attlee's path, a generation earlier, had been similar, although the analogy cannot be pushed too far. Having got into Parliament, Joseph found that his ideas went on evolving, sometimes faster than his intellectually less agile colleagues were able to keep pace with.

But first there was the immediate question, when he returned from the Army in 1946, of a career. He had been in uniform for more than six years. He launched himself into the postwar world with all the urgency of a man making up for lost time. His zeal was no greater than was to be characteristic throughout the rest of his career, but there was a twist to it in 1946 that must have been disquieting for those who knew him.

In his first year at home he set himself three tasks. As a member of the family firm, he set out to qualify as a licentiate of the Institute of Building, studying on the job, which meant digging holes and laying bricks by day and reading up the theory by night. Next, by way of carrying his law studies at Oxford to a logical conclusion, he read for the Bar exams. Third, he decided also to take his Oxford education a stage further by sitting for a Fellowship of All Souls. He succeeded in all three of these endeavours within the year – the Fellowship, incidentally, identifying him as a high-flier, because with the return of the ex-servicemen there had been a particularly large number of candidates that year.

The twist was that in doing all this he damaged his health, potentially disastrously, not by mental over-exertion but because he had meanwhile put himself on a near-starvation diet.

A Jewish friend, hearing of this, smiled knowingly and remarked: 'That's very Jewish.' He had come home from the Army plumper than he felt he should be, but plumpness could only be part of the explanation for what seems to have been drastic self-punishment. There was evidently an urge to live on as little money as possible. The conscience of the rich. . . .

Whatever the motivation, he had to live with the physical consequences. He developed an ulcer, which gave him hell, on and off, for the next ten years. When the attacks came on, he found he could restore himself by drinking milk – and a dreary feature of the next phase of his life was the flasks of milk that had to go everywhere with him. Then the sheer quantity of milk he drank brought on further complications of body chemistry. Eventually an operation, which removed half his stomach, cured him, and by the time he became a public figure his health was in fact reasonably good. As a minister he was physically, as well as intellectually, able to see off less robust politicians and officials.

His digestion suffered further problems later when he developed a hiatus hernia, and the stories abounded of his dietary eccentricity, providing a foundation on which it was all too easy for the media to build up a reputation for general eccentricity.

Fairly early in the postwar years he seems to have decided that his destiny did not lie in the building industry. (As for the Bar, he got as far as being called by the Middle Temple but never practised.) His father had never pushed him into committing himself to the family business; there were plenty of good people running Bovis, some of them cousins, some not. Nevertheless he carried on in the firm in one capacity or another until he entered government.

He started work on the site. One of his memories was of the foreman taking him aside to tell him, in terms appropriate to an exchange between a Fellow of All Souls and a building-site foreman, to take things easy: it was one thing to rush at the job of digging holes if you are the boss's son, and know you are not going to be doing it all your life; but it spoiled the market for nature's hole-diggers with nothing else to look forward to. It was the kind of moral that appealed to him. As a minister he passed on a version of the foreman's advice when a colleague told him proudly that he had proved that levels of social security were adequate under the Conservatives, by living on £x for a whole week; the real test, Joseph told him briskly, was not how you survived on £x for a single week, but how you managed week after week and month after month.

He became a Bovis foreman himself (and then a manager, a director and for a time chairman of the company). Meanwhile – and still coping with his dietary problems – he was working on his All Souls thesis. It was never completed, possibly because the topic he chose was uncompletable. The subject was tolerance, and the idea had been to differentiate between tolerance and indifference: he wanted to make the point that conflicting views can be held strongly, even passionately, but can coexist. (*Passion* was a word he often used; it fitted ill with his subsequent reputation as a cold intellectual.) Failure to complete the thesis provided, in due course, added ammunition for those who accused him of never being able to make up his mind because he insisted on seeing so many sides of every argument.

Even before his struggles with the thesis he apparently decided that academic life was not for him. He turned down an offer from his old tutor of a job at Oxford to teach law.

It was not all the striving and starving that brought what was probably the most important development at this stage of his career. The real opportunity came simply because he was his father's son. In 1946 he was invited to stand as Common Councilman, and then alderman, for the ward of Portsoken. Election was a formality. The fact was that, compared with other returning ex-servicemen hesitating between one career and another, he was a young man with advantages and a secure background that went beyond financial security.

Portsoken gave him a base, and the push he was looking for. The young alderman – youngest in the history of the City, it was said – was delighted with his parish. It was a place with more of the character of the East End than of the City. Petticoat Lane provided an exotic version of cockney chirpiness.

The inhabitants had their share of poverty, and he engaged in various projects to remedy it. He was active in a charity for the elderly, on which he worked with a remarkable physically handicapped woman, Mrs Rita Cohen. He had qualifications that could prove useful to any charity. He had energy and he had contacts. Over the years he learned how to use the contacts to raise money and to harness talent. He could be persuasive and persistent.

His charitable concerns went beyond material deprivation and expanded geographically. He joined the Howard League for Penal Reform. He became chairman of a Nuffield Foundation committee on senility, which provided him with a foretaste of what he tried to do in the geriatric wards when he became Secretary of State for Social Services.

One of his favourite charities helped women in the classic situation of missing out on life because they had stayed at home looking after aged parents. This was the organisation that eventually became known as the National Council for Carers and Their Elderly Dependants, and it had been founded by the Reverend Mary Webster, a Congregationalist minister with whom Joseph worked as her honorary treasurer until her premature death. On behalf of middle-aged spinsters he found himself making speeches about the case for marriage bureaux and the importance of beauty parlours.

Some of his early utterances, dug out by the profile-writers when he became a public figure, read very oddly. But if there was a grand theme that inspired him it was perhaps that no group of people should necessarily be excluded from the good things of life.

In 1949 he resigned as alderman, giving as his grounds ill health. But he was probably also beginning to be bored, and to realise that there was more show than substance in that branch of government. His eyes were now turning to 'real' politics where he could get his hands on levers that would actually move things. Meanwhile his horizons were about to expand in another direction. He was thirty-three when, at a tea-party, he met Hellen Guggenheimer, an American studying in London. About six months later they were married, on 7 July 1951, at the West London Synagogue. The reception was at Claridge's, the best man was the architect Denys Lasdun, and an address was given by Sir Basil Henriques, the celebrated East End magistrate who was one of the grand figures known to everyone who did good works in London.

The wedding took place during the last weeks of the postwar Labour government. On 25 October 1951, as the couple started married life, the Conservatives under Churchill returned to power. Over the next few years, Keith Joseph became confident enough to take the next step in his political ambition. He applied for and was taken on to the Conservative candidates' list. In one sense he had an excellent curriculum vitae to offer: he was now a director of Bovis; he had been an alderman; he was involved in good works. On the other hand he had never made any effort to attach himself, as had other bright young men of his generation, like Reggie Maudling or Iain Macleod, to the network of Tory committees and study-groups that had been busy rethinking Tory policy to suit modern fashions. Joseph may have been part of what later came to be called the postwar consensus, which took the Welfare State and the commitment to full employment for granted, but he never had even a minor part in analysing or formulating it. Nevertheless he was an eligible enough young politician, now backed by a photogenic wife, to present himself to Tory constituency officers. He showed none of the self-doubt that became manifest in the later stages of his career. By the time of the 1955 general election he had been adopted for a seat that was possibly winnable by the Tories: a London constituency, newly created by boundary changes, at Barons Court.

This was the general election which followed quickly when Churchill eventually retired, and Anthony Eden stepped into the shoes that had been kept warm for him for so long. Eden himself visited the constituency during the campaign. Joseph failed to win the seat, but he kept the Labour majority down to 125. It was a performance that put him in a strong position to offer himself at any by-election that came up.

The one that came up for him a few months later was in the safe Tory seat of Leeds North-East. He had no particular connection with Leeds, and he made it clear that he had no intention of moving to Yorkshire if he was elected. He undertook to come north once a month. The local Tories – latterly they had seen their previous Member much less than that – were happy enough. And they were delighted, Joseph always made a point of saying, with his wife, who had no desire to involve herself in politics on her own account but who charmed the Tory ladies of Yorkshire. (The *Yorkshire Post* noted the young Lady Joseph's resemblance to Audrey Hepburn.)

The Jewish connection was no disadvantage; Leeds North-East had a substantial Jewish vote. The Labour candidate was a local Jewish solicitor.

In those days party managers did not avoid winter by-elections, as they usually tried to do later. Polling day was fixed for 9 February 1956. During the campaign it was noted that Joseph preferred to call himself a 'Tory', which was less common then than later – 'no Conservative he,' noted the *Times* special correspondent elliptically.

The political context was that Anthony Eden's honeymoon with the electorate had not lasted long. The new year had opened with a much discussed attack in the columns of the *Daily Telegraph* under the headline 'Time for the smack of firm government' which had sent Eden into a fury. So Keith Joseph was in the position of defending a government that was in difficulties – although nobody foresaw that within a few months the Prime Minister would have been destroyed by the Suez disaster.

If the Suez Canal seemed far away, however, the Middle East was in fact a live by-election issue in a constituency where a substantial proportion of the electorate had a keen interest in the state of Israel. British Jewry had been watching government policy on the Middle East closely. Churchill had been regarded as a friend, most of the time, of Zionism, whereas Eden was seen as a friend of the Arabs, and the Labour candidate at Leeds North-East devoted a substantial part of his election address to the policy of arms exports to the Middle East. Joseph retorted by reminding voters that the postwar Labour government had never done the things that Zionists wanted: Labour, after all, was 'the party of Bevin, who left Israel without adequate protection'. There was more he could have said about Ernest Bevin to reopen old Jewish wounds, but even that much of an argument *ad hominem* was uncharacteristic of him.

On polling day the weather was appalling. Snow swept across Yorkshire, and most of the electors stayed at home. On a turnout of only 39.9 per cent, Joseph had a majority of 5,869 in a straight fight, putting the Conservative share of the vote up marginally to 63.2 per cent.

It had not been a by-election that hit the headlines nationally. The big news in the papers the next day was the weather. Another big news item was the complex arrangement for financing the Aswan Dam, on which President Nasser of Egypt pinned his hopes for pulling up his country's economy by the bootstraps. As it turned out, Joseph's first year as a Member of Parliament was dominated by the events that followed when those financial arrangements collapsed.

CHAPTER THREE

SUEZ AND THE SUPPLY SIDE

We have always known that heedless self-interest was bad morals; we know now that it is bad economics.

Franklin D. Roosevelt

Keith Joseph's parliamentary career divides neatly into two parts, before and after his 'conversion to Conservatism'. The first began in the year of Suez, 1956, and in a sense it came to an end when another Middle East war, on Yom Kippur 1973, helped to precipitate another British political crisis.

Over Suez, rather surprisingly, he was a rebel. It was one of his very few essays into foreign affairs in thirty years in the House of Commons. His maiden speech was very much on home affairs. It was delivered during the debate on the 1956 Finance Bill, implementing the only budget introduced by Harold Macmillan (the budget which was best remembered for inventing the premium bond).

The maiden speech makes interesting reading, coming from a man who was to be 'converted' in his economic thinking eighteen years later. Give or take a few points of emphasis, the 1956 speech would have fitted easily enough into the celebrated series of speeches in the 1970s which were credited with having launched Thatcherite economics. At the time it was regarded not as controversial but as a highly competent piece of common sense. ('I do not know,' said the Labour Member who followed him, 'that I have ever listened to a clearer, more logical and more interesting maiden speech.') His starting-point, after the formalities of appealing for the indulgence due to a new Member, was to take for granted the importance of dealing with inflation:

It is generally agreed that inflation will not be brought to an end until demand and supply are equal to each other. I welcome the Chancellor's pledge to cut Government expenditure, his savings drive and all his

13

other measures to reduce demand, but it would, of course, be much
more agreeable if part of the job of defeating inflation could be done by
increasing supply.

The word 'supply' would have been a flashing red light in the Thatcherite
years when 'supply-wide economics' was regarded as an extreme ideological
import from the United States. As it was, he led on from this elementary-
textbook introduction to the case for increasing supply through industrial
efficiency: 'It is far more sensible to criticise management than it is
to criticise wage earners.' Management must have its 'proper reward'.
Meanwhile the workers must be reassured that increased productivity
meant better jobs and more jobs, not fewer jobs. The aim was wealth
creation for the benefit of all (with a surplus to help the Third World).

All this sounded like thinking, caring, progressive Toryism, and there
was a natural home for such Tories at that time in the One Nation Group.
The group welcomed him with open arms when they realised that he was
interested in the social services. In 1956 bright young Conservatives tended
to be prospective chancellors or foreign secretaries, or defence secretaries
or Commonwealth secretaries. There was a vacancy for any eager beaver
willing to sit down with boring reports on things like hospital waiting-lists.
He got himself elected secretary of the party's Health and Social Services
Committee and threw himself into a study of the working of the Welfare
State. He became known as a note-taker. In conversations he would
produce a notebook, or the back of an envelope, to write down things that
interested him.

One fairly representative Tory of the time, who was fond of Joseph,
described how he nevertheless always regarded the new colleague as
something of a mystery, almost alien, 'although he had an English sense
of humour – nothing wrong there'. The affection he undoubtedly enjoyed
among fellow-Conservatives seemed to have some of the quality of the
sense of relief in a crowd of hearties realising at the end of a hard night's
drinking that among them is a teetotaller able to drive the car.

When Eden ordered British forces to attack Egypt on 4 November, there
were plenty of Tory MPs with doubts. The excitement, and the bitterness
of the feeling pro and con, reached heights that were hard for later
generations to comprehend. Suez divided families. At Westminster it
needed either courage or foolhardiness to risk accusations of lack of
patriotism. In this fevered atmosphere the new Member for Leeds North-
East joined a small group of Tories who questioned the need for military
action. They called for British troops to be placed under United Nations
control. Without reading too much into Joseph's rôle, it can be said that

it indicated several things about him as a young MP: there was an instinct to take the 'liberal' side; and as a Jew he certainly did not automatically side with the Israelis – indeed, his Jewishness probably inhibited him from being even more critical than he was of Eden's preoccupation with the threat posed by Nasser. Joseph was not pro-Nasser; he simply felt that if Nasser were destroyed he might be replaced by something worse.

The other significant point was that Joseph, not for the last time, took an anti-establishment line – and got away with it. Some of the Tory Suez rebels were never forgiven. In Joseph's case a moderately senior member of the Government (the Earl of Selkirk) took him to lunch, and politely heard him argue his case. That more or less ended his excursion into foreign affairs, but the aftermath helped to shape his political future.

On 6 November the British action was halted in humiliation. The pound plunged. The United States ambassador turned up at the Palace of Westminster to tell Eden personally that the Americans refused to support it unless there was an immediate cease-fire. Conservative morale plunged, too. And Eden's health collapsed.

There followed the most memorable episode of Joseph's first year as an MP. The Government was now temporarily in the hands of Rab Butler, to whom fell the task of confronting the Tory backbenchers of the 1922 Committee. Joseph found Butler's intricate skills of advocacy unimpressive; but Butler – imprudently, since it was so obviously on the cards that Eden was on the way out, and there would have to be a contest for the leadership – had decided to take along to the party meeting with him, for moral support, the Chancellor of the Exchequer, Harold Macmillan. Macmillan, when invited to say a few words, proceeded to talk for half an hour. The young Joseph was enthralled.

Others at the meeting, on that gloomy November evening, were less starry-eyed. To the mordant Enoch Powell the Chancellor's performance was simply 'one of the most horrible things that I remember in politics. . . . Harold Macmillan, with all the skill of the old actor-manager, succeeded in false-footing Rab. The sheer devilry of it verged upon the disgusting.' It had apparently been agreed that Rab's job was to try to pacify the Tory right, outraged by a sellout to the Americans; Macmillan was to mollify the left, and the old actor-manager certainly pulled it off with Joseph. What to Enoch was the kitsch of ham acting, to Keith was inspired rhetoric. Thirty years later he could still recall how Macmillan 'peppered his brilliantly effective monologue – if you can apply peppering to silences – with long pregnant silences in which you could have heard a pin drop in that packed committee room'. Joseph was a Macmillan man rather than a Butler man. As an aspirant Tory MP he had not been in the charmed circle around the Research Department, where Butler's skills mesmerised those who came in contact with him. On the other hand, Macmillan, the Housing Minister who had built those famous 300,000 houses for the Churchill government – that was something Joseph could warm to, with his building background at Bovis and, more important, with his anti-poverty background.

What Macmillan had grasped in November 1956 was that the more idealistic wing of the party, no less than the sabre-rattling right, had been devastated by the evidence that Britain was no longer in the first league of world powers. The balm they needed to have rubbed into their wounds was not military victory but something subtler. For his speech to the 1922 Committee, Macmillan chose as his theme the story of Greece and Rome. Just as Rome's power was built on the intellect of the Greeks, the future of the world might depend on the economic might of the Americans on the one hand but on the brains of the British on the other. The relevance of all this to the harsh realities of Britain's needs over the next quarter-century may not have been clear in the cold light of morning after the 1922 meeting, but the impression of Macmillan as a man of vision was an important element in the next phase of Keith Joseph's career.

He was not disappointed that it was Macmillan, not Butler, who succeeded as prime minister when Eden's health finally gave way a few weeks later.

To others, in a nation picking itself up after the trauma of Suez, Macmillan seemed, of course, so far from being an inspiration, simply a sign that the old gang were still in power. Quite apart from Suez, 1956 was a kind of turning-point of revulsion against the past. It was the year when John Osborne's *Look Back in Anger* crossed a new frontier in the theatre. It was the year when another young man called Colin Wilson published *The Outsider*, briefly regarded as an important seminal work. To the angry young men, the Conservatives at Westminster seemed to sum up much that was wrong with the country. The Tories were still to a large extent Churchill's party. The old man still sat there in the Commons, saying nothing but possibly all too conscious that the main reason that Eden had reached Downing Street was that he, Churchill, had put him there.

The close world of the Westminster Tories in the late fifties was portrayed lightheartedly (in *Westminster Blues*) by Julian Critchley, who entered the House not long after Joseph:

The party still retained something of its pre-war sleekness; elderly gentlemen in Trumper's haircuts, wearing cream silk shirts and Brigade or Old Etonian ties. Everyone seemed related to everyone else. . . . Many had had 'a good war'.

*

To angry young men, this was a party run by rich selfish people. In fairness, rich though they may have been, the charge of selfishness was in a sense irrelevant. On social services – and this was Joseph's initial interest – the reality was that most policies simply did not personally concern average Tory politicians at all. Housing policy was about council houses they were never going to live in; education policy was about schools their children were never going to attend. Most of these smartly dressed old gentlemen were willing enough to accept the principle of providing houses and education and pensions and so forth for other people; to that extent the Welfare State was now part of consensus politics, although they might grumble about it. It was an 'us and them' world, in which there was an accepted, if ill-defined, responsibility on 'us' to look after 'them'.

Superficially, Keith Joseph fitted into that world. His background was the background of the traditional Tories. He was rather a smart dresser himself. If his had not been a 'good war', it certainly hadn't been a discreditable one. He shared the consensus view about the Welfare State, but he put his own twist on the case for maintaining it. For one thing, he was unhappy about an 'us' and 'them' mentality: that was why he had busied himself in his various charitable works.

A One Nation pamphlet entitled *The Responsible Society*, dated March 1959, has a chapter on the social services which, although anonymous, has a Keith Joseph ring to it. In British society, the pamphlet noted with approval, wage-earners were beginning to enjoy 'the same freedom that middle and higher income people have always had'. Some wage-earners would abuse that freedom, just as some of the middle and upper classes had always abused their freedom. What was important was that the faults in society should not become an excuse for challenging the principle of the Welfare State. Of course, the provisions of the welfare services must be topped up by private savings, but

> the social services for the most part are here to stay. . . . Surely it is not seemly for critics – sometimes secure other than by their own efforts and seldom thereby demoralised – to seek to deny some share of security to their fellow citizens. Security, even automatic or unearned, is not necessarily demoralising. It is as much a spring-board for vigour and family devotion as insecurity; the whole history of the middle class is evidence of this.

It was early days, however, the pamphlet concluded, to judge the impact of the social services on the moral fibre of the British people: 'Judgment must wait until better education has had time to teach how a more secure life can be enjoyed – and lived, to the full.'

A secure life . . . a civilised, educated life . . . life lived 'to the full'.

There was a noble pattern to the Joseph dream of the British society of the future; but there was a sense in which he was blind to the realities of the existing class structure, in the way that people with liberal views on race like to think they are colour-blind.

He continued to talk and write fluently about social class, but the two biggest political storms he was ever responsible for could both have been avoided if he had taken advice on the class-conscious sensitivities of the British: the storm over his pronouncement in 1974 about birth control for the lower classes; and the very different storm almost exactly ten years later when, as Education Secretary, he failed to grasp how much the middle-class ethos had become wedded to the idea of highly subsidised higher education for middle-class children. The first of those two storms caused him to give up his bid for the leadership of the Tory Party; the second was the only occasion when he felt strongly enough about political developments to offer his resignation as a minister.

His enthusiasms as a young MP sometimes sounded odd, as his enthusiasm about the rights of middle-aged spinsters sounded odd. An anecdote from a later period gives the flavour of what seemed his unworldliness. He came back from a trip to his constituency, where he had visited an old people's home. It had saddened him, but not because the inmates were physically neglected. Ample money available, but so little imagination! Their idea of giving the old folk a treat was fish and chips! It made him angry: with better management, those old people in Leeds could be dining off . . . well, why not *bœuf bourguignon*?

Although that anecdote dates from later, even in the 1950s some of his Tory colleagues found his views disconcerting. One of them thought he had found a key to the thinking of the young Member for Leeds North-East when he was invited to a lunch-party that Joseph gave at the House for Sir Simon Marks, of Marks & Spencer, on his seventieth birthday. Marks gave a little speech setting out how at Marks & Spencer they believed that sound business economics went hand in hand with respect for the customer on the one hand and for the company's staff on the other; there must be due respect for human dignity.

Some of Keith Joseph's philosophy matched that of Marks & Spencer in being a mixture of liberalism and a strong sense of the importance of running a business efficiently. In 1959 he was a co-founder of the Foundation for Management Education. In the Commons, on social issues he tended to come down on the 'liberal' side. He voted against hanging and in favour of reform of the law on homosexuality. When race relations became an issue during the Harold Wilson régime, the Conservatives decided to vote against the Labour legislation on the grounds that it would make race relations worse, not better; Joseph abstained.

If human dignity was the aim, Joseph tried to put action where his mouth was in his own business career. He had a view that there was a social function in the employment of building workers. Men between jobs, men coming out of prison could pick up labouring work; but the casual nature of the work brought hardship. When, in 1958, he became chairman of Bovis, one of the monuments he hoped to leave behind him was a scheme for decasualisation of building labour. One firm might be laying men off in a region while another was recruiting elsewhere. The obvious thing, it seemed to him, was to offer a guaranteed contract for a proportion of workers. He talked to his fellow-chairmen of other construction companies, he talked to the unions, but the scheme came to nothing, and before long he had to give up the chairmanship on entering the Government.

In 1957 he had become a Parliamentary Private Secretary. He could scarcely claim that he was being recognised as a high-flier, because the minister who took him on as PPS was a mere Parliamentary Under-Secretary of State (at the Commonwealth Relations Office): Cuthbert ('Cub') Alport. Alport, who was to become a pro-consul in Central Africa, was a conscientious and thoughtful politician, a founder of the One Nation Group, which is how he had got to know Joseph. Alport was also a shade on the pompous side, and no great orator. Socialists saw him as a fuddy-duddy old Tory. His right-wing colleagues saw him as a boring liberal, with unsound ideas on how to handle blacks in the Commonwealth. After a punishing round at the dispatch-box, he would retire to the smoking-room to lick his wounds. His PPS went with him, expected to give words of comfort. Like the best man at a wedding, a PPS is a glorified messenger-boy and bag-carrier, but an important part of the job is simply to be *there*, a moral support.

In the smoking-room there would be gloom. It hadn't gone very well, Alport would say. What did you think, Keith? No, it didn't go well, Keith would reply bleakly. Not at all well. There was no guile in Keith. He was a kind man and a thoughtful man, but neither as a young MP nor as a minister did he acquire the small change of the politician which consists of telling people, or at least seeming to tell them, what they want to hear. He seemed to relish bad news; not least about himself.

It was while he was a PPS that Macmillan rode out the storm caused when his Chancellor of the Exchequer, Peter Thorneycroft, resigned in January 1958, taking with him his two junior ministers at the Treasury, Enoch Powell and Nigel Birch, in protest against what they saw as a dangerous financial policy being wished on them by the Prime Minister. Macmillan, famously, dismissed the multiple resignation as 'a little local difficulty'. It was in fact the first battle in the war between the neo-Keynesians and the advocates of 'sound money' which was to preoccupy Joseph in the seventies, but he seems to have had no premonition of that. Like most of his colleagues, Joseph was prepared to trust the Prime Minister.

CHAPTER FOUR

NO HESITATION

There are only two sorts of people, the efficient and the inefficient.

George Bernard Shaw

The general election of October 1959 was a triumph for Harold Macmillan, leader of a party that had been tottering on its feet less than three years earlier. It was in what was now a self-confident government that Keith Joseph got his first ministerial post. In Leeds, his own majority, with no snow to keep the voters at home that time, was up to 11,531, and he put his share of the vote up a point to 64.1 per cent.

Macmillan appointed him Parliamentary Secretary at the Ministry of Housing and Local Government. There was a complication about him becoming a minister in the Housing Ministry when he was a shareholder in a building company, but there was a recognised procedure, which involved putting his shares into trust, to remove possible conflict of interests. When he was summoned to the Prime Minister's room at the Commons he had omitted, in the excitement of being offered a job, to raise the matter, which occurred to him only as he emerged into the corridor. He paused, wondering whether he ought to go straight back in. In the corridor, as he recalled, there was one of those fatherly policemen who are part of Commons folklore, who looked at the hesitant figure and decided he needed advice. 'Never 'esitate, sir,' he said. 'Never 'esitate.'

On which note, Keith Joseph began his ministerial career. The mechanics of being a minister came easily. He loved being a minister. Maybe there was almost a sense of coming home. Later, a fellow-minister, comparing him with colleagues, spoke of Joseph as a thoroughbred among cart-horses.

The thoroughbred quality went down well in Whitehall. If, as was sometimes said, he was in many ways a mandarins' minister, it could be a back-handed compliment; over the years there were to be plenty of accusations that he simply lay down before his officials. He accepted willingly – indeed, to a fault – that a minister is the front man who takes the blame

21

when officials get things wrong. One of his cabinet colleagues put it simply that he was always 'winged' by his various departments; that he would have been better off as a minister without portfolio. Another of his associates commented drily that the ideal cabinet post for him would have been as 'Minister for Thought'.

Meanwhile, however, he proved an impressively effective junior minister, and at that stage it probably helped that he spoke the same language as the best of the mandarins: a language always civilised, but based on a hard-headed understanding that power is everything in government. He had the mandarins' faith that intelligent men sitting round a table can reach intelligent solutions to most problems. He had their instinct that decisions ideally relate back to principles.

Someone once described his conversation as being like fine dry sherry served up on a silver salver. In the right atmosphere he was a stimulating and congenial companion. His courtesy was legendary. That said, there were those whose tastes did not run to dry sherry and who thought there was a thin dividing-line between courtesy and condescension.

He was an impressive performer at the dispatch-box, always well briefed and courteous, determined to make points by rational argument, not by assertion. It was not a style calculated to dazzle, but occasionally it could reach the heights, when the sheer competence, backed by the impression of integrity and sincerity, could annihilate opposition. There was always an undercurrent of nervous energy, of passion even. Never, in thirty years, was he entirely easy speaking in the Commons. (As he sat down after his first front-bench speech, Macmillan, who was beside him, patted him on the hand and whispered urbanely: 'If it's any consolation, it will get worse.')

On the whole, he was happier speaking outside the House, provided it was a serious occasion. His wit was considerable but it was not the kind that lent itself to the classic after-dinner speech. In due course he developed a technique for the occasional oratorical blockbuster, composed with immense care and with much help from officials or other speech-writers. It is on his big speeches in the country in the 1970s that much of his reputation stands or falls. Lesser speeches – at luncheons of a trade association, say – might be a matter of jotting notes down on a menu-card or paper napkin. He enjoyed informal speeches where he was heckled. With a certain kind of small audience he liked bringing them in to participate. There tended to be a strong educational streak to his speaking.

Not all his speeches went down well with everyone. What came over to some listeners as impressive command of the facts came over as arrogance to others. What one listener might applaud as a brilliantly original piece of intellectual insight seemed to another to be airy-fairy evasion of unpleasant facts.

He accepted that part of a minister's job was to be a link between the Department and the real outside world. This never meant that he was happy as a talking head on television, a rôle which by the 1960s had become a basic for even junior ministers. The Joseph attitude to television was engagingly antediluvian. Once, after tying himself in knots during an interview, he turned to the producer, immediately the camera was switched off, to ask please could they start all over again: it had all gone so horribly wrong – 'Not your fault of course; my fault entirely.' The producer was scarcely sure how to answer this. 'I thought you realised, Sir Keith,' he said, 'that this was to be a live interview?' 'Yes, yes, I know that,' said Sir Keith. 'That's why I want to do it again.'

It was no wonder that Whitehall public relations men had their problems with Sir Keith. His political career had started about the same time as television, but his love of the medium certainly did not develop as it developed. In the early days, when studio lights were harsher, he was once persuaded to appear with Rab Butler in a performance which caused a member of the production team to remark afterwards that it was the best recording of perspiration he had ever seen.

As the parties became more sophisticated about television, he was sent on a media training course but did not take to it – 'I was too stubborn, I suppose,' he recalled. Yet one of the consultants employed to train Conservatives to face the cameras, Stanley Hyland, speaking critically of the Tory leaders' performances during the election of October 1974, actually rated Joseph the best of an imperfect bunch. 'He is very nervous of television,' said Hyland. 'I don't think he has any reason to be. His intellect is obviously high-quality. But he is not persuasive because he tends to regard it all at too high a level. He is not talking to common people.'

Actually, Joseph did not mind the longer interview, with, say, Brian Walden – that could be an intellectually satisfying experience for him – but he abhorred the short encounters where he was expected to condense issues to a few sentences. He liked to think that his platform style, when he stumped the country at elections, belonged to the pre-television age. Apart from anything else, it meant that a single speech could last the whole tour – 'I was a sort of Harry Lauder going round before radio was invented.'

It was well known that he never invested in a television set for himself or his family. The most often quoted television anecdote was about how, when he was being shown round a television studio, he earnestly asked somebody: 'Do you think television has come to stay?' Such remarks were all too apt to slip out, to the horror of his entourage: they were sometimes merely his way of asking whether it had occurred to people to challenge accepted wisdom. There is in Keith Joseph a lot of the innocence of the child in the story of the Emperor's new clothes.

He entered ministerial life resolved to keep a firm hold of his private life. It went beyond his determination to protect his family from Whitehall – so far as he could, given the appalling hours to be worked and the demands of 'the boxes' to be read at home. There sometimes seemed to be another part of his life kept meticulously away from his officials. By the time he became a minister he had built up a network of contacts in the business world and elsewhere, and his skill at picking their brains was one of his major contributions in government. But some at least of the officials would have liked to know more about who and what influenced his decision-making. There was an old Gladstone bag he brought to the Private Office, with a combination lock, that they would sometimes have liked to get their hands on and bring the contents into the intricate games that civil servants play with their ministers.

His officials in his different departments over the years were in fact mostly devoted to him, even if their tidy minds would have preferred everything to be in a form that could find its way into the files. He kept up a private correspondence as a minister, which did not go through the Private Office machinery. Occasionally he would go out and post letters himself, sometimes queueing up at the post office to buy the stamps. There was nothing sinister in this, and no lack of trust. And in buying his own stamps he was following the example of Gladstone. It was his nature not only to keep his private life separate from his public life but also to keep different strands of his public life in compartments. He also, in an age of leaks, had old-fashioned attitudes about the importance of observing confidentiality.

The result was that politically interesting material went unrecorded. This took on considerable importance after 1979, when Joseph was one of those closest to Mrs Thatcher. Instead of writing minutes, or making the kind of ministerial telephone call when the Private Office listens in on the extension and takes notes, he might phone Number 10 or Number 11 and say: 'Could I come round for twenty minutes?' So the full extent of the Joseph influence in the Thatcher government will not be revealed when the cabinet and departmental papers are released under the Thirty-Year Rule.

On the whole, though, he was a minister who fitted easily into the Whitehall way of doing things. He read the documents the civil servants laid in front of him. He would go off every evening with a couple of fat boxes, and at the weekends with twice as many. He read letters before signing them, and where his signature could be little more than a rubber stamp, as in routine decisions on planning matters at the Ministry of Housing, he had a technique of extracting every nth document and studying it in detail.

His method of decision-making was to start by listening to every point of view. It was a process that appealed to the civil service mind, if not to some of his fire-eating political colleagues who believed in government by banging a fist on the table. It tended to mean that a ministerial day was a succession of meetings, with the diary getting farther and farther behind, and that the paperwork had to be put off until he got home at night. It was, as one of his advisers put it, the Socratic way of government. On the other hand, it also laid him open to the charge of taking the side of whoever he had spoken to last.

Socratic it may have been, but life in the Private Office was seldom relaxed. Typically the atmosphere was of sometimes frenetic intellectual and nervous energy. A bluebottle in a jam-jar, someone called him. At a certain point of nervous energy there was a vein on the forehead which would vibrate alarmingly.

It was as Parliamentary Secretary at the Ministry of Housing and Local Government that Keith Joseph first worked with Margaret Thatcher, who had entered the House in 1959. She was immediately lucky enough to get a place in the ballot for private members' bills, and was persuaded to take over a measure that the Cabinet wanted to see enacted but preferably not as a government bill. The topic was a curious one in view of her later relations with the media: a bill to give the press the right of entry to local-authority meetings. The motivation was more strictly political than seemed on the surface: during a printing strike, some Labour councillors had barred journalists who, in defiance of the print unions, had tried to go on reporting council meetings.

On 5 February 1960, Mrs Thatcher moved the second reading – it was her maiden speech – and, as minister at the relevant department, Joseph helped her see her bill through the committee stage. She did not, at the time, make any dramatic impression on him.

In 1961 he was promoted to be Minister of State at the Board of Trade. This was a job that he relished. It fitted in with all his ideas about wealth creation and industrial efficiency. This was an age when it was assumed that a major responsibility of government was fostering exports. Feeling very daring, he approached his family's old friend Simon Marks and suggested that Marks & Spencer might consider going into the export business; subsequently they did in fact open up in France.

He became a great exhorter and facilitator. Managers were invited to London for pep-talks which followed the theme of his maiden speech. He toured factories, bringing with him, in the words of *The Times*, 'a modern look to a Ministerial visit. He probes and criticises as well as praising. He asks about their design departments and their apprentice schemes (if any), and how can Government help?'

The day had not yet come when Tory ministers learned to say that it was not for them to tell industry how to do its job; and the 'white heat' rhetoric of the interventionist era of Harold Wilson was around the corner. In the early sixties Keith Joseph looked the very model of a modern politician. Further promotion was assured. He fitted into the Harold Macmillan form of government, although he apparently failed to come up to the old actor-manager's high standards of style: 'the only boring Jew I've ever met,' Macmillan called him. Joseph could console himself with the thought that Macmillan, with the worlds of statecraft, publishing and country-house society at his command, could pick his Jewish friends exactingly.

Politically Macmillan was moving from the crest to a trough. Wage settlements were running too high for the good of the economy, and the Government instituted a 'pay pause', one of many during the sixties and seventies. The first half of 1962 saw discontent among workers ranging from railwaymen and dockers to nurses and university teachers. The extent of government unpopularity was dramatised on 14 March 1962 at a by-election in suburban Orpington, where a Conservative majority of 14,760 was turned into a Liberal majority of 7,855.

This was, so it was said, the revolt of the new middle class: the 'young marrieds' who had taken on heavy mortgages and now found that their incomes were not keeping pace with inflation. There were other by-election reverses, and the Liberals did well, too, in the local elections. On 12 July yet another by-election, at Leicester North-East, saw the Conservative candidate in third place. The following day the Prime Minister acted, or over-reacted. July 13th, 1962, was the 'night of the long knives' when one-third of the members of the Cabinet were dismissed. Joseph was among the beneficiaries, joining the Cabinet, only six years after entering the House, as Minister of Housing.

The key to what was in Macmillan's thinking lay in the replacement of the Chancellor of the Exchequer. Selwyn Lloyd, who symbolised the belt-tightening that upset the young marrieds of Orpington, was super-seded by the more spaciously minded Reginald Maudling. The night of the long knives upset many Tories, including those whose views on Macmillanite economics were voiced by Nigel Birch, who had resigned from the Treasury in 1958 along with Thorneycroft and Powell and who now wrote a characteristically terse letter to *The Times*: 'For the second time, the Prime Minister has got rid of a Chancellor of the Exchequer who tried to get expenditure under control. Once is more than enough.' Getting expenditure under control was certainly not the overriding priority of the Cabinet that Joseph now joined.

CHAPTER FIVE

ONWARD AND UPWARD

Government is a contrivance of human wisdom to provide for human *wants*. Men have a right that those wants should be provided for by this wisdom.

Edmund Burke

Keith Joseph's first day in charge of a Whitehall department started with an early ring on his doorbell in Chelsea. 'There's a man from the undertaker's,' his wife told him. This was the Private Secretary, in the days when private secretaries still dressed in black and wore bowler hats, come to take him to his desk. They decided in the Joseph household the Department must be in mourning for his predecessor, Charles Hill.

Dr Charles Hill was in some ways a symbolic figure. (Mourning, as it happened, was premature: he went on to become a vigorous chairman of the Independent Television Authority and then of the BBC.) Hill had entered politics after making his name during the war as the 'Radio Doctor', purveying homespun advice about keeping healthy on rationed food. His departure marked another break in the links with the politics of the wartime coalition which had dominated the Conservative Party for two decades.

It was a big department that Joseph took over in the summer of 1962. His full title was Minister of Housing and Local Government and Minister for Welsh Affairs. (The last part involved joining in singing 'Land of My Fathers' in Welsh at an eisteddfod.) Given the blows that Macmillan's prestige had suffered in the first half of the year, the job contained a major political as well as administrative challenge. He was one of the ministers specifically expected to prove to the party and the country that the Macmillan government had got its second wind. The Prime Minister made the point in more formal language in a letter to the Queen shortly after the night of the long knives: 'I have been very glad to have had the opportunity to bring in men like Sir Edward Boyle and Sir Keith Joseph, who represent active and energetic youth.' The first set-piece occasion for the young men was the Conservative Party Conference in October in Llandudno. Morale was not high: the abruptness of the cabinet dismissals had upset many of the faithful, and in the gloom the new Housing Minister's contribution was received as a shaft of light. He got a tremendous ovation. *The Times* described his success thus: 'Instead of debate, the members got direction; instead of magisterially phrased sentences, carefully qualified by this and that, they got machine-gun bursts of fire.' It was at Llandudno that the party really became aware of Keith Joseph. Political success depends very much on being in the right place at the right time. Keith Joseph, it has to be said, had his share of that luck. He is often portrayed as having been a solitary figure swimming against the tide, a man who enjoyed unpopularity. There is in fact another side to him. For all the supposed unworldliness, there is in part of him the astuteness of the politician who knows how to sniff the wind and set his sails appropriately.

The strategy for housing that he outlined to the 1962 conference was for the biggest slum-clearance programme of all time. It would be a worthy sequel to Macmillan's own housing drive of the fifties when he was directed by Churchill, with tears in his eyes, to provide 'homes for the people'. Moreover, the Joseph housing drive was going to give the taxpayers value for their money. The latest techniques, including prefabrication, would be faster and more cost-effective; and by building upwards rather than outwards there would be more cost-effective use of land. It was the message the party of the time wanted to hear: the power of government was to be used, with Tory efficiency, not socialist dogma, to house the homeless.

The speech got a splendid press. The *Observer* commented that 'few people newly appointed to the Cabinet can ever have built up a favourable public image more swiftly.' Joseph himself was apprehensive that he had raised hopes too high. He also suspected, with good reason, that there was going to be a fundamental flaw in his housing policy. Council housing was important, so was the increase in owner-occupation; but the peculiar problems of British housing would never be solved until there was a healthy private rented sector. Homes to rent were taken for granted in every other Western country, whereas in Britain private investment in housing had been all but destroyed by the rent-restriction laws. But Joseph knew that he was unlikely to get Parliament to seize the nettle of rent restriction.

Macmillan's first Housing Minister, Henry Brooke, had nibbled at the problem. The relaxation in the law had not been enough to attract serious investors but had been exploited at the sleazy end of the market by people who bought property, forced out the tenants and put up the rents or sold the house. This, plus natural decay, created a substantial problem of replacement of housing stock. On rents legislation Joseph did some more nibbling, but decided that this was a classic case of a political dead-end: if financial institutions were to be persuaded to invest in bricks and mortar, they needed long-term assurance that their money was safe; but any Conservative reform could be overturned by the next Labour government. This is precisely what happened when Joseph was replaced in 1964 by Richard Crossman, who put an even tighter straitjacket on landlords' rights. Getting back to a viable private sector in housing was like finding the road to Tipperary: you had to start from somewhere else.

The failure to tackle rent control was one of the many things for which Joseph blamed himself ever after. It did not help his peace of mind when the media decided that one of the archetypal figures of these later years of the Macmillan government was Peter Rachman, the most notorious of the new, sleazy, post-Brooke landlords. (According to Richard Crossman, Rachman kept photographs of Keith Joseph and Henry Brooke on his wall as the men who kept him in business.) It was now that Keith Joseph became accustomed to facing chanting demonstrators, who used to beat a path to his Chelsea home.

There was an easy theoretical solution, from the Conservative point of view, to all that Rachman represented: the answer was to give more, not less, freedom to private landlords; then the sleazy ones would be squeezed out by a new respectable breed of landlord. The Tories of 1962 were not ready for such radical reasoning.

So the onus remained largely on publicly provided housing. Given the political realities, the Joseph years at Housing fitted into the philosophical consensus of the time. For instance, up to a point he shared the fashionable suspicion of property developers. (He dabbled with the possibility of a land-betterment tax.)

He was a consensus man, too, in his faith in technology, and was much struck by a development on the doorstep of his own constituency. Three local authorities, Leeds, Sheffield and Hull, had set up the Yorkshire Development Group to exploit the benefits of scale building. They had calculated that if they mounted a joint five-year programme for at least 4,500 housing units they could provide housing faster, and no more expensively, than conventional building methods could. The pioneer scheme was at Hunslet Grange on the south side of Leeds. Several streets of small houses were cleared, to prove how space could be used more economically. The old homes were replaced with a 1,250-unit complex. It was the last word in technical efficiency, at a time when Leeds had 20,000 names on its housing waiting-list.

Hunslet Grange also claimed to represent the fashionable idea of community participation. It was not only what people needed, it was what they desired. 'We are involving the tenants on the estate at every stage,' said the city's housing chairman. 'The scheme is their choice.' It was indeed a common complaint about traditional slum clearance that the tenants re-

sented being plucked away from the cosy intimacy of the old slums. The
sprawl of the postwar estates had been much criticised. High-rise living
was supposed to bring back intimacy. At the opening ceremony at Hunslet
Grange, a Leeds councillor who blurted out that he himself would not care
to live there was asked by the chairman to keep his voice down.

The Leeds scheme was hailed as the way for the future. It seemed to
solve two of the problems of mass housing: high cost and shortage of land.
But twenty years later Hunslet Grange was demolished and the 1,250 units
replaced by 400 houses not all that different from the ones pulled down to
make way for the high-rise flats.

In fact defects in the factory construction had become evident almost
from the start: water had seeped in through joints, and condensation
was a major problem; the concrete panels which were the basis of the
construction were liable to crack and shift.

Nevertheless system building was the consensus way in the sixties. It
was fostered by Joseph, and the policy was carried forward enthusiastically
when the Labour government took over in 1964. A circular from Richard
Crossman in 1965 told local authorities that system building was 'the only
way to build the number of houses we need'.

But the Joseph years at Housing were not all high-rise flats, nor indeed all
publicly financed building. Under his régime there were some imaginative
developments, privately financed, like New Ash Green in Kent. What the
consensus certainly never grasped was that there might be an argument
for preserving, not pulling down, the old terraces where the business of
living had once been carried on on a human scale, and could have continued
to do so. Joseph envisaged the restoration of 'saveable' housing, but looking
back in 1987, he summed it up sadly: 'I didn't have a philosophy. I was
just a "more" man. I used to go to bed at night counting the number of
houses I'd destroyed and the number of planning approvals that had been
given. . . . Just *more*.'

He was always busy. Housing chairmen from the cities and the shires
were summoned to London to be exhorted. If they complained (as Labour
chairmen did) that government was not providing them with enough
money, they were told the answer was to be more cost-effective. But the
funds he did provide from the taxpayer were huge.

He was forever visiting housing projects, with an eye for detail. Dustbins
interested him. Sanitary arrangements he regarded as fundamental for
human dignity; he was a great puller of chains. He was regarded as
eccentric for talking about how the two-bathroom home should become
the norm: it would be a symbol of the working classes catching up with
the middle class.

★

In political terms, housing policy was made more difficult to discuss rationally not only because Rachmanism was so emotive but also because the Rachman issue interweaved with one strand of the greatest political scandal of the period, the Profumo affair: a War Minister who shared a girlfriend, Christine Keeler, with a Soviet attaché did not help the government image; and Keeler, as it happened, was also involved with Peter Rachman. It all added up to create an air of moral, political and economic corruption and decadence. Macmillan's handling of the Profumo crisis seemed to indicate that he had lost his old touch.

During the Profumo case it was reported that several ministers were contemplating resignation, and that Joseph was one of them. This he denied. When the Government faced a censure motion in the Commons over housing in July 1963, Joseph accused the Leader of the Opposition, Harold Wilson, of exploiting the link with Profumo. But it was typical of the Joseph debating style that, when a Conservative backbencher helpfully intervened to suggest that protests against housing policy were 'communist-inspired', *Hansard* records Joseph as dismissing this with: 'No, no. There is a real evil here somewhere.' The Henry Brooke Rent Act had not caused Rachmanism, he argued. It had been caused because there were not enough houses, and he could claim that the housing supply was 'immeasurably better' than when the Conservatives had come to power. 'The limitation is not finance. . . . It is not even land. The imperative necessity is to increase the output of the building industry and to achieve somehow more decentralisation from our big cities.'

In October 1963, Harold Macmillan announced his resignation, because of ill health. In a sense it was an unnecessary resignation. His illness turned out to be less serious than he had thought. The political health of the administration was something else.

Macmillan's resignation was announced, in the most dramatic circumstances, at the Tory conference in Blackpool. There followed what was for the Tories an extraordinarily public struggle for the succession. Joseph found the 'theatricality' of it all distasteful – 'Very vulgar scenes'.

This was the last of the Tory leadership changeovers to be carried out under the old arrangements whereby leaders were not elected but 'emerged'. (One observer, William Rees-Mogg, noted that at Blackpool 'the Conservatives ceased to be gentlemen without becoming democrats'.)

Macmillan himself had the initiative, masterminding matters from his hospital bed, where he decided that the man 'emerging', as a compromise among the rivals, was Alec Home, although he would have to renounce his earldom to do so. Back in London from Blackpool, Joseph was among ministers called to the sickbed on Wednesday, 16 October before

Macmillan made his submission to the Queen. Senior members of the Cabinet had been there on the Tuesday. Macmillan noted in his diary: 'Practically all these Ministers, whether Hoggites or Butlerites or Maudling-ites, agreed that if Lord Home would undertake the task of Prime Minister the whole Cabinet and the whole party would cheerfully unite under him.' Joseph saw Home as the right choice, simply in terms of 'integrity', which was the need of the times. After a year in the Cabinet he still had not fallen under the spell of Butler. As for the other candidates who had been flaunting their talents at Blackpool, he admired but had reservations about Quintin Hogg; he was suspicious of Reginald Maudling.

So Joseph was a Home man: in the four leadership changes during his thirty years in the Commons – the changes that brought in Macmillan, Home, Heath, Thatcher – he was on the winning side, so to speak, each time. He was much more of a mainstream Tory than his reputation often indicated.

CHAPTER SIX

WHITE HEAT

It is enterprise which builds and improves the world's possessions. . . . If enterprise is asleep, wealth decays. . . .

J. M. Keynes, *Treatise on Money*

On 15 October 1964, Sir Alec Douglas-Home, as he had become since stepping down from his peerage to become prime minister, went to the country. He came nearer to winning than seemed likely. As happened at several general elections, Keith Joseph contrived to convey a message of pessimism to some who watched him during the campaign. Tony Benn, who was near the heart of the Labour campaign, noted in his diary for Wednesday, 7 October:

> David Butler and Tony King [writers on politics and psephology] called. They told me that the Tory Party was in a state of great disarray and that the NOP on the marginal constituencies is showing a terrific swing. They said that Sir Keith Joseph, amongst others, was completely dejected by the way the Tory campaign was going and thought it might be a Labour landslide.

In the event, Labour got a Commons majority of only five seats. After thirteen years – the 'thirteen wasted years', as Labour propaganda had it – the Conservatives were out of office again. At Leeds North-East, Joseph's majority was down to 8,325 in a straight fight with Labour, who had put their share of the vote up from 35.9 per cent in 1959 to 39.3 per cent.

Harold Wilson came to power with a kind of respectability in *bien-pensant* quarters that Attlee never had in 1945: it was not just traditional Labour voters who suspected that the Tories had wasted those thirteen years. But Joseph, if he had been acquiescent in 1945 in his attitude to the Labour victory after the war, was not neutral now. There may have been a superficial similarity between Keith Joseph's zeal to apply new technology to the housing shortage and Harold Wilson's vision of a new Britain to be forged, as he expressed it in words much quoted, in the 'white heat' of the 'scientific revolution'; but Joseph had refined his views on socialism since

34

1945. Some of his fellow-Tories of 'One Nation' leanings were more sympathetic to what Wilson was trying to do as he introduced his National Plan, which implied a new relationship between industry and the State. But Joseph had become aware – if only 'spasmodically aware', as he put it later – of what he called the 'demotivating' effect of reliance on the State. During the Wilson years he moved to the right.

Within a few months of the election there were murmurings about the need for a change in the Conservative leadership. Alec Douglas-Home, having emerged quietly from the background in 1963 to do his duty, decided in the summer of 1965 that it was time to return to the background. On 27 July the Tory members of the House of Commons, for the first time in their party's history, elected their leader, under rules drawn up after the old arrangements had been discredited at Blackpool in 1963.

The choice offered was not as wide as some of them would have liked. Two obvious names were missing, although this did not create problems for Joseph, because he was not attracted to either of them as a leader. One was Rab Butler – at sixty-two still in the prime ministerial age-range – but he had finally decided a few months earlier that he had had enough. The party had rejected him twice, and he accepted an invitation from the Labour prime minister to be nominated as Master of Trinity College, Cambridge, and to move from the Commons to the Lords (where he sat as an Independent). The other missing candidate was Iain Macleod, who had a core of almost fanatically loyal supporters, but who knew there was a core of disproportionately more influential enemies, some of whom had never forgiven him for giving away much of the Empire when he was Colonial Secretary; and he suffered from his reputation, in a party always suspicious of intellect, of being 'too clever by half'.

In the event there were three candidates. The favourite was Reginald Maudling, who, it was widely assumed, was a more up-to-date version of Harold Macmillan. Second was Edward Heath, less well known to the public, but who had built up a solid reputation in the parliamentary party as Chief Whip and then for the painstaking work he had performed in the last government on the bid (so far unsuccessful) to get Britain into Europe. And his prewar record at the Oxford City by-election established him in the tradition of Churchill rather than of the Tory appeasers.

Joseph was emphatically for Heath. Not a natural lobbyist, he nevertheless entered enthusiastically into the spirit of this first election. One of the votes he swung behind Heath was that of Mrs Thatcher.

He apparently discounted the third candidate, Enoch Powell. If the party had collectively wanted an ideological transformation in 1965, the choice might have been Powell. As one of the trio who had resigned from the Treasury in 1958, he was admired by those who thought Macmillan had played fast and loose with the economy. But he, like Macleod, was not helped by being clever, and in any case the party was not ready for an ideological revolution. Over the next few years, however, Powell advanced notably in influence if not in office.

On the morning that the MPs voted, the *Daily Mail* came out with a National Opinion Poll that showed that Maudling was still the choice of electors at large. The MPs voted differently:

Heath	150
Maudling	133
Powell	15

Under the rules, which required an overall majority of at least 15 per cent, Heath had not secured enough votes to be the outright winner, but Maudling announced that he would not go forward to a second ballot. When the result was announced, Joseph rejoiced in a way that was uncharacteristic of the man to whom partisanship did not come naturally. As he recalled at the age of seventy: 'I was a Heath man. Heath had been very good to me . . . listening to me. He had the right ideas on management. I remember the sheer excitement when he won.' The pattern of parliamentary confrontation was set for a decade: Heath leading the Tories and Wilson Labour. It was, some said, a little like Gladstone and Disraeli.

With the Tories in opposition, Joseph returned to Bovis, as deputy chairman. He evidently had not thought, however, of relinquishing politics for business, although he regarded himself as being useful to Bovis. He knew he had a talent for identifying the areas where the company ought to be expanding, but he had long since decided that the rôle of 'entrepreneur' – which he was coming to see as the key to national prosperity – was something he was better at advocating, and defining, than at practising himself.

He also engaged in an important new charitable venture. At the Housing Ministry he had become attracted by housing associations as an arm of the campaign to house the homeless. He founded, and was until 1969 chairman of, the Mulberry Housing Trust. It was less successful than he had hoped (and was eventually absorbed in another housing association). As with other Joseph ventures, he perhaps set his sights unrealistically high. He was depressed, for instance, when a social survey carried out among Mulberry tenants indicated that they tended to feel they actually had more problems in their personal life, including marital problems, after moving to their pleasant new homes than when they were in their unsatisfactory old ones. Most social scientists could have told him that this was unsurpris-

ing, that it is when people's material problems diminish that they realise
that they have less tangible problems. It was very typical of Keith Joseph
to be saddened when the underprivileged didn't seem to be able to make
use of the privileges they were offered: it was like the old people who
preferred fish and chips to *bœuf bourguignon*.

Another interest he took up in opposition was the chairmanship of the
research board of the Institute of Jewish Affairs.

On the political scene he was now quite high up in the pecking order.
Joseph is one of the relatively few politicians who grew in stature during
opposition. It was the Tories' next spell out of office, in 1974–9, which
earned him his place in history; but it is often forgotten, by others and by
himself, how much influence he had during this earlier period when
Edward Heath was Leader of the Opposition.

Opposition, it has been said, is the real test of a politician, just as
defence, not attack, is the real test of a general. The leaders of a defeated
party are weary – and often perplexed by the problem of how to earn a
living. Fresher pastures, in the City or in academia, look attractive to
defeated politicians even if they have no financial problems on losing their
ministerial jobs, as Rab Butler had shown. Joseph's fellow-baronet in the
Shadow Cabinet, Sir Edward Boyle, took the opportunity to become a
university vice-chancellor.

Any leader of the Opposition has a thankless task in trying to keep a
vigorous team together. The recriminations that are almost bound to follow
an election do not help. Joseph's special kind of energy actually seemed to
leave him with extra resources of energy when he moved from ministerial
office into opposition. His distaste for the conspiratorial side of politics
saved him from some of the jealousies and point-making of opposition
politics.

A word constantly applied to Joseph was *anguish*; and, indeed, he
devoted immense quantities of nervous energy to decision-making and to
squaring his conscience. Equally it was said, truthfully, that he lacked
the toughness to trample on his opponents. But the other side of his
conscience-driven personality was the innocence which insulated him from
a whole range of the tensions of a traditional politician. Virginity carries
its own protections and its own rewards.

In the Heath Shadow Cabinet he held the portfolios for Labour and
Social Services. He was 'busy, busy', as he would say when he looked back
later and wondered how much the busy-ness had actually achieved. He
was a great study-group man, producing papers on future social policy.
Outside advisers were drafted into service. It was in this context that he
really got to know Margaret Thatcher, who impressed him with her speed

at absorbing the detail of the tangle of welfare-benefit rules, and by how, once she sniffed out some absurdity, she would heap ridicule on it.

Keith Joseph brought a degree of intellectual rigour to policy formulation that was not always taken for granted in politics. One young MP, Patrick Jenkin, a future cabinet minister, who was signed on to do some of the research, was taken aback by the standard expected and wondered whether he would ever make the grade.

Meanwhile the Labour government had launched itself, with its tiny majority, on undoing what was seen as the damage done by the thirteen wasted years. The 'white heat of revolution' seemed to appeal to the electorate, and by early 1966 Wilson felt able to go back to the country to reinforce his electoral base. He called a general election for 31 March, when he increased his majority to ninety-seven. The swing to Labour was reflected at Leeds North-East, where Joseph's majority fell below 5,000.

Wilson was now in a powerful position, able to dictate the terms of the political argument. The years when Ted Heath led the Opposition, with Joseph now influential in the Shadow Cabinet, were the 'Swinging Sixties', the years of the Beatles and miniskirts, when people did their own thing, and any self-styled Conservative Party was automatically at a disadvantage.

But if Britain was a jolly, swinging place, the sixties did not seem so relaxed internationally. They came to a climax in 1968, which opened with the 'Prague spring', after which the Russians showed again their determination to stamp out dissension in the satellites. That same year saw the celebrated French student revolt in Paris. Meanwhile the Vietnam war rolled on, with awful results not only in South-East Asia but also in the fabric of American life. Martin Luther King and Bobby Kennedy were assassinated. There were Americans convinced that it *was* a good time to preach conservatism; among them a group of rich Californians who put up a moderately well-known actor, Ronald Reagan, as Governor of California.

In Britain the Heath Shadow Cabinet was struggling to find a distinctively Conservative theme to appeal to the electorate. It seemed that first they had to find a way of appealing to the opinion-forming media – one of the slogans of the sixties was that the medium was the message – and the media seemed largely enamoured of the idea of planning: National Plans, indicative planning, fine-tuning of the economy and all the rest of the fashionable politics of the Wilson years. Joseph, looking back from his Thatcherite period, felt there had not been enough rethinking of basic economics in the sixties. Nevertheless:

Heath led a very active opposition. Very, very active. . . . It was still a statist approach, though with a huge emphasis on releasing entrepreneurship, on reforming trade unions and on sharpening competition. So to that extent Ted Heath injected much more of a cutting edge into the policies connected with economic competitiveness.

Joseph recognised that Heath, as Trade Secretary in the last government, had solid qualifications on competitiveness. 'He had, after all, taken the morally very courageous decision to abolish resale price maintenance.' The abolition of resale price maintenance (RPM), pushed through by Heath in the face of fierce opposition from vested interests working through the Tory Party, had been as substantial a contribution as any Tory politician had made for years to bringing the benefits of market economics to the consumer. But in doing it Heath had left scars in the party. The hostility against him was obviously masked for the present, but it meant that when things went wrong he did not have reserves of support to call upon.

There was another area where there was suspicion about Heath. It was a suspicion concerned with economic theory and therefore also of no immediate practical importance, but, again, it was to be significant later: the suspicion among a small nucleus of right-wing backbenchers that Heath – despite his bold move on RPM – was not really committed to a real free-market economy. The hero of this small nucleus was Enoch Powell, whom Heath had given a shadow portfolio that kept him safely away from economics; as Shadow Chancellor, Heath had chosen Iain Macleod. During the Wilson years, this small band of market-economy zealots formed a sort of ginger group watching suspiciously for signs that the Heath Shadow Cabinet might accept too many of the assumptions of the Wilson government. They were certainly convinced that some members of the Shadow Cabinet, notably the ex-Chancellor Reginald Maudling, leaned too far to the left.

Where did Keith Joseph stand at this time in terms of economic ideology? The point is important in the light of his later explanation that he was not converted to 'real Conservatism', the Conservatism of market economics, for another decade. One right-winger, who arrived in the House in 1966, recalled that although Joseph was now 'part of the Heath establishment' he always seemed to be on 'our' side, that is, on the side of the ginger group. This view is reinforced by Iain Macleod's biographer, Nigel Fisher, who saw Joseph as representing an economic extreme in the Shadow Cabinet while Macleod as Shadow Chancellor was somewhere in the middle: 'Over the whole field of economic policy and particularly taxation, Heath and Macleod saw eye to eye, and steered a middle course between the two lines of thought represented respectively by Maudling and Joseph.'

Both Tory and Labour parties at this time were much exercised to find the best way to control inflation by not allowing wages to get out of control.

Incomes policies, and the powers of trade unions to determine incomes, dominated the political thinking of the sixties and the seventies. Keith Joseph certainly believed that it was folly to try to flout the market in fixing pay according to some absolute formulae. On the other hand, one close observer of the Tory scene in the later 1960s noted that Joseph 'was always very keen on the educational side of an incomes policy – that you tried to educate and persuade people of the dangers of inflation'. This observation came from Jim Prior, in his memoirs, *A Balance of Power*. Prior, as Heath's PPS, was in a good position to assess how the doctrinal battle-lines were being drawn up in the party, and he was to be an important figure in the Keith Joseph story over the next twenty years.

At this time Joseph was indeed an admirer of Enoch Powell, but he was also anxious to make it clear that he had not changed his ideals as the caring Tory. In May 1967 he was writing to *The Times* to complain about his views being labelled 'virtually laisser-faire'. He was inspired, he wrote, by two main causes. One was 'a much more vigorous private enterprise economy – with more rewards for success and with more bankruptcies for failure'. 'More rewards – and more bankruptcies' was a favourite theme of his and it dated back, actually, to his maiden speech. His other main cause, he explained to *Times* readers, was that 'there should now and urgently be more help for people in need'. These objectives, he said, 'require continuing Government activity – in the fields of demand-planning, procurement, restrictive practices, social policy and much else. The purpose is to release energies for another, but this time a humane, industrial revolution. . . . Surely these are not "virtually laisser-faire" policies?'

Joseph's admiration for Powell was confined largely to matters of economic philosophy. The two men differed on the Common Market, for instance, which Powell had now turned against. They differed in the area where Powell made his most notorious impact during the Wilson years: Commonwealth immigration and race relations. Powell on race relations provided one of the more spectacular explosions in the explosive year 1968. It was on 20 April 1968 that Powell told an audience in Birmingham, in a speech to be quoted, or more commonly misquoted, for years to come: 'Like the Roman, I seem to see the River Tiber foaming with much blood.' In the words of the historian of the Conservative Party, Robert Blake:

> The speech was varyingly regarded as an irrevocable blow to racial harmony or a catalyst for freedom to discuss openly a subject hitherto swept under the carpet. The 'classes', to use the categorisation of the third Marquis of Salisbury, were shocked, but the 'masses' were delighted. Five thousand dockers went on strike to demonstrate support for Powell.

If Powell, in the 'Tiber' speech, was speaking for the 'masses', Joseph, with his refined instincts, and his dreams of a society where different kinds of Englishmen could live together in happiness, was a model of the enlightenment of the 'classes'. Indeed, he was already uneasy about the middle-of-the-road line that the Shadow Cabinet were trying to follow on immigration. Early in the Wilson administration the Government had introduced a race relations bill which the Shadow Cabinet opposed on the grounds that racial harmony was not something to be legislated for. Joseph abstained on that vote. Now, shortly before the 'Tiber' speech, the Labour government had brought in a second bill, on which the Shadow Cabinet line was similar, but this time their reservations were expressed through a reasoned amendment arguing that to threaten to punish people guilty of prejudice would actually make race relations worse. In that vote – which took place just three days after Powell spoke – Joseph abstained again.

By that time Heath, 'with great regret', had dismissed Powell from the Shadow Cabinet. To quote Blake again:

> One may wonder how great the regret really was. Powell had become something of an embarrassment. There was his espousal of extreme laisser-faire economics; there was his contempt for incomes policies and planning; there was his hostility to the Common Market and his scepticism about the value of the Commonwealth (itself a factor in the Birmingham speech).

But of course each of those 'embarrassing' policies had its attractions to some Tory backbenchers. Moreover, all those marching dockers, and other evidence that Powell had a strong populist appeal, provided food for thought about how the Conservatives should reshape their policies before the next election. Inside the Shadow Cabinet the centre of gravity of Conservative policy-making shifted with the departure of Powell. If there was a vacuum, Joseph was in a position to fill part of it.

Heath, often accused of being authoritarian, in fact encouraged widespread policy-discussion in the Tory Party of the mid-sixties. Open discussion, some of it spurious, was of course a feature of the Swinging Sixties. On the left it was the great era of 'teach-ins' on the Vietnam war, for instance. On the right it was a time of study-groups and seminars and pamphlets, reflecting Conservatism old and new. Joseph was in the thick of it. One of his pamphlets, published by the Conservative Political Centre in 1967, sought to apply the rigour of market economics to his old field of housing: 'We have slums . . . we have homelessness . . . we have long waiting-lists. . . . Yet we have done so well in other problems of production and distribution. Car ownership has spread dramatically. Television ownership is nearly universal. . . .' And he went on to argue the classic case for incentives for private capital to be put into providing housing.

Part of the difficulty the Tories had in this period was that, although the Wilson revolution had scarcely shown itself yet to be white-hot, the general perception tended to be of Labour as the party of the future; the Tories still as the party of reaction. A Joseph speech in January 1970 tried to make the point that he was preaching something which was the very opposite of reactionary:

> Competition is a bold concept – and a highly artificial state of affairs. Left to themselves, most businessmen would share the market and keep newcomers out. To maintain competition calls for determined, tireless Government action.

The significance was picked up by a *Guardian* writer:

> Competition is of course an old favourite among Conservative slogans. But most Conservatives talk about it as if it were some noble state of nature to which the economy would readily return if it were not for Socialist interference. Sir Keith is more realistic, and, therefore, more threatening. In fact, he is a revolutionary.

That speech was one of a series on trade and industry which he delivered in January–February 1970 as the time approached for the next election. The texts were in fact largely the work – for Joseph was still making use of his capacity for picking brains – of a journalist called Alfred Sherman, who had got to know him by interviewing him as Housing Minister.

Sherman assumed a very much bigger rôle in Joseph's life later. At this time he was doing work for the *Daily Telegraph*, which had been edited since 1964 by Maurice Green. Green, whose background was in economics and City journalism, had decided to give a new, more intellectual cutting edge to the paper's traditional rôle as a Conservative newspaper. Part of this was to provide a platform for writers, from the London School of Economics and elsewhere, who would challenge many of the economic assumptions of both parties since the war. The *Telegraph* picked up the 1970 Joseph speeches and used them as texts for its own thoughts on the need for the next Conservative government to turn its back on some previous Conservative policies. The ideas – for instance, that the economics of Keynes and the post-Keynesians needed more critical assessment – were not new. Many academics had been worried about the corruption of Keynesian economics – but it was unusual for a daily newspaper to take up the theme: most of the media at this time were often preoccupied with the mechanics of Harold Wilson's politics.

There was an American dimension to the anti-Keynesian movement. The Chicago professor Milton Friedman, still largely unknown in Britain, had recently given the presidential address to the American Economic Association which gave impetus to what came to be known as the monetarist approach to political economy. He could give an earthy touch to the dismal science: 'there is no such thing as a free lunch'. Friedman's ideas were filtering across to Westminster.

But the Shadow Cabinet now had to move from open-ended debate to drawing up a platform on which to stand at the 1970 general election. They met for a weekend strategy meeting at the Selsdon Park Hotel at the end of January. The choice of hotel was probably strictly practical: it was easy to get to, and had spacious grounds which gave privacy. But to some the place was symbolic. It was no remote country-house setting. Selsdon, just south of Croydon, is in the heart of the commuter belt, and the hotel was the sort of place associated with sales conferences and training sessions for junior executives. The Tories were not only turning their back on the grouse-moor image of the old party, but also showing they were not afraid to acknowledge that their power-base was now the more or less affluent owner-occupied south-east of England.

After Selsdon Park the word went out that the party leadership had come down firmly on the side of the free market rather than on that of the interventionist economy. Peter Walker, who came to be regarded as one of the more left-inclined Tories, recorded (in *The Ascent of Britain*) that at Selsdon, when Iain Macleod came down on the side of dismantling the apparatus of state economic influence which had been built up under Harold Macmillan and augmented under Wilson – pay boards and the like – only three members of the Shadow Cabinet raised their voices in dissent: Walker, Maudling and Sir Edward Boyle.

Selsdon took place while Joseph was delivering his series of speeches about the invigorating effect on industry of the free-market economy. 'Selsdon Man incarnate', one commentator called him. Labour seized on this image. Over the coming months Joseph was portrayed as the wild man who wanted to pull down all of society's safety-nets, the ogre who would seize bread from the mouths of starving children. Whatever effect he had on the Opposition, he did tend to terrify his own side. The suspicion with which he was viewed by some colleagues helped to shape the next stage of his career, when the Tories in fact got back into power. Significantly, however, about this time, Harold Wilson was reported to be telling associates that Keith Joseph was the man who could provide the most effective challenge to him.

The general election was fixed for 18 June 1970, when Wilson was sure he would win. The opinion polls agreed with him.

Joseph was invited by the *Daily Telegraph* to sum up the Conservative case, which he did under the headline 'We are the radicals now'. The election was notable if only because it proved how the opinion polls can get it wrong. Heath won a majority of thirty-one seats.

During the campaign, it had been widely assumed that Joseph, guru of the competitive-market economy, would go to the Department of Industry; and, if the wild men of Selsdon had truly been as wild as they were portrayed, that might have happened. There were those who would have liked to see him at the Exchequer rather than Iain Macleod. In the event Heath kept him away from economics and appointed him Secretary of State for Social Services.

CHAPTER SEVEN

HEALTH OF THE NATION

This is a very fine country to be acutely ill or injured in, but take my advice and do not become old or frail or mentally ill here.

Sir Keith Joseph, as Secretary of State for Social Services

Heath's government got off to a tragic start when his Chancellor of the Exchequer, Iain Macleod, died within a few weeks of moving into 11 Downing Street. Joseph's name was mentioned as a possible successor. Looking back at the age of seventy, he was emphatic that he had never wanted the job: 'I never wanted to be Chancellor. I'm not an economist. I don't have any self-confidence in that field. And, energetic though I am, I dreaded the drudgery. I've always thought of the Chancellor as "poor chap".' To replace Macleod, Heath picked Anthony Barber. We have no way of knowing how much his record in the Heath government of 1970–4 differed from what Macleod's would have been. There is no doubt, though, that the sudden removal of such a powerful figure as Macleod, on top of the removal of Enoch Powell, weakened the party leadership. Arguably it created another vacuum which Joseph might have sought to fill in part. His economic contribution to policy-making was less than some people thought it should have been.

One of the first people Joseph had got in touch with when the unexpected result of the 1970 election came through was Professor Alan Walters of the London School of Economics. Walters was already an important figure in the anti-Keynesian monetarist movement gathering force in the universities of Britain and the United States. Walters, whose talents were in demand in various places, had just landed in Israel when Joseph telephoned him, explained that he had got the Social Services job rather than an economic department, but said that he wanted Walters to come and work for him.

Walters said he had too many other commitments. He then experienced

45

what he came to think of as a classic example of the Joseph charm and guile in trying to land a fish that he wanted. 'Well,' he said, 'at least come and have lunch when you get back.' At lunch he produced a paper from his pocket and said this was something that might interest Walters. It was the Bonham-Carter report on the size of hospitals, and, as Joseph had known, it was calculated to tickle Walters's intellectual fancy. 'I don't believe this,' he said.

The report proved, with apparently impeccable logic, that a hospital could not support the appropriate size of medical team with less than 2,000 beds. It was the kind of logic that in some ways was typical of the 1960s and 1970s: the case for bigness, reorganisation and a more complex hierarchy. (An important factor in the medical evidence to Bonham-Carter seemed to be the need to enhance the career structure of doctors.) Over the lunch-table, Walters was hooked to the extent that he agreed to work temporarily, part-time, for Joseph, and helped to produce reasons for keeping the number of beds in a hospital down to about 600.

Walters, one of the most energetic, politically conscious economists capable of providing critical analysis of the new government's economic policies, also worked temporarily for the new 'think-tank' which Heath established in the Cabinet Office.

After leaving Whitehall he kept in touch, and became alarmed at the economic drift of the Government under Barber's chancellorship. Later he submitted a detailed paper to Joseph showing how the Government was turning its back on the economic principles of Selsdon Park. Joseph passed this on to the Prime Minister, and passed the reply back to Walters – the reply being that Heath and his Chancellor realised the economic risk they were taking but were convinced it was worth taking. This was the 'dash for growth' which, in the event, failed.

There appears to have been little debate in the Cabinet on the merits of the general policy. Partly this was because of the powerful presence of Ted Heath. Joseph, in a 1987 interview for the Institute of Contemporary British History, in which he conceded that he had 'never been a very effective Cabinet member', said this of the 1970–4 government with the benefit of hindsight: 'We were – with the best of intentions – tending to make things worse rather than better. I cannot exaggerate the good intentions of Ted Heath or of us under him. But I failed to lift up my eyes.'

He was number eight in the official order of seniority in the Cabinet list, which gave him reasonable clout if he had cared to use it. But the duties of his vast department preoccupied him.

If there was one word used more than any other, not always in a complimentary way, to describe the Heath government of 1970–4, it was *managerial*.

This was symbolised by bringing Derek Rayner, of Marks & Spencer, into the Ministry of Defence to raise the efficiency of its purchasing methods.

Management was to be a key word in the offices of the Department of Health and Social Security at the Elephant and Castle from which was controlled the apparatus of the Welfare State as it had grown since its creation under the postwar Labour government nearly twenty-five years before. The National Health Service, which in England and Wales employed more than 800,000 and had a budget of some £3 billion, was often described as the envy of the world, but was creaking at the seams. During the pre-election debate inside the Tory Party there had been much talk of sweeping away the existing financial structure of the NHS and moving towards a system where people paid for some services as they used them.

When the new Parliament met, the Labour Opposition selected the future of the NHS for one of its first set-piece attacks in the Commons. The Welfare State, Mrs Barbara Castle noted, was now in the hands of 'the arch-apostle of the abrasive new style of Toryism'. Sir Keith, replying to her, was at his most disarming. *The Times* parliamentary sketch-writer observed that 'Anyone rushing to the Commons today on the basis of the Labour Party's X-certificate billing of Sir Keith Joseph as the original Selsdon Man would have been sorely disappointed'. He had already, earlier that month, introduced a bill which provided financial help for various groups hitherto neglected by the social security system, including an Attendance Allowance for those looking after severely disabled people. None of this looked like a crazy axeman at work.

Nevertheless the new government was hastening to produce a programme for immediate cuts in public spending, and behind the scenes Joseph was examining fairly drastic changes. The idea of charging for every visit to the doctor was considered and rejected; so were charges for staying in hospital. He was attracted to the idea of shifting the cost of the Health Service away from general taxation by increasing the cost of the National Insurance stamp, but was dissuaded by the Treasury, always suspicious of taxes earmarked for special purposes. His ingenuity in reforming the structure may have been blunted by the fact that his own homework for the past couple of years had been concentrated not on the social services but on trade and industry.

In any event, within a few months of his taking over the Department, radical change in the financing of social services, such as some of the right-wing backbenchers would have loved to see, was effectively ruled out. As at Housing in the early sixties, at Social Services in the early seventies what he did was not to destroy the Attlee welfare provisions but to try to bring them up to date. And he did this while conscious – as frequent remarks to the staff at the Elephant and Castle made clear – that he had made plenty of mistakes at Housing. Again, he was a *more* man. As he recalled later about the Department of Social Services: 'I used to try my Private Secretary beyond endurance – say to him, "Only 970 days to the next election" almost every day . . . feverishly impatient to create Utopia.'

The package of cuts that the Government worked out within a few months of getting into power in 1970 certainly contained changes in the social services that the Opposition did not like; prescription charges were raised. But the Secretary of State's image as the caring Tory was largely untarnished, and he had enhanced his reputation as a minister in a way that some of his colleagues had failed to do. When the House debated the cuts in November, the same writer in *The Times* was reporting how Joseph had

> wound up the debate on Mr Barber's expenditure package with the flair and parliamentary expertise that has been so missing from the Tory front bench for the greater part of the two-day debate. . . . With just the right balance between toughness and humanity, Sir Keith laid clearly on the line what the new charges and exemptions would mean to the people they would affect most.

He was helped by the fact that the Treasury had agreed to a new social security benefit, the Family Income Supplement, for the least well off. This was open to criticism on a variety of ideological grounds – it was argued, for instance, that it was a licence for employers to keep down wages – but it was further evidence of how the 'abrasive new style' was to be qualified at the DHSS.

Indeed, Joseph's faculty for persuading the Treasury to provide the funds he wanted for the social services was to be a feature of the next few years. At this period of his life he saw no conflict between investing money in the Welfare State and his rigorous views on the rôle of government: government should withdraw from trying to run industry; that was the way to prosperity, but the prosperity could then be legitimately used on social services. At least one Conservative commentator, Ronald Butt, writing in November 1971, was not displeased with the record: 'Sir Keith Joseph's conduct of the Department of Social Security since he took it over is almost a model of this Government's general attitude in practice towards its doctrine, and its obligations to the facts of political life. . . .' From a contrary political viewpoint, the *Guardian* expressed it differently. The Social Services Minister was 'almost single-handedly presenting the smile on the face of the tiger'. Elsewhere he was described as the Heath government's 'statutory humanitarian'. It was an irony of the 1970s that Keith Joseph started the decade as the humanitarian among a pack of hard-faced Heathites, and ended it being screamed at as the hardest of the hard-faced men while the Heathites had become the caring Tories.

His three and a half years at Social Services, working in one of the less-attractive government offices, at the Elephant and Castle, produced four major innovative projects: one of them did not get beyond the planning stage because the Conservatives lost office before it could be implemented; the second came to be regarded, by him among others, as a disaster; but the other two were widely seen as lasting successes – even he himself could be persuaded, after his 'conversion' and all the regrets about his earlier career, to concede that he might have been constructive.

The plan which was scrapped by his Labour successor, Barbara Castle, was for a massive reform of the state pension system.

The disaster area was the administrative reorganisation of the Health Service. It was a well-meaning disaster and, indeed, an impeccably planned one: much of the planning was in the hands of McKinseys, then regarded as the last word in management expertise. Not that the pre-Joseph structure of the NHS had many defenders. It had been devised a quarter of a century before by the architect of the Health Service, Aneurin Bevan, who was constricted by his understandable fear that the medical profession, left to themselves, could not be trusted to implement socialist medicine. Consequently, in the words of one of his biographers (John Campbell, in *Nye Bevan and the Mirage of British Socialism*, 1987): 'He insisted that he, as Minister of Health, should be accountable for every dropped bedpan in the NHS.' As a result, by 1970 it was generally agreed that the gap between the Elephant and Castle and local decision-taking was too wide. It was also felt that there should be closer links between the family doctor service, the hospital service and the clinics and other services which in those days were still provided by the local authorities. The last of these elements was particularly important in keeping people out of hospital, by prevention of illness and by providing care in people's own homes (as did the Attendance Allowance).

What emerged from the Joseph review was a 'three-tier' structure: first, the Department at the Elephant and Castle; second, regional boards, to which much of central power would be devolved; and, finally, local area boards. From the political point of view, what was significant was that Joseph was wedded to the idea of a *national* health service, albeit a decentralised one; he was not prepared to experiment with privatising hospitals. Instead he was putting his faith in 'boards', with a substantial lay presence. This would be the way the British people would control their health service. It presupposed the availability of a substantial number of able men and women – 'generalists' was the word used – who would be able and willing to provide their time.

It was Joseph's way of resisting pressures from interested parties, who wanted to reshape the structure in ways that suited them. One such group was the doctors. A Conservative minister was in a stronger position here than Nye Bevan had been. We have already seen how Joseph challenged medical interests on the size of hospitals. Professor Rudolf Klein, in *The Politics of the NHS*, noted a striking contrast in this respect between the original set-up and Joseph's structure: 'While Bevan had had to make extensive concessions to the leaders of the specialists, Joseph was able virtually to ignore the special pleadings of the consultant élite.' The Health Service trade unions and the local authorities constituted other interested parties anxious to get their hands on NHS management. The Joseph arrangements, whatever else they did, tended to keep them at bay, too.

On what he himself saw later as the credit side of his stewardship of the Welfare State was his attack on 'the afflictions'. He once observed that 'Doctors can be remarkably selective in choosing the ills they regard worthy of treatment'. He agonised over the misery of the deaf and of the rheumatics and arthritics who got a poor deal out of the Health Service because their affliction, from doctors' point of view, 'has no sex appeal'.

When he arrived at the Department there had been a number of horrific stories about conditions, sometimes reaching downright neglect and occasionally criminal cruelty, in hospitals for the old and for the mentally ill. 'More than anything else on the Health side, this was a running torment to me. . . . If I were faced with incontinence . . . cabbages . . . day in, day out, I'm not sure I would behave all that impeccably.' The reports of the Hospital Advisory Service on long-stay institutions became his weekend reading:

> I would get say three reports, one 90 pages, one 40, one 70. After reading them I would have put a cross against say 170 different items. Ideally, if I were in business, I'd call in a management consultant – but he would have the power to say: fire this person, seek a new managing director. You can't in a health service. You can't find anyone better to run a geriatric hospital. No discredit to the physicians – they hadn't been trained as managers. So the readings were exercises in self-mortification.

In fact he achieved more than self-mortification. In increasing the total expenditure on the Health Service he diverted proportionately more of the funds to the 'afflictions' and to the long-stay hospitals. As a proportion of gross national product, social expenditure rose from 23.4 per cent in 1970 to 27.3 per cent in 1974 when Joseph ended his tour at Social Services. The expenditure included, in his last year, what was known in Whitehall as 'the queerest billion ever'; it was the most spectacular triumph Keith Joseph ever scored over the Treasury and it was for personal social services for the disabled and the sick, made available through local authorities. Meanwhile he earmarked funds for centres for the treatment of arthritis and rheumatism and of cancer. Characteristically he harnessed various voluntary organisations to fill gaps in the Welfare State. He encouraged the then new hospice movement for the dying.

He also – and this counts as the fourth, separate, main area of his passions as Secretary of State for Social Services – launched his campaign against the 'cycle of deprivation' – a phrase that earned him a place in the *Penguin Dictionary of Modern Quotations*. (He is credited with two entries in the *Dictionary*; the other is 'We need inequality in order to eliminate poverty'.)

The cycle of deprivation, for a time, preoccupied him, and it is easy to see why. It was about the quality of life, and how that quality was being denied to innocent sufferers. It was about unnecessary suffering passed on from parents with problems to children who perpetuated the problems. He felt stimulated by it as a challenge to the Welfare State, a challenge not only to break the cycle but also to arouse the public conscience. He tried to transmit his sense of urgency to his officials. When it was made known that he planned a major speech, the cycle of deprivation swirled through the corridors at the Elephant and Castle. The speech went through eleven drafts. (Some of his later speeches, on monetarism, went through more than that.)

The final text, drawing on research which covered the United States at one extreme and the Soviet Union at the other, became required reading for a generation of social workers. His immediate audience was the Pre-School Playgroups Association, which fitted in with his conviction that the way out of the cycle was through education, which had to begin as early as possible. Deprivation, he said, 'takes many forms, and they interact. It shows itself, for example, in poverty, in emotional impoverishment, in personality disorder, in poor educational attainment, in depression and despair.' The cycle transmitting the problems of one generation to the next could affect all social classes, but families at the bottom of the social scale were most vulnerable. 'When a child is deprived of constant love and guidance, he is deprived of that background most likely to lead to stability and maturity.' The speech did not hit the headlines in the way that his series of speeches on industry had done before the 1970 election, but it established him as a thoughtful observer of social policy. And, whereas the industry speeches had made him a hero of the political right, all sides could find ammunition for their cause in the Playgroups speech. The

Conservative commentator Ronald Butt, welcoming 'a remarkable and philosophically penetrating speech', said its real point was summarised in the words 'The family is under attack'. Farther to the left it was welcomed as pointing to the collective duties of the community and the State. He was said to be the only minister of any party who had been given a standing ovation by the Child Poverty Action Group.

Whatever the standpoint of the enthusiasts for dealing with the cycle of deprivation, a major theme was planning for parenthood; and this projected the debate into the minefield of 'family planning' in the technical sense. In March 1973 the *Sunday Mirror* (who labelled him in their headline as 'A man of strange contradictions, the Tory Minister who really cares') interviewed him on the subject of problem parents, and quoted him as saying: 'What the devil are we to do about them? . . . First of all, to make sure that all parents – and potential parents – know about family planning so that they needn't have children by mistake.' He was speaking, of course – in what was very much the age of the Pill, in a Britain emerging from the Swinging Sixties – of the Pill. But the sophisticated young people who were most conscious of the Pill were not the problem Joseph had in mind. It was people who didn't or couldn't know how to use family planning clinics:

> They don't organise their lives well enough. . . . They are so poor they can't afford the fare. . . . Though they might like to go, their underclothes aren't clean enough. . . . They can't leave their other children.
>
> We have got to take it to them, to knock on their doors and ask *politely* if we may help.

He moved on into much more dangerous territory:

> One is entitled, really, to say: 'Don't have a child at all if you're not going to take some trouble.'
>
> Indeed, one of the things one feels is that some women see having a baby as almost inevitable. But some women don't have a flair for maternity at all, and, if they haven't a flair, and aren't going to take trouble either, why bring a child into the world at all?

He was now coming near to the theme that was going to get him into overwhelming trouble only a matter of months later – he was going to be pilloried by the left-wing media as a monster – but here he was still accepted by a left-wing Sunday paper as a 'Tory who cared'. What he was saying seemed to represent progressive thinking. In a sense, the National Health Service was still geared to the moral climate of the days when contraceptives were something purchased in seedy barbers' shops. This was to be changed only under the NHS reorganisation which went through Parliament in 1973. But there was no unanimity about how the NHS ought to change in regard to family planning.

The debate on contraception was more heated than later generations could find easy to understand. It took up a substantial amount of parliamentary time in 1973. It aroused the Catholic conscience and the Nonconformist conscience, as well as the libertarians of both left and right. It provoked a confrontation between the two Houses of Parliament. The episode is discussed in detail in *Parliament and Health Policy* by Stephen Ingle and Philip Tether (1981): 'Right-wing Tories could support comprehensive birth control measures as promoting social responsibility or indeed for "eugenic" reasons.' On the other hand there were peers who were shocked by the implications of 'immorality at the taxpayer's expense'. Again, the Upper House contained a substantial proportion of peers with social-work experience who knew about the social consequences of unwanted pregnancies.

Joseph was in no doubt that contraception should be a normal part of the Health Service. The problem was money. The plan he came up with was that normally the service should be paid for by those who could afford it. He reached this decision apparently not on any ideological grounds but simply because there were so many other things he preferred to spend the taxpayer's money on. But the House of Lords jibbed at this; for a combination of reasons, they came down on the side of free contraception. In the Commons, the Government eventually conceded a compromise. Contraception would be available for the normal prescription charge, remitted for poorer people. The cost would be £13 million. (A completely free service would have cost another £3 million.) Joseph, it was noted by Ingle and Tether,

> was not moved by the arguments of some Catholic MPs that free contraception would lead to greater immorality; 'loose and casual people are not made loose and casual by the availability of contraceptives whether free or for 20p'. For him the real problem was to 'break the cycle of deprivation', of which unwanted children was one manifestation.

Sixteen years later, he could talk about the issue in the way which showed the ultra-honest approach – disarming or infuriating, according to your point of view – that made him so different from the normal politician:

> I'm ambiguous. You need to be fairly self-assured, theologically and anthropologically, to be convinced that abstention is entirely right or on the other hand that contraception is entirely right. I don't come to any conclusion at all. . . . I was going to say that marriage is the answer.

> On the other hand there are perfectly stable relationships. . . . I finished
> up with a resounding statement of a dilemma at the end.

This was when he was reminiscing, at the age of seventy, for the purposes
of this book. He laughed, and went on to say he reminded himself of the
story of the Labour minister who kept putting off a difficult decision, and
one day found a sharp memorandum on his desk from his Permanent
Secretary, saying: 'You have a simple choice – you can do A or you can
do B.' The minister annotated it at the bottom: 'Agreed.'

While these theological and anthropological issues were being debated, a
sharper debate was developing. The Heath government had now made its
famous U-turn. As the party's historian, Robert Blake, put it in *The
Conservative Opportunity* (1976):

> The Cabinet began with the intention of 'getting government off people's
> backs', but, lacking any clear intellectual mandate to do so, somehow
> ended with an even larger number of public employees in the non-
> productive sector than ever before. It began with a determination to
> abandon lame ducks and avoid all forms of intervention in wage-fixing,
> but it ended by capitulating to the sit-in at Upper Clyde Shipbuilders
> and by trying to impose the most complete statutory wage policy ever
> attempted.

The statutory wage policy was an attempt to offset inflation, for which the
Government itself, as well as the trade unions, had to accept responsibility.
The Government had decided to risk a dash for growth, with what was
known as the 'Barber boom' – although the Chancellor of the Exchequer,
Anthony Barber, was less responsible for the slackening of monetary
controls than some of his cabinet colleagues. There was little dissent inside
the Cabinet. The two members, Joseph and Thatcher, who were later to
be the sternest critics of the Barber boom, stuck largely to their departmental areas of responsibility (Thatcher was at Education); both were safely
away from the central economic area, and both were large spenders.

On the backbenches there was plenty of protest about the levels of
government expenditure. There was a group – 'Enoch's Privy Council',
they were sometimes called – who included future ministers like John
Biffen and Jock Bruce-Gardyne and who were now convinced that the
Government was failing badly by the one economic test that was relevant,
which was not pay policy or wage controls but the money-supply. One of
this group, Richard Body, combined at this time with two monetarist
economists, Alan Walters and Brian Griffiths, to produce two open letters

to the Prime Minister. This was the same message that Walters had tried to convey a little earlier, without success, through Keith Joseph.

Enoch Powell was an important figure in the background. *The Economist* noted on 16 June 1973 that 'It is a rare Tory MP who doesn't have a Powell group of some real consequence in his local association'. *The Economist* itself was solidly on the Government's side – an earnest of how the establishment of the time was confident that the risks of the Chancellor's policy would pay off in the end. (Looking back, Joseph was convinced that without the solid weekly support of *The Economist* the Cabinet might have been much more worried than it was.)

Meanwhile the Government went on spending, not least at the Department of Social Services. Shortly before the Government fell, Joseph had to announce some cutbacks in Health Service spending but he pointed out (on 28 January 1974) that 'Over the last three years we have spent, on average, in real terms, 30 per cent more each year than the average of Labour's last three years'.

The autumn of 1973 brought further economic complications when the latest twist of Middle East politics, after the Yom Kippur War in October, accelerated the increase in oil prices already being determined by normal market forces; this was to bring advantages to Britain when North Sea oil came on stream, but that was still far over the horizon.

The more immediate difficulty was the breakdown of pay restraint, with the miners' union in the forefront. The Heath government found itself facing what all British governments had always feared, a miners' strike, made worse by taking place in winter and at a time of world fuel shortages. At the turn of the year Britain was formally in a state of emergency; there were power cuts, and industry was on a three-day week. There was much talk of the Dunkirk spirit. Heath decided that he could not go on without a vote of confidence from the electorate – the theme was 'Who governs Britain?' – and he called a general election for 28 February 1974.

CHAPTER EIGHT

CONVERSION

It was only in April 1974 that I was converted to Conservatism.
I had thought I was a Conservative but I now see that I was
not one at all.

Sir Keith Joseph, *Reversing the Trend*, 1975

The year 1974 was a year when political goalposts were visibly shifting.
Compared with some of the year's upheavals, a single Conservative deciding
that he had never really been a Conservative might have seemed a fairly
small earthquake. The year saw two general elections. The first of them
took place, unprecedentedly, amid bitter industrial conflict; when it produced no clear majority, there followed a serious attempt to put together a
coalition government. When that failed, Britain had a minority government
for seven months. The disorientating effect which that sequence of events
had in high places was considerable. The extent of the disorientation may
have been largely forgotten within a few years, but it was important in
making the next stage of Keith Joseph's career so influential.

The industrial bitterness, accompanied as it was with extremism on the
left of the Labour Party, alarmed many voters and, indeed, Labour
front-benchers. The strikes – directed effectively against the Government
rather than against employers – gave the first of the 1974 elections the
theme: 'Who governs Britain?' When the election seemed to provide no
clear answer to the question, there was a further disturbing development
in proposals to raise a 'citizen army' to maintain essential services in the
event of a breakdown of order: an idea which had an appeal for many
public-spirited citizens but had sinister overtones. The best-known pro-
ponent of this idea, General Sir Walter Walker, a retired NATO com-
mander, did not enjoy high political credibility, but a few politicians,
including the experienced Conservative Geoffrey Rippon, were attracted
to different versions of it.

Behind all this was a very real feeling among ordinary people of having
been let down by the traditional politicians. A 'government of all the
talents' was much talked of.

In this confused and clamorous situation, Keith Joseph behaved in the way that the most effective innovators throughout history have often behaved: he walked off in what seemed to be a completely different direction from everyone else. He underwent his famous 'conversion to Conservatism' in April 1974 – the precision of the date was characteristic – and went on walking. By the time most politicians, and most commentators, were aware of what he was up to, he had helped to set in motion something that had a greater impact on Britain than some of the more dramatic solutions that were being contemplated in 1974. Moreover, within a few years of becoming a 'real Conservative', he had gone a long way to providing his own distinctively 'Conservative' interpretation of the concept of 'government of all the talents'.

The mental turmoil which led to the 'conversion' seems to have developed during the grim winter of 1973–4 as the evidence accumulated of the consequences of the financial policies of the past few years, evidence which was brought home to him personally because there was a link with the financial troubles of the family firm, Bovis.

The trouble was not on the company's building side, but because Bovis had chosen, as many firms in the property sector had done, to go into 'fringe' banking. It happened in October 1971, when Joseph was in government and had no executive rôle in the company (and if he had had one, he later emphasised, there was no reason to suppose the decision would necessarily have been any different). Bovis bought, from the First National Finance Corporation, a secondary bank called Twentieth Century Banking for £6.5 million, and injected a further £4.5 million.

After the deal, Bovis seemed to be going from strength to strength. It was a mark of how high they were riding that in 1972 they were in the position of offering to go to the rescue of the shipping group P & O, then in troubled waters; but the move was blocked by P & O's shareholders. Then – and under the régime of the government of which Joseph was a member – the secondary-banking bubble burst, and Bovis were left holding £45 million of guarantees in respect of Twentieth Century.

By late 1973 they had a vast liquidity problem, which was solved in a bitterly ironic way: only fifteen months after the P & O episode, the positions were reversed, and Bovis were saved by a rescue bid from P & O.

At one point during the negotiations in 1972, Bovis had been valued at over £160 million. The 1974 rescue bid put the value at less than a sixth of that, at £24.6 million. There was a clear link in Joseph's eyes between the rashness of Bovis's attempt to cash in on secondary banking and the rashness of the Heath government's dash for growth.

The takeover of Bovis was completed in January 1974, in the midst of the crisis that brought down the Heath government. It was in the middle of the crisis that Keith Joseph had what proved to be his last real social contact with Ted Heath, when the Prime Minister invited him to dine *à deux* in the mess of the Honourable Artillery Company: Heath had served in the HAC and knew that Joseph had a tenuous HAC connection going back before the war. It was a kindly gesture, but the occasion was gloomy. Joseph was conscious that, given their respective characters, he had no comfort to offer. It was like that uneasy relationship with Cub Alport years before. He had no direct involvement with the miners, or with the management of the economy. The only comment he was inclined to make about the economic state of the nation would have been in general terms about the need to change cultural attitudes about how money was earned, and this was scarcely the right time or place.

There were no further opportunities for socialising that winter. The Prime Minister decided to go to the country and fixed the general election for 28 February. Relations between the two men were now about to become strained, to say the least.

In the election on 28 February 1974, Joseph was faced for the first time at Leeds North-East with opposition from a Liberal as well as from Labour, and the Liberal took rather more votes from Labour than from him. Over the country as a whole, the Liberals had their best showing for half a century. They had won a quarter of the votes cast, but still only a handful of seats. The Tories had won more votes than any other party, but ended up with fewer seats than Labour:

Labour	301
Conservative	296
Liberal	14
Others, including Nationalists and Ulster Unionists	23

So no party had a clear majority in this the first of the two 1974 elections. Nor did the Liberals hold the balance, because of the good showing by the Scottish and Welsh National Parties and the Ulster Unionists. 'We are all minorities now,' said the Liberal leader, Jeremy Thorpe, 'but some of us are more minorities than others.'

When the election results came in on Friday, 1 March, Heath decided, with constitutional propriety, that there was no immediate requirement on him to resign. Apart from anything else, the fact that he had more of the popular vote than Labour provided some moral advantage. He opened negotiations with Jeremy Thorpe, but by Monday it was evident that a coalition with the Liberals was not on. Heath resigned, and Harold Wilson was back in Downing Street.

A major consideration among Joseph's colleagues in what was now the Shadow Cabinet was that since the country had moved towards the Liberals the Conservative Party should be turning its eyes towards the 'middle ground' of politics. In thinking differently, Joseph was in a minority, a minority which also included the relatively junior Margaret Thatcher. A fellow ex-minister, Peter Walker, described the situation later (in *The Ascent of Britain*) thus:

> I regret to say that after our defeat in 1974 there was a growing and genuine difference in view between Keith Joseph and Margaret Thatcher on one side and Ted Heath, myself and the majority of the Shadow Cabinet on the other. It was a difference devoid of personal hostility.

If there was no 'personal hostility', the difference was over basics: whether the Heath government had got things fundamentally wrong. And Heath and the majority of his ex-ministers would have been less than human not to become angry as they listened to retrospective criticisms, over the coming months, from two colleagues who had sat with them in cabinet for three and a half years without challenging general policy. The fact that one of the critics was a woman and the other a man with a somewhat other-worldly, almost saintly reputation added to the irritation. With other personalities involved, the air might have been cleared with a blowing off of steam. But during 1974 much of the pressure which eventually caused an eruption was building up under cover.

An air of astonished innocence coloured much of Joseph's life during these months. For three and a half years he had had his head down at his desk at the Elephant and Castle. In March 1974, expelled from his desk and from the cloistered world of red boxes, ministerial cars and civil service entourage, he returned to real life, blinking like a Rip Van Winkle.

His sensitivities were shocked when he went to call on Alan Walters, whom he regarded as an old friend, at the London School of Economics. No, Walters said bluntly, he didn't feel like shaking hands. How on earth could a man of Joseph's intelligence have allowed himself to be party to the economic folly of the Heath government?

We come now to his 'conversion to Conservatism' in April 1974. 'Conversion' can hardly be the right word. The philosophy to which he now devoted himself had largely been there, in his speeches and writings and his arguments at Selsdon Park, for instance, years before. On the other hand, he was not unique in waking up in a state of shock after being forced out of office. The Whitehall system, with the fearful discipline of the red boxes, can indeed prevent a Cabinet minister from raising his eyes from his desk. At least two of Joseph's cabinet colleagues, more worldly-wise, later blamed themselves, in just the way that Joseph did, for not appreciating what was going on in the real world in the early seventies: Willie Whitelaw and Francis Pym. In their case they put part of the blame on the spells they each spent at the Northern Ireland Office.

In any event, it was a particularly puzzling world for an ex-minister to wake up in. Some of the political signposts had been twisted round by 180 degrees. Enoch Powell – 'I was born a Tory and I shall die a Tory' – had been telling people to vote Labour at the February election. (And the Conservatives had in fact done especially badly in the Powell country, the West Midlands.) Admittedly Enoch was his own man. He had his own reasons, not least his passion for keeping out of the Common Market, for loathing Ted Heath and all his works. Nevertheless the traditional definitions of left and right seemed to be in the melting-pot.

Nowhere was this demonstrated more dramatically than in the background of the man who was now moving on to the stage to be one of the most important influences in Keith Joseph's life.

CHAPTER NINE

THE BURIAL OF KEYNES

What is the advice I have to offer you? The first is this – that
you have to clean your slate.

Lord Rosebery

Like Joseph, Alfred Sherman was a Jew who grew up in the London of
the twenties and thirties with an ambition to do something about social
injustice. Sherman, however, was an East End Jew. When Joseph was at
Harrow he was at the Hackney Downs County Secondary. His father was
a Labour councillor. In the East End, Sherman liked to say, people were
not converted to socialism, it was simply natural to be a socialist, and he
himself did not believe in half-measure politics; when Joseph was at
Magdalen, playing cricket and visiting the poor of Yorkshire with his
Quaker friends, Sherman went off to the Spanish Civil War, as a machine-
gunner alongside the communists.

After the war – or, rather, after two wars in his case – Sherman was still
a Marxist. He took a degree at the London School of Economics, then
became disillusioned and turned his undoubted revolutionary skills in
other directions. He had a gift for polemical journalism and found a natural
target in the bumbling municipal socialism of the 1950s, particularly in
the London boroughs. One of his subjects was council housing, and he
originally got to know Joseph by interviewing him as Housing Minister. By
that time Sherman had developed a contempt for many Labour politicians,
without losing any of his contempt for the cosy old traditions of Conservatism.

By the 1970s his loyalties lay firmly in a new faith: in the free market.
He belonged to the group of New Right commentators who saw market
economics as the key to sweeping away the ineffectiveness of socialism on
the one hand and of the Tory old-boy network on the other; doing away,
above all, with the woolliness of the postwar consensus of watered-down
Keynesian economics. The New Right had briefly hoped that Edward
Heath might prove to be the instrument for the radical changes they
wanted in the British economy. They were all the more bitter when the

61

Heath government, as they saw it, seemed to go the same way as previous Conservative governments.

If most of the Cabinet had proved a failure, however, Sherman still saw hope in Joseph. During the confusion of the three-day week and the miners' strike, Sherman sought him out to tell him where the Heath government had gone wrong. In March, after the election results, he was invited to the Joseph home in Chelsea, and arrived bubbling with ideas about how every government since the war had gone wrong with their economics. 'You don't understand,' he cried. 'Keynes is dead. Dead.' Sherman had his critics – who were to increase in number and in virulence over the months and years to come – but few of them denied that he had a fertile mind. He produced political suggestions in the way that stand-up comedians produce one-liners.

In the spring of 1974, each of the two men fulfilled a need in the other. Sherman as a journalist had access to outlets for his ideas but had no *locus standi* in the Conservative Party, or in any other party. Joseph, in some ways an intellectually lonely man, always needed other brains off which he could bounce ideas. After eighteen years in the Commons he had friendships there, and political alliances, with various colleagues, but he had never built up close intellectual relationships. Sherman's were in fact only one of the many sets of brains on the fringes of politics that he picked during 1974, but it was to Sherman, more than to anyone else, that he attributed his 'conversion' that April. Sherman's fecund mind was the 'prism', he said, through which he now saw clearly the political reality that had eluded him in the previous twenty years.

The relationship prospered, notwithstanding – perhaps because of – the all too obvious contrasts between the two of them. To Joseph, politics was a high-minded exercise in principle, ideally practised without descending to the distressing level of personalities. Sherman, gnomic grin on his face, relished the level of personalities; he was deeply concerned with principles, too, but he liked to put a name to every bit of villainy he uncovered.

They argued differently. Joseph had the austerity of a certain Westminster style of understatement, of conceding the maximum number of the opposition's points he could concede, and then courteously setting out the other case. Sherman could be an urbane debater, too, but there was a style to much of his argument that was once described as being in the knockabout tradition of shouting matches in the boulevard cafés of central Europe.

Then there was the contrast between the two men physically: the one slim and dapper and fairly obviously the product of an English public school; the other short and round, and looking like most Englishmen's idea of an alien.

Sherman's intellectual brightness attracted Joseph. So did his gift of popularising arcane concepts like monetarism which, it was becoming clear to Joseph, were going to be at the heart of politics: Sherman could think in headlines. There was also the fact that he was prepared to make the time and had the energy that qualified him to work for somebody like Keith Joseph. But the secret of the bond that linked them – often uneasily and certainly not permanently – was possibly that Joseph now had a new element of passion in his politics, under the smooth exterior, a passion which matched that of a converted Marxist. In the spring of 1974 there seems to have been in Keith Joseph's heart plenty of what any psycho-analyst would identify as 'anger': anger at how his party, and the whole establishment of which he was part, had fallen into ignorance of economic basics; and anger at his own part in it. The way that Bovis had come face to face with economic facts may have helped.

Sherman was at his elbow during the weeks when the Tory ex-ministers picked themselves up after defeat and contemplated what their tactics should be as a Shadow Cabinet. Even without Sherman's influence, Joseph would have been determined to push to have his voice heard on economic policy. The ex-Chancellor, Tony Barber, was pulling out of politics (and a few months later became chairman of the Standard Chartered Bank), but it seems unlikely that Heath would have been any more likely to give the Shadow Chancellorship to Joseph than he had been to give him the substantive job in 1970. Robert Carr became Shadow Chancellor. So Joseph asked for, and was given, a roving commission on party policy.

Heath declined his request, however, that the Shadow Cabinet should get back to the drawing-board on economic policy. It was perhaps an unrealistic request to have made. This was not the case of a party looking forward at leisure to a general election four years hence. There was a hung Parliament; there might be another election any day; every division in the Commons was potentially a cliffhanger. (A major, rather unseemly, row in the early weeks of the new Parliament was over the rôle that the Queen would play if the minority government was defeated on a vote of confidence.) It was small wonder if the majority of the Shadow Cabinet were more preoccupied with the short term than with the long. The Tory instinct was not to go into another election campaign proclaiming doubts about the policies they had been following just a few months before.

The thoughts of any other politician, thwarted by his colleagues like this, might have turned to conspiracy. Joseph was not a natural conspirator – at least, not in the sense of canvassing support in the corridors of Westminster for bringing down the party leader. Characteristically he thought in terms of persuading people, not of manipulating them, and decided, equally characteristically, that he must start with self-education.

One of his first ports of call was at the headquarters, in the Georgian enclave just south of the tourist-ridden part of Westminster, of the Institute of Economic Affairs.

The IEA had been generating its own criticism of the economics of the Heath government. Its rôle since its establishment in 1957, as the kind of research organisation better-known in Washington than in London, was to counteract the tendency of postwar economics to put too much emphasis on governmental planning and too little on the workings of the free market. In 1974 its director was still Ralph Harris, an economist whose recreations included doing conjuring tricks and whose moustache looked as if it had escaped from the Battle of Britain. More important, he was a congenial and lively writer and speaker who had done as much as anyone to argue the case for market economics and to lay it in front of lay audiences. He knew Joseph slightly, as he knew many MPs of all parties.

Joseph explained his mission. Could the IEA help with his self-education? Harris told him to feel free – this was an educational charity, and they had helped worse cases than Sir Keith.

Over the following weeks, Harris found that they had on their hands a mature student whose diligence was an inspiration and whose modesty was almost embarrassing. Could they spare him fifteen minutes? He promised not to keep them longer. What time would suit them? Precisely on time, he would turn up with his questions. Value Added Tax, he might say (or university finance, or town and country planning, or wages policy): who were the authorities worth reading? And, if the authorities were all on the one side, was there somebody worth reading to get a different view?

His reading appetite was gargantuan. When he came back next time he would not only have studied the recommended texts but would also be brandishing some other book or pamphlet that he had discovered. This man's theory, he would say, was it original? Surely things couldn't be as simple as the pamphlet made out? There must be more to it. Was there a book that gave the background? When he found an idea that excited him, he wanted a critique of it: not a socialist critique – that would be too simple – but who else was there who could argue about it? And off he would go with more lists of books, and more lists of people whose brains he could tap. The IEA were good at supplying names, and Joseph was drawing on other sources as well. Always, Sherman was in the background, with names, and ideas, and interpretations of issues.

When he heard Joseph saying that he was only beginning to learn what it was to be a Conservative, Harris felt bound to point out that it would be more accurate to say that what he was really learning about was Victorian Liberalism.

It was eventually 'Conservatism' that Joseph was convinced he was being converted to, and the British voter had to be persuaded of the importance of market economics. The IEA was all very well, but he decided to set up his own institute to give fresh political edge to the argument. It was now, with Sherman, that the decision was taken to set up the Centre for Policy Studies.

Years later, Willie Whitelaw, who was Conservative chairman during 1974 and had a reputation for being one of the shrewder political observers of the time, regarded it as one of the great political mysteries that the Centre for Policy Studies was allowed to come into being. He blamed himself for not being aware of what was going on inside the party; he was weary from a spell as Secretary of State for Northern Ireland and then as Employment Secretary during the horrors of the pay policy and the miners' strike. If the party leadership was unaware of the sea-changes taking place among Conservatives, equally it did not grasp how the Centre, over which the party leadership had little control, could influence the direction of those changes.

Since two members of the Shadow Cabinet, Joseph and Thatcher, were involved in setting up the Centre, approval was required from Ted Heath as leader. He gave it with no great enthusiasm after it was explained that the object was to examine how the market system worked in the various economies of the world: a point he seems to have seen in its favour was that it would do both Keith and Margaret good to learn more about business economics – and part of his criticism of them over the next ten years was that they continued to lack practical knowledge of the real business world. Meanwhile he allowed the CPS to go ahead, with the proviso that he could nominate a director (Adam Ridley); and he allowed his name to be used in the Centre's fund-raising activity.

Joseph became chairman of the CPS and Mrs Thatcher a director. Sherman was appointed 'Director of Studies'. Another director, to handle administration, was Nigel Vinson.

Vinson was a fine example of a fairly new breed: a man who can think up a new product – in *Who's Who* he gave his profession as 'inventor' – but who also has the business skill to make money out of it. The story was that the idea that made his fortune went back to a day at school when he had organised a science club outing to the local plastics factory. When he got his first job, in a factory making hosepipe, he worked out that there was a large range of products that could be improved by coating them in plastic. When his boss didn't seem to be interested, he started on his own in a Nissen hut. Twenty years later he was employing two thousand people coating plastic, a classic entrepreneur.

He floated his company and found himself at a loose end, only just in his forties, but anxious to propagate the ideals of entrepreneurship. He was recommended to Joseph by Ralph Harris and by one of Joseph's business friends, Jack Hawkins.

Vinson was an admirer of the German economic miracle. 'What this country needs,' he said, 'is fewer faint hearts and more Erhardts.' It was the kind of phrase that fitted into the philosophy of the Centre. But phrases were not all that the Centre needed in the spring of 1974. Vinson set to the workaday tasks of raising funds and finding premises. Funds were a problem because they had to lean over backwards not to be seen to be tapping the same sources as the Conservative Party. Joseph had contacts, and Vinson had others. One benefactor was Sir James Goldsmith.

Most of the contributions were not enormous. Shoestring economics was to be a feature of the Centre. The premises Vinson found (in Wilfred Street) were easy of access to the political world, but not in the grandest part of Westminster.

Vinson also had the rôle, as a man of considerable if slightly eccentric charm, of trying to keep the peace among the powerful personalities who found their way to Wilfred Street. The Centre attracted people anxious to change the world, and they were not always easy to live with. Handling personality problems was not something the chairman wanted to spend time on.

The choice of a converted Marxist as organiser of the main creative effort emphasised, although it does not seem to have struck Joseph in that light, that they were in a radical business. Nobody at Wilfred Street believed they were going to be any more than a research institution studying the nature of the Continental economies. Five or six years later Joseph and Sherman had parted, the latter bitter at what he considered Joseph's pusillanimity when it came to putting his brave words into action in government. For his part, Joseph always went out of his way to say his 'conversion' would never have happened but for Alfred. Alfred was a demanding and stern schoolmaster. Visitors to the Centre often thought it odd to find Sir Keith – the man who was by then talked of as a prime minister *manqué* – sitting with his head in his hands being verbally lambasted by Alfred.

The aim of the CPS was to get at the fairly small number of people who influence the thinking of a nation. It was comparable to the Fabian Society, almost a century earlier, which had changed the British intellectual climate sufficiently to make socialism acceptable, working through the educated classes. The major task of the CPS was to make market economics acceptable in a society that had for years taken a measure of socialism, or at least of state intervention in the economy, for granted.

There was much discussion in the early days whether it might be too daring to talk overmuch about the 'market economy': one school of thought was that it would be better to talk of the 'social market economy'. This was the literal translation of *Soziale Marktwirtschaft*, the system that had been so effective in Germany – roughly speaking, the philosophy that market economics, allowed to operate freely, provides the goods and services that people want, and does so more democratically than any system of central planning can do.

'Social Market' had an important appeal on two grounds. One was that the word 'social' conveyed the idea that market economics was not in conflict with social idealism; indeed, that social idealism was unrealistic *without* market economics. The other advantage came from the connection with West Germany: it gave credence to the reputation they wanted to maintain *vis-à-vis* Tory Central Office that they existed simply to study the workings of business economics internationally.

Fourteen years after the event, when Keith Joseph was questioned about his 'conversion' for the purposes of this book, he replied by telling first a story about Lord Rothschild, the man who set up the Cabinet 'think-tank' under Ted Heath. The think-tank was supposed to take a long view of government policy. Rothschild, he recalled, had once been 'rapped over the knuckles by Ted'. 'Now, you don't rap Victor very easily. But he was rapped over the knuckles for saying that we were likely to become the poor man of Europe. Well, I'd been saying that for *years*. But because I wasn't very forceful I suppose nobody paid any attention.' What, then, had happened in 1974? 'I was more and more concerned. Put it down to a mixture of impatience with our slow progress and envy of our neighbours. I never focused on America – I thought they were outside our culture and our reach – but our ruddy *neighbours*. Why should they do so much better, particularly when they had been prostrate and flat on their back after the war?' So 'conversion' was perhaps the wrong word, he said. It was 'a sharpening of views and willingness to seek attention for them'. This was why he was such a willing listener when Sherman had come to him to propose the idea of a Centre for Policy Studies.

The argument that a Centre was essential ran something like this: to pull itself out of the rut, Great Britain needed a change of culture; the change could come only under the Conservative Party, but it was useless to rely on the Tory Party machine to inspire that change – the party machine was designed to win elections, not change a culture, and tended to be in the business of pragmatism and consensus. What Sherman wanted, and (from 1974 onwards) what Keith Joseph wanted – and then what Margaret Thatcher wanted – was conviction politics, not consensus politics.

CHAPTER TEN

POLITICS AND
PERSONALITIES

We know what happens to people who stay in the middle of
the road. They get run over.

Aneurin Bevan

If Keith Joseph in 1974 was determined to find distinctively 'Conservative'
answers to the questions the electorate were asking, there were few of his
colleagues who saw things in such clear terms. Writing of the same period
when the Centre for Policy Studies was taking shape, David Butler and
Dennis Kavanagh (in their *British General Election of October 1974*) described
policy at Conservative headquarters – where everything was geared to the
knowledge that another general election could come at any time – in these
terms:

> There was a determination not to appear abrasive. The one million votes
> that had been lost to the Liberals had to be won back. It was, indeed,
> not only a question of winning back Liberal votes but of preventing
> further encroachments, for, as private polls showed, there was Liberal
> potential for taking more Conservative seats.

In the February election, Heath had been in aggressive mood, but it
had been aggression based on conviction that he was fighting a national
cause that went beyond party interest. The theme of 'national unity' took
shape throughout 1974, and called for a reassessment of traditional party
loyalties. By June one of Heath's senior colleagues, Peter Walker, was
talking about a 'government of national unity', which would represent
most of the Conservative and Liberal parties – and as much as one-third,
Walker predicted, of the Labour Party. It was well known that a substantial
number of Labour MPs were concerned about the wild men who were
part of their party (although it took another seven years before the Labour
moderates took the plunge and broke away to form the Social Democratic
Party).

In so far as the Conservative Party was divided over coalition policy, it was not a division between the left and right wings: it had an obvious appeal to middle-of-the-road Tories, but the idea of dishing the Labour Party appealed to right-wingers, too. One young MP who was to become Mrs Thatcher's Chancellor of the Exchequer, Nigel Lawson, produced a paper during 1974 on the advantages of reaching an arrangement with the Liberals in a limited number of constituencies. One advocate of a national government was Maurice Macmillan, MP, usually thought of as being moderately leftish, but another was Julian Amery, emphatically on the right. The importance of that particular alliance was somewhat vitiated by the fact that they had a common link with Harold Macmillan, one as his son, the other as a son-in-law, and the notion that the old man might be trying to influence events from retirement in his country home at Birch Grove did not really go down well in any camp. Yet the dream of what Maurice Macmillan called 'a ministry of all the talents' appealed to a wide range of Conservatives.

In the early summer, while the Labour government soldiered on in the House without a majority, and while Joseph was beavering on at founding the CPS, there were informal contacts between Conservatives and Liberals. They seem to have broken down over the personality of Ted Heath. On the case for removing Heath, Butler and Kavanagh observe: 'Some advisers thought that it was essential if the unity theme was to be made credible. One brave Shadow Minister did raise the subject with Mr Heath and was met with a blunt "*Et tu, Brute?*"'

Meanwhile conviction politics was taking shape at the Centre for Policy Studies, which was building up a tiny staff, and even beginning to pay them. The existence of the Centre was formally announced by Joseph in a speech on 22 June in Upminster. He emphasised that its mission was to learn from the economic experience of other industrialised countries.

> Compare our position today with that of our neighbours in Germany, Sweden, Holland, France. They are no more talented than we are. Yet, compared with them, we have the longest working hours, the lowest pay and the lowest production per head. We have the highest taxes and the lowest investment. We have the least prosperity, the most poor and the lowest pensions.

The only conceivable basis for prosperity rested on 'a healthy competitive private sector – a market economy within a framework of humane laws and institutions'.

The Upminster speech was recognised as rocking the boat, as putting too much stress on the theory of the market economy at a time when the party establishment wanted not to get involved in too much theory. The speech was recognised as a significant political event. The political correspondent of the *Daily Telegraph*, Sir Harry Boyne, got in touch with Sherman to point out that from the Centre's point of view they might have done better if they had circulated the full text in advance. The fact that such advice was necessary indicated how the Joseph campaign at this stage was not marked by the kind of professionalism that an American politician in his position would have taken for granted.

Meanwhile the parliamentary situation was on a knife-edge. MPs went off on holiday at the end of July knowing the odds must be on having an election before they met again. During August (the month, incidentally, when Richard Nixon resigned, to prove the fragility of politics in the Western world, if that were necessary) Britain's three main parties worked on their manifestos, dealing as best they could with the question of how much, in each case, they were prepared to co-operate with others.

Heath finally came down firmly on the side of 'national unity' to the extent of a pledge that if he won the election, even with a clear majority, he would bring non-Conservatives into his ministry. The Conservative manifesto was already in proof form when he took this decision, but the pledge was written into the draft on 3 September.

Two days later the extent of the disunity in the party, and the part played by the Centre in fostering it, became all too clear, in Joseph's next speech, in Preston. As it had taken shape during the early summer, the Centre scarcely looked like a power to start a revolution. By the late summer, it was ready for a major attack. The Preston speech on 5 September 1974, which turned monetarism from an academic into a major political issue, was the most important speech in Joseph's career, and one of the seminal speeches in political history.

When the party leadership got wind of what was happening, Joseph was asked in Shadow Cabinet not to make his speech. It was clear that effectively it would disown much of the economic policy of the previous government, and thus challenge much of Heath's current policy – and this with another election just around the corner. Joseph replied that he felt bound to express his doubts about the Heath policies publicly since he had been denied the internal reassessment of policy that he had asked for. Heath, who could have forbidden the speech, merely stipulated that the text be vetted by colleagues: it was apparently mutually agreed that responsibility for vetting should fall on Geoffrey Howe and Margaret Thatcher. There were two significant points here: first, that Heath felt unable to assert greater authority; and, second, that he did not realise how close these two colleagues were to Joseph's thinking – the alterations they suggested to the Preston speech were in fact minimal. Once again it was proved how the leadership in 1974 did not realise that Joseph was speaking for more than a cranky minority.

When it was eventually published, as one of the major texts of Thatcherism, the speech – given the title 'Inflation Is Caused by Governments' – read as a polished piece of work, which was remarkable, considering how many pens had contributed to it and how much midnight oil burned at Wilfred Street. It was largely Sherman's work. Alan Walters had helped. Samuel Brittan of the *Financial Times* – no Tory but one of the gurus of monetarism – gave advice. Draft after draft was passed around for comment.

It opened, without preamble, on an apocalyptic note: 'Inflation is threatening to destroy our society. . . . The distress and unemployment that will follow unless the trend is stopped will be catastrophic.' There was a minimally polite reference to colleagues: 'Mr Heath and Mr Carr [the Shadow Chancellor] and all of us say that inflation is the most important issue before the country.' So far so good. But the speech went farther than Heath and Carr would have done in accepting the monetarist interpretation of inflation: 'Incomes policy alone as a way to abate inflation caused by excessive money supply is like trying to stop water coming out of a leaky hose without turning off the tap; if you stop one hole, it will find two others.' Inflation was now raging – as a result, Joseph believed, although he did not say so in so many words, of the 'Barber boom'. 'Why did successive governments for the last score years, led by well-intentioned and intelligent people advised by conscientious officials and economists, take a course which led inexorably and predictably to the present nightmare?' The answer was the fear that jobs would be destroyed unless money was pumped into supporting industries which were out of date:

> Our post-war boom began under the shadow of the 1930s. We were haunted by the fear of long-term mass unemployment, the grim, hopeless dole queues and towns which died.
>
> So we talked ourselves into believing that these gaunt, tight-lipped men in caps and mufflers were round the corner, and tailored our policy to match these imaginary conditions. For imaginary is what they were.

There followed the section of the speech that was to look sadly complacent a few years later when his monetarist theories were put into practice. What he said at Preston was in effect a continuation of the theme in his maiden speech, years before, that workers had nothing to fear from industrial change:

> Since the war until this present critical period there has been virtually no unemployment on Keynesian terms on a national as opposed to a

regional scale. . . . Indeed, for much of the time we have had negative real unemployment, that is a shortage of labour – what you might call fuller-than-full employment.

To understand the concept of 'fuller-than-full employment', one had to look, of course, beyond the crude unemployment figures. One had to disregard workers between jobs – what Keynes called 'frictional' unemployment; then there were the unemployables, the 'voluntary' unemployed who regarded spells between jobs as others might regard holidays, and retired people who still kept their names on the unemployment register. That left the 'real' figure of unemployed: 'During the post-war period, their numbers will have fluctuated between 100,000 and 300,000 or so. They tend to be unskilled, semi-skilled or less skilled, older than average, and a substantial proportion of them are in the less prosperous areas.' In this section of the Preston speech analysing the nature of British unemployment he was setting out to counter allegations that 'monetarism' meant losing jobs: 'Let me emphasise that I am not saying, have never said and do not believe that we need a certain level of unemployment to avoid inflation. . . . A healthy economy in a world with normal trade conditions should sustain full employment. . . .' Some jobs would disappear, but others would be created by the health of the economy; and some displaced workers would find jobs 'in the public utilities which are crying out for more staff'. 'This prescription will not be easy nor enjoyable. But after a couple of years we should be on to a sounder basis and be able to move forward again. . . . If I had to give a personal guess about the total time horizon of a successful anti-inflation policy, I would say three or four years.'

His reply to the current talk of a government of national unity came in the peroration: 'We, the Conservatives, are not without blemish, I freely admit; but how much of this derives from bi-partisanship, from middle-of-the-road policies, from confusing a distinctive Conservative approach with dogmatism?'

This was a flouting of the party line by a leading member of the Shadow Cabinet at a time when it was known that the next election could only be a few weeks away. The colleagues were apprehensive. Jim Prior has recorded, in *A Balance of Power*:

> A number of us tried to stop Keith giving his speech. I even had a word with Margaret Thatcher, who by then seemed to have become one of Keith's followers: 'You know this is a disastrous speech – can't you stop him giving it?' Margaret replied that it was the work of Alfred Sherman: she felt that Keith did not always understand the political impact of arguments, but that she did not have much influence over him.

*

The impact of the Preston speech was twofold. It was a challenge, at the highest level, to Heath's leadership. The fact that Joseph got away with it – in the party that rates loyalty so highly – was a tribute to his reputation for integrity. It was a discontented party, and there had been mutterings ever since the February election about changing leaders. He had belled the cat; and, arguably, there was nobody else in the party who could have done it.

The other half of the impact of Preston was in the message of monetarism. The Centre had now got its public relations act together. Enough news had been leaked in advance to allow the speech to cast its shadow before it: the media knew that something big was coming. The text was circulated in advance. If this was battle, it was like one of those classic naval battles where the gunboats are seen taking up their positions on the horizon and the world waits for the explosions to start. The formality of the occasion was another reason why it would have been imprudent for Heath to stop it. Too many people knew.

The coverage of the Preston speech was spectacular. Joseph expressed himself amazed when the quality newspapers printed the text in full (which, in terms of postwar newspaper practice, put the speech in the Winston Churchill class). His henchmen were less surprised. They simply knew they had pulled off a competent public relations operation.

It was not just the quality papers. Editors of the tabloids decided that it was possible to make news out of the political philosophy of the Tory Party. The *Sun* devoted two of its pages – a vast proportion of that paper's verbal content – to Preston.

Comment was mixed. *The Times* believed that 'the main lines were unquestionably right'; it saw Joseph as carrying on the campaign 'once associated with the name of Enoch Powell', but the Joseph analysis seemed preferable to Powell's 'because it shows a deeper understanding of the difficulties of the argument'.

Powell himself was sardonic at the sight of this belated acknowledgement of economic arguments he had been using for years: 'I have heard of death-bed repentance. Perhaps it would be more appropriate to refer to post-mortem repentance.'

For the Labour Party, Michael Foot, who was now Secretary of State for Employment, described the speech as one of 'rare intellectual distinction', but also of 'reckless courage'. Denis Healey said the nation could at least be grateful that the issue of the next election had been made clear; Healey added, not being a man to miss an opportunity to make mischief, that Joseph's views seemed to have more support in the Conservative Party than 'the demoralised mumblings of his colleagues'.

After Preston, the policy arguments that had been simmering inside the

Tory Party now had a focus, but the debate was shortly interrupted: within a couple of weeks Wilson announced the date of the election, 10 October. It had been the shortest Parliament since 1681.

The issue of monetarism did not go away during the election campaign. Inflation was a grim reality for all voters. The monetarist interpretation was helped along by a broadcast by Milton Friedman, who told his British audience that of course there was no mystery about why they were suffering from the miseries of inflation: it wasn't the present government's doing – it was simply that the Heath government had churned out too much money, and the excess money-supply of eighteen months ago was now showing its effect in inflation, precisely as the economic textbooks said it should.

In the campaign, price controls and pay policies were discussed, but Conservative candidates reported that voters on the doorstep, without being able to quote Friedman, were also talking about dealing with inflation by 'turning the tap off'.

An odd feature of the Tory campaign in October 1974 was the performance of Margaret Thatcher. Mrs Thatcher was Opposition spokesman on the environment, a remit that covered housing and local government (and local rates), and she presented a policy which was at variance with the financial rectitude that her Centre for Policy Studies was promoting. She announced that a Tory government would provide funds to protect house-owners from the worst of inflation by limiting mortgage rates to 9½ per cent – a very generous figure in the light of the current inflation rate. The reason she found herself doing so was described years later by Hugo Young in the *Guardian*:

> In the summer [of 1974], at a meeting in Ted Heath's house in Wilton Street, he urged upon his shadow Environment Secretary the desirability of rates abolition as an eye-catching idea to lift the Tory profile, and also suggested a mortgage ceiling of even less than 9.5 per cent. Those present recall her fiercely arguing against each policy, and especially against the irresponsibility of advancing them both together. It was, they say, a brilliant performance, matched only by the dramatic bravura with which, at the election, she advocated both ideas.

The episode was perhaps an indication that at that stage her grasp of the theory of monetarism was less sophisticated than Joseph's. A view from the left came in the *New Statesman*'s 'Election Diary', which noted that, as a result of Edward Heath's slackening grip on his party, Tory policy 'oscillates wildly between the lavish spending promises of Mrs Thatcher and the austere Powellism of Keith Joseph'. The irony of this comment is that the author of that 'Diary' was Paul Johnson, who was soon to move from the left to the right and whose later writing about Mrs Thatcher was to approach the hagiographic. He was one of the more spectacular converts of the next few years.

Aside from the 9½ per cent mortgages, it was noted during the campaign, however, that she, along with Joseph, was notably unenthusiastic about the party line on the subject of a government of national unity.

Presenting himself to the Leeds Tories as their candidate, Keith Joseph introduced a note of whimsy. He recalled how, back in 1956, they had chosen a keen young man:

> But was he not inexperienced? When you first chose me, we disagreed about almost everything. As the years have gone by, we have got closer together. What I had in those years was book-learning, but what you had was life experience. Bit by bit, I have come to see the book-learning in the light of the judgement of life.

Heath campaigned on his pledge to try to create a government of national unity. He even set out the timetable he would observe once he won: on Friday, once the election result was clear, he would see the Queen; on Saturday he would consult with the leaders of the Labour and Liberal parties; the following week they would get down to serious discussions on how to deal with the national crisis.

The 'national unity' dream caught at least a part of the national imagination. One newspaper columnist, on the eve of the election, set out his personal choice of a national government. He would have had Shirley Williams as Prime Minister; Keith Joseph as Chancellor; Jeremy Thorpe as Home Secretary; Margaret Thatcher as Social Services Secretary; Enoch Powell as Minister for the Environment; Edward Heath as Secretary for Industry; and Len Murray (TUC General Secretary) as Secretary for Transport. But on polling day Wilson scraped together an overall majority for Labour. Coalitions and governments of all the talents were off the agenda for several years.

In Leeds, Joseph's majority was reduced to 5,628. The Labour vote had stayed firm since February; his figure had fallen from 20,822 to 18,749.

The election had been the fourth national confrontation between Wilson and Heath. Heath had won only one of them, and lost three. His replacement was now only a matter of time.

CHAPTER ELEVEN

THE TWO UNMENTIONABLES

Had I become party leader, it would have been a disaster for the party, country and for me. . . . I know my own capacities. Adequate for some jobs, but not for others.

Lord Joseph, 1987

The process, sometimes painful, sometimes illogical, sometimes ludicrous, by which the Conservative Party got rid of its leader during the winter of 1974–5 marked the start of the Thatcher era, with all the implications of a change of national culture which that implied. But the leadership debate was scarcely a battle between rival interpretations of Conservative philosophy. For all the talk of monetarism, of incomes policies, of the case for coalition, the overriding factor in the leadership battle was simply the desire to replace Ted Heath.

Heath still had important backers, he had the loyalty of almost the whole Shadow Cabinet; but, as one MP put it, by the autumn of 1974 the real division in the Parliamentary Conservative Party was not between left and right, or monetarists and non-monetarists, but between those who wanted Heath to go at once and those who wanted merely to give him notice that he would be replaced as soon as the party had decided whom they wanted to lead them into the next election. There was no obvious successor at that time.

The last government's U-turn had upset many Conservatives. Heath's 'managerial' style, which had seemed right for the sixties, now looked to be a recipe for failure; and he was guilty of the unforgivable crime of being a loser. Perhaps most important, his personality, once a great strength, had now made him many enemies. And he tried his friends sorely. The stories of his lack of tact and grace were legion. Three backbenchers long remembered being at dinner at the Commons, when the Members reassembled after the October election, with Jim Prior. The ex-Prime Minister entered, exchanged a few words with his colleague Prior and went off without a word to any of the others. Prior shook his head sadly. What could you do with a man like that? Here were a group of his back-benchers just back from the hustings where, not without difficulty, they had been loyally defending the Heath record – and he didn't even say thank you.

There were other backbenchers who felt equally piqued at never getting any thanks, and gave their votes, a few months later, to Margaret Thatcher. These were anti-Ted, not pro-Margaret, votes.

But the leadership issue was well launched long before the new House met. On the Monday morning, 14 October, after the Tory defeat in the election, the executive of the 1922 Committee met at the home of the 1922's chairman, Edward du Cann. The name of du Cann himself had already been mentioned, as it happened, as a possible successor to Heath: he was a powerful backbencher, with a higher profile than most 1922 chairmen had had; added to that was a high profile as a City businessman.

The media predictably took a ghoulish interest in how far the 1922 Committee would go in seeking to get rid of Heath. The comings and goings at the du Cann house that Monday were recorded in detail. The executive decided to continue their discussions the following day, more discreetly, switching the meeting-place to du Cann's office in Milk Street in the City. Friends of Heath at Tory Central Office – this was symptomatic of the atmosphere in the party – saw no reason to make things easy for the committee and tipped off the media. The 1922 officials, emerging from the office on Tuesday, 15 October, found the photographers waiting for them, and the next day's newspapers were full of gleeful stories about the 'Milk Street Mafia'.

The Heath entourage had good reason to see the 1922 as effectively an anti-Heath conspiracy. All the signals they were getting from the backbenchers were that Heath was a liability. The committee's problems were, first, how and when to persuade him to go; second, if he refused to go voluntarily, whether a realistic candidate could emerge to stand against him, given the famous Conservative instinct of loyalty. The likeliest candidate, Willie Whitelaw, would never stand against his colleague; if Heath stepped down (as Douglas-Home had done ten years earlier after being defeated), it would have been a different matter.

There were at least two other Heath-men from the 1970–4 government being mentioned at this stage: Jim Prior and Robert Carr; then there was du Cann, who had the advantage that his ministerial experience had ended ten years before, so he was untarred by association with the Heath government; there was Joseph, who was *sui generis*; and the name of Margaret Thatcher had been mentioned but not widely or very seriously.

Years later, Keith Joseph frequently emphasised that he 'had never taken himself seriously'.

But when people urged me, I flirted with the idea. . . . At that point I tended to dismiss the idea. I had my area of concern . . . very narrow. No foreign experience at all. No defence experience. A few people approached me. I don't recall taking it as sensible or likely. Three or four people spoke to me, as far as I remember. I certainly didn't make any effort whatsoever, nor would it have been *suitable* in my very modest assessment of my own suitability.

There is evidence that he talked in the same self-deprecatory way in 1974. To several people he mentioned particularly his lack of expertise on Northern Ireland (1974 was a year when the IRA were tragically active with their bombs). On the other hand, lack of experience was less important than it might seem: anyone who had worked with Joseph knew that he was a quick learner, far quicker than most of his rivals. The candidate most obviously lacking in experience was Mrs Thatcher, whose only senior post up to that time had been at the Department of Education.

The self-deprecation may have caused some colleagues to decide against him as a leader. Some may have taken him at his word. Others felt that the very fact that he talked himself down showed he lacked the steel needed in a leader. But he was certainly flattered when the 'three or four people' spoke to him. And he must have taken the possibility of the leadership seriously if only because he was a man who took most things seriously. If proof were needed, he provided it when he received this letter from a young MP, dated 15 October, the day of the 'Milk Street Mafia' meeting:

I dined with Geoffrey Howe last evening and had the impression from him that if the situation was to arise, you might be reluctant to allow your name to go forward as a candidate for the Leadership of the Party.

This note is just to say how very much many of the younger Members of Parliament hope that you will allow your name to go forward.

I enclose a copy of a letter which I have sent to my own Whip. I know that this letter reflects the views of many of our colleagues in the House.

If Joseph had wanted to discourage talk about him becoming leader, this was the chance to do it. In fact, when he replied the following day, it was in these terms:

Thank you for taking the trouble to write to me yesterday such an encouraging letter.

If Ted does decide to resign, I shall certainly allow my name to go forward, but of course he has not yet made any decision.

Your kind references to me in your letter to the Whip are most heartening. I shall do my best, whatever happens, to live up to the comments you make.

This was becomingly modest, but it was a letter from a serious candidate – grateful for 'encouraging' and 'heartening' expressions of support. So we have to assume that, at least on 16 October, Barkis was willin'. If Geoffrey Howe (who was eventually a candidate himself) was giving colleagues the impression that there might be reluctance, Joseph was ready to contradict it in the most specific terms. His willingness to stand was not in question. The question mark hung only over whether Ted would decide to resign.

At the Centre for Policy Studies in Wilfred Street, there were certainly no doubts that he was a leadership candidate. In a sense, their work was a nonsense unless he did stand.

So he knew that when the House reassembled the following week the new Parliamentary Conservative Party would be sizing him up as a potential leader. The realisation added to the anxiety that he would have felt anyhow about returning to Westminster. He was out of touch. Much of his energy between the two elections of 1974 had been expended away from the precincts of the House. In any case he had never been involved in the kind of tea-room gossip at Westminster that would have given him a feel about which way the party was moving.

He did know, though, that some of his colleagues considered that the speeches he had been making had scored own-goals against the party. For that reason he had been happy to have another desk to work at, away from the House, in Wilfred Street.

Assuming that he was a candidate, what happened next? This sort of thing did not come naturally to him – but, then, it did not come naturally to anyone in the Conservative Party. This was only the second leadership election the Tories had had, and at the first the process was set in motion when Douglas-Home stood down voluntarily. There was no counterpart in the Tory Party of what is taken for granted in American contests for office, where Democrats campaign openly against Democrats and Republicans against Republicans in primaries, and then shake hands before the real election.

What the Conservatives had always been good at was fixing things quietly behind closed doors. But that was not Joseph's way, either. When he was asked, fourteen years later, whom he was consulting at this stage, his reply was:

Oh, no one. Not a soul. It may be unusual, but I didn't, as it were, seek or encourage or have political intimates. I had political *allies*, on different subjects. I didn't take any of this [the leadership] seriously enough to seek advice when my name was being bandied around. I wasn't a lone horse in the sense that I keep myself away from others, but in the sense that I was a leadership candidate I had sought no allies.

He had no recollection of having sought advice from his co-founder at the Centre, Mrs Thatcher.

With such a man, it is easy to see how frustrating his would-be allies must have found him. It is also easy to imagine that such conversations as he engaged in about the leadership may have had a slightly unreal quality.

Meanwhile, word got around that there was another great speech on the way. This, it was said, was to be specifically his 'bid for the leadership'. It was to be made at the dinner of the Edgbaston Conservative Association in Birmingham, on Saturday, 19 October.

As with Preston, the text was released in advance and newspaper leader-writers primed to comment. The day of the week, Saturday, was important. It would be reported and commented on in the Sunday papers, and the Monday-morning papers would take it all a stage further.

This should have been his great day. It turned out to be a nightmare. The press arrangements backfired: if journalists are provided with the full text of a detailed speech, it allows them time for full coverage, but it also gives them the chance to look for 'angles' that make headlines. That happened with the Birmingham speech even before it was delivered.

But the speech is worth looking at for itself before looking at the headlines. It was designed to show that Joseph's 'conversion to Conservatism' went far beyond monetary rectitude. His passion for the quality of life, which had been the hallmark of the first part of his career, was unchanged, but the emphasis was now shifted away from the collective community, to the individual and the family.

The Birmingham speech, on the moral and spiritual state of the nation, was largely the work of Sherman – but not wholly his work, which was part of the problem. It opened in relaxed style with a funny story ' – apocryphal I am sure – about the Regular Army officer, at the end of the First World War, saying "Thank goodness, now the war is over we can get back to real soldiering".' Now that the general election was over, Joseph said, we could 'get back to real politics: Tory politics'. Politicians had an unhealthy preoccupation with economics: the public knew that economics was not everything. 'Would it not now be better to approach the public as whole men rather than economic men?' His theme was 'the tone of national life'. On the face of it, this was good politics. It met the obvious criticism that a monetarist government must be unfeeling and amoral. But a moral theme would also tap a great reservoir of conservative feeling in the country, among people who were not interested in monetarist or any other kind of economics but who in 1974 were distressed by what they saw when they looked at the schools and universities, and society generally, in the aftermath of the Swinging Sixties.

Self-discipline, said Joseph, had been out of fashion since the war. There was now a 'new establishment' which had preferred 'the permissive society and at the same time the collectivised society. . . . Are we to be destroyed from inside – a country which successfully repelled and destroyed Philip of Spain, Napoleon, the Kaiser, Hitler – are we to be destroyed by ideas, mischievous, wrongheaded, debilitating, yet seductive because they are fashionable and promise so much on the cheap?' His more sophisticated political friends might shy at such an uninhibited appeal to what in the United States was called the moral majority; but it may have rung true in humbler homes. Conversion to 'Conservatism' had, in that sense, moved him down-market as a politician.

He was not afraid to devote a substantial section of the speech to the best-known British spokeswoman of the moral majority, Mrs Mary Whitehouse:

> I do not accept all her ideas; she will not accept all mine. Yet we can see in her a shining example of what one person can do singlehandedly when inspired by faith and compassion. . . . Look at the scale of the opposing forces. On the one side, the whole of the new establishment with their sharp words and sneers poised; against them stood this one middle-aged woman. . . . Her book, *Who Does She Think She Is?* took its title from the outraged cry of an acolyte of the new hierarchy, who asked how an unknown woman dare speak up against the BBC, the educators and false shepherds.

Intellectually this was distancing himself, as it happened, from some of the most vigorous propagandists of free-market economics. His friend Sam Brittan, for instance, who had helped with the Preston speech, was instinctively a social libertarian as well as an economic liberal.

The Birmingham speech portrayed the anti-socialist cause and the anti-libertarian cause as fitting into a coherent whole, and worthy of a crusade: 'We must fight the battle of ideas in every school, university, publication, committee, TV studio even if we have to struggle for our toehold there. . . . We shall need intellectual as well as moral courage.'

That was as good a peroration as he could have wished, and if he had stuck to Sherman's draft he would have left it there. But he went on to illustrate the need for courage: 'I shall confine myself to one example,' he told the Edgbaston Conservatives, 'because I have been talking longer than you may have bargained for already.'

He drew the single example from an area where he was convinced he was on sure ground: the cycle of deprivation.

During the summer, he had been shown an article in *Poverty*, the magazine of the Child Poverty Action Group, and he met its authors: Arthur and Margaret Wynn. Mrs Wynn was author of a number of books on deprivation as a threat to family life. Her husband, after retiring from the Government Scientific Service, had been carrying out statistical work for her researches. The article in *Poverty* set out evidence indicating how poorer families produced larger families; the middle classes were better-organised at using birth control.

This fitted in with all Joseph's work on the cycle of deprivation, but it appeared to reveal a disturbing trend, not hitherto noticed, in the changing balance of the population. After reading the article he sent it to the Government Central Statistical Office for their comments. Their initial response was that it seemed to indicate nothing new, but they promised to produce detailed figures. The figures had not arrived in time for the speech. Relying largely on the Wynns' article, he expressed the message – this was his 'one example' of a social trend that called for courage to deal with – in these terms:

> The balance of our population, our human stock, is threatened. . . . A high and rising proportion of children are being born to mothers least fitted to bring children into the world and bring them up. . . . Some are of low intelligence, most of low educational attainment. They are unlikely to be able to give children the stable emotional background, the consistent combination of love and firmness, which are more important than riches. They are producing problem children. . . . Yet these mothers, the under-20s in many cases, single parents, from classes four and five, are now producing a third of all births.

He cited the *Poverty* article as showing that social groups four and five (semi-skilled and unskilled workers and their families) made far less use of birth control. Here were very large numbers of vulnerable people at the mercy of the permissive climate.

> Yet proposals to extend birth control facilities to these classes of people, particularly the young unmarried girls, the potential young unmarried mothers, evoke entirely understandable moral opposition. But which is the lesser evil. . . ?

The substance of this argument was no different from his enthusiasm a couple of years earlier for breaking the cycle of deprivation. Later, much later, he could laugh wryly at the folly of having brought together in a few sentences the two topics on which the British are supposed to be most hypocritical: sex and social class.

That apart, he had made two serious blunders in drafting the speech, a speech he knew was going to be fully reported, and that he *wanted* to be fully reported, and fully analysed, phrase by phrase. One was to have failed to check the statistical background – and over the next few weeks the public were to be bombarded with figures that showed up statistical shortcomings in his argument. The other mistake was to introduce a weasel phrase like 'human stock'. Somebody at the Centre should have stopped him using 'human stock'. (From now on the CPS staff went through his speeches with a fine-tooth comb to get rid of words like that.) But this was very much his own part of the speech: Sherman had advised against putting it in. On the cycle of deprivation he was his own man. Maybe it was Joseph's Jewish background that subconsciously blinded him to the Nazi, the *Herrenvolk* connotation of the word 'stock' when he was going on to talk about birth control.

The fact that he had a serious problem on his hands emerged at lunchtime on the Saturday, hours before the speech was to be delivered. The press, with their advance texts, were on to him. He tried to reach Sherman on the phone for advice on tactics, but Sherman was away on a speaking engagement of his own.

The *Evening Standard* was first off the mark. The Saturday edition, bought largely for its sports coverage, treated the speech, not yet delivered, as the second most important story of the day. (The top story was 'Spurs Win the Crunch'.) Below that came the news item that set the tone of the next few weeks:

SIR KEITH IN 'STOP BABIES' SENSATION

Sir Keith Joseph will make a sensational speech tonight about the decline in moral standards in Britain. One of his controversial proposals is for much more extensive use of birth control by people of low intelligence and morality.

By the time he had got to Birmingham to make the speech he tried to limit the damage by inserting a few sentences 'in view of misunderstandings', but the dangerous words were still there.

In fairness, the Sunday newspapers next morning did not ignore the broader issues of the Birmingham speech, but they regarded the birth control issue, to use the fashionable media word of the time, as the 'sexy story'.

Comment gushed in. This was 'castrate or conform', said a Labour MP. Over the next few days the media projected thousands of words of reaction, from politicians, bishops, sociologists, educationists, family planners. The

A father to live up to: Sir Samuel Joseph as Lord Mayor with Winston Churchill (Lady Joseph behind).

Growing up between the wars: the privileged child.

The artillery officer who came home determined to lose weight.

Rising star in the Macmillan team of the sixties.

'I didn't have a philosophy. I was just a "more" man. I used to go to bed at night counting the number of houses I'd destroyed and the number of planning approvals that had been given . . . . Just *more*.'

'Heath had the right ideas on management . . . . I remember the sheer excitement when he won.' Joseph with the new party leader in 1965.

Campaigning in Leeds in the October 1974 election, when he was a front-runner for the party leadership.

It all went wrong after the speech on birth control – but the bulk of the letters flowing in were friendly.

By the autumn of 1974, relations with the party leader were strained. Heath had just been rejected by the electorate for the second time in seven months.

Mrs Thatcher in the early days as Leader of the Opposition with Keith Joseph, recognised as policy co-ordinator and chief campaigner in changing the intellectual climate.

The 1976 conference: the Tories were now moving away fast from what Heath represented, but it was considered important to get a smiling picture of him with the new leader – Keith Joseph at her elbow.

The campus campaign to win youth away from the old 'consensus' politics. Some audiences were huge. This one, at Hatfield Polytechnic, was tiny because protestors had put up notices saying the meeting was cancelled.

Thatcherism takes over – and the steel workers strike. It was Joseph who bore the first brunt of confrontation in state-subsidised industries.

Mrs Thatcher was Keith Joseph's primary concern as he went down the fire escape after the bomb in the Grand Hotel, Brighton. Unlike colleagues, he was careful to take his red box with him.

public were instructed by media commentators on the official definitions of Social Classes I, II, III, IV and V.

At the Department of Social Services, Joseph's old staff were put to work by his successor, Barbara Castle, to produce figures which would pour cold water on the *Poverty* statistics about birth rates among the different classes. Mrs Castle had a speech scheduled for the following Friday in Liverpool, and decided to turn it into a major attack on Joseph, which the media seized on. Her contemporary account went into *The Castle Diaries*:

> It was a rather snooty cleric who greeted me when we arrived late at the rendezvous with the Family Service Council. He was obviously not too pleased at the incursion of the TV. A hurried bit of back-combing by the make-up girl and I was on my feet – and potentially on the air. . . . Surprisingly extensive coverage of my speech on TV. I hadn't expected this. Slept a satisfied and relaxed sleep.

A footnote is worth adding to the part played by the *Evening Standard* on Saturday, 19 October. The following month, its owners, who were going through financial troubles, announced that as a necessary economy the paper would no longer be published on Saturdays.

A lot of people enjoyed themselves with the Birmingham speech. Enoch Powell observed, predictably: 'It's great fun to see somebody else getting into hot water over a speech. I almost wondered if the River Tiber was beginning to roll again.' He claimed to have found the emphasis on morality in the Birmingham speech rather strange: 'After all, in the 1970 Parliament there was not a single resignation from a government which reversed almost every undertaking and promise on which it was elected.'

One attempt to put the fuss into good-humoured perspective came from a commentator not noted for sympathy for the Joseph brand of politics, Alan Watkins. Writing in the *New Statesman* a week after Birmingham, Watkins was indulgent, if patronising:

> In essence he said no more than the Child Poverty Action Group, the Family Planning Association and other estimable bodies have said: that by and large, taking one thing with another, admitting exceptions, conceding that no one can really generalise, least of all about these personal, intimate and, yes, sacred matters, but on the whole – it is not their fault mind you, we are all responsible and let no one cast the first stone – the largest families do seem, somehow, to get born to those least fitted to cope with them. . . .
>
> The national 'stock' is an unfortunate phrase, perhaps; but to me it

is redolent of 19th-century crankiness – vegetarianism, national dress and so forth – rather than of Nazism.

Meanwhile there was ample evidence, not least in Joseph's postbag, that people around the country thoroughly approved of the moral tone of the speech; the outrage was concentrated among professional opinion-makers. To accuse Joseph of committing a self-evidently grievous political blunder was merely to accept the folklore of the sophisticated classes.

Something else that passed into folklore was that immediately after Birmingham a shattered Joseph instantly withdrew from the leadership contest. In fact he remained a candidate for another month.

At the CPS office in Wilfred Street on the Monday morning after the speech, all was indeed gloom, and it was at this point, rather than in choosing the words used in Birmingham, that his judgement could be seriously called in question. His colleagues were unable to persuade him to follow the old political maxim, 'Never apologise, never explain'. He apologised profusely for not making himself clearer. He explained at length, with statements and press interviews and a letter that filled more than a column in *The Times*, complaining about 'grotesque misrepresentation'. Apart from anything else, he was deeply hurt that he could be so misunderstood after his long years of trying to do something for the underprivileged. A different kind of politician would have shrugged his shoulders, told himself it was a rough old world, and assumed that the storm would have blown over within the week.

He agreed, on the morrow of Birmingham, to expose himself to questioning by the doyen of newspaper interviewers, Terry Coleman, then working for the *Daily Mail*.

> Sir Keith was, I believe, a little distressed. . . . 'I thought that I still had some, ah, repute from my work at the Department of Social Services.' He paused, and then, a trace bitterly, picked up the pamphlets on his desk, and then, dropping them, said as if to himself, and as if that was all the thanks he had received for them: 'Thank you very much for your studies.'

On the party leadership, he proposed to go on avoiding the question whether or not he regarded himself as a candidate, but Coleman persisted.

> Well, if he were a candidate, his speech would not have helped him? – 'Jolly clumsy,' he said.
> And it would have delighted Mr Heath? – 'If he regarded me with any seriousness, and thought I might be a candidate, certainly. It's a very damaging speech, as it has come out; it wasn't intended to do more than advance the cause in which I believe.'. . .

I said he sounded disappointed, and disenchanted. He said: 'I think I may have damaged – things in which I rather deeply believed. I hope not.'

Some of those who had been most enthusiastic about Joseph after the Preston speech were to be heard expressing the wish that he could have stuck to economics. At the end of a cruel week, *The Economist*, which had been and still was a supporter of Ted Heath, was magisterial. After noting that after the election this was the moment to search for 'policies that have deeper roots than the cheap mortgages offered by Mrs Thatcher', the paper commented sourly:

The trouble Sir Keith takes to leave no confusions undispersed, no misunderstandings of his pronouncements unexplained, has become well known ever since, after the Tories' February defeat, he was lumbered with the roving job of refining, redefining – or re-somethinging – Conservatism. . . . A political sage must be clever as well as holy.

Nevertheless at the end of that week Joseph was giving a long television interview in which, although he still said there was no leadership contest until Ted Heath chose to resign, he said enough to indicate that he was still in the running: Sir Keith Joseph, reported the *Daily Mail*, had 'swept away virtually all pretence about his own ambition'.

CHAPTER TWELVE

IF YOU DON'T, I WILL

Infirm of purpose! Give me the daggers.

Shakespeare, *Macbeth*

The Members of the new House of Commons elected in the October 1974 election were now assembling at Westminster, and an important figure moved on to the stage – or, rather, moved powerfully behind the scenes: Airey Neave. Airey Neave's view of Ted Heath was said to have been firmly fixed at the time when Heath was Chief Whip under Macmillan and Neave a junior minister. He had to resign because of minor heart trouble. The story was that when he reported his medical problem to Heath the Chief Whip had tersely commented, in effect, 'That's the end of your political career, then,' and Heath had acquired yet another enemy.

Neave had never taken much part in the party's ideological debates. His skills lay elsewhere, and owed something to his distinguished war record, when he escaped from Colditz and thereafter helped, at MI9, to organise the escape of shot-down airmen from occupied Europe. It had been a job that called for ingenuity, boldness, and circumspection to prevent information reaching the enemy. He had an engaging personality, but with a suggestion of mystery and secrecy behind it. His skill at keeping secrets was soon to be a major factor in winning the leadership for Margaret Thatcher as her campaign manager.

But Mrs Thatcher was not actually the first horse for which, so to speak, Neave offered his services as trainer. He first tried to advance the candidature of Edward du Cann, but it soon emerged that the party was not ready to pick a man with such a high profile – a controversial profile – in the City. Neave's eyes then turned to Joseph. Whether a specific offer was ever relayed to Joseph is not clear. The two were not really on the same wavelength. (Joseph was a man who was at home in an atmosphere of privacy, not of secrecy.)

In so far as there was a Joseph campaign, the nearest thing he had to a campaign manager was his old PPS, David Mitchell. At the Department of Social Services, Mitchell had become a Joseph devotee. He now proved his loyalty; but, as with all his political helpers, Joseph confined him to a large extent in one compartment of his political activity. Mitchell had not been consulted, for instance, about the Preston speech.

After the election, Joseph remarked to Mitchell that *somebody* had to stand against Ted Heath if there was to be a change to the policies set out in Preston. Mitchell took this as authority to act on his master's behalf. He equipped himself with a card index and made soundings. It was all appropriately informal, but he arranged for his man to be available to individuals or groups of MPs who wanted to hear his views.

There was no doubt that Mrs Thatcher was an important Joseph backer. The idea of a Thatcher candidacy had indeed been floated by a small number of people, including journalists at the *Spectator*, who would have liked to campaign for her; the *Spectator*'s then political editor, Patrick Cosgrave, has recorded how she 'practically ordered them' to support Joseph.

Where else did the Joseph camp draw its support from?

Much of Westminster comment since the Preston speech had taken for granted that the Tories, if they ditched Heath, had a choice broadly between Willie Whitelaw, the 'moderate', and Keith Joseph, the 'right-winger'. (Part of the case put forward on behalf of du Cann was that he represented a compromise between these two.) One point that emerged on Mitchell's card index, however, was the volume of support enjoyed by Joseph on the liberal wing of the party. This reflected the goodwill he had built up over the years with his interest in social services, not to mention the amount of money he had directed into the Welfare State as a minister until eight short months ago. That support, added to the right-wing backing he attracted – and added to the urgency felt by many Members about the need for change – put Joseph in a powerful position in October 1974 even after the Birmingham episode.

The position of Tory right-wingers could not be seen in isolation from the departure of the grand old man of sound money, Enoch Powell. Powell's supporters in the party had kept candles alight for him for years. He had often embarrassed them, but he had provided a sort of benchmark for one important strand of Conservatism. The idea of his returning to lead the party had been no more than a pipe-dream for years. Now even the pipe-dream had been blown away in 1974. Having opted out of the February election, Powell in October had returned to the Commons as an Ulster Unionist, as Member for South Down. Forthright individualism was one thing in the Tory Party; Ulster politics was going a bit far, even for Enoch. The old Powellites were in the poignant position of parents who have been clutching at the hope that their son, posted missing, will turn up, and then hear that the body has been found: nothing has changed in reality, but there is a lot of emotional adjustment called for.

Joseph was picking up the old Powellite mantle, and was providing a new benchmark. His Preston speech provided a respectable theoretical framework for the many Tories who simply felt instinctively that Ted Heath had got the economy wrong. The Tories might be the Stupid Party, but they could respect, and use, people able to express plausible rationalisations for their gut feelings.

There was another point about Joseph. The monetarist case, the anti-Heath case and the case for a radical reappraisal of Conservative policy might have been argued as vigorously by others, but it would have been easier to have written them off as wild men on the fringes. Joseph was an eminently respectable Tory. To borrow the phraseology of electing a new Pope, he was manifestly *papabile*. There was a reputation for eccentricity, perhaps, but the gossip-writers had not begun to build it up in the way they were about to do in the later seventies; and he certainly did not have the sinister strangeness of an Enoch Powell. He was proof, apart from anything else, that 'right-wing' financial policies could come from somebody with a social conscience.

It was not a question of being universally regarded as a saintly character. He had plenty of enemies on the political left who regarded him as representing the worst features of Conservatism. And there were radical Tories who admired the Preston speech but had serious doubts about his abilities to put his theory into practice. One such was Ferdinand Mount (a future head of Mrs Thatcher's Policy Unit at Downing Street), who wrote a newspaper article about this time suggesting that Joseph's celebrated powers of analysis fell short of political genius: 'Sir Keith, despite his brilliance, is inclined when in doubt to call for more paper as looser men will call for more wine.'

Nevertheless there was the widest respect for his integrity. If there had not been the two strands to the Joseph candidature – that he represented respectability on the one hand and Tory radicalism on the other – it can be argued that the party would not have chosen the radical path, would not have taken a turn to the right, as it did eventually by electing Mrs Thatcher. The cards were being dealt one by one that autumn into Mrs Thatcher's hands, and several were dealt to her by Joseph. Without him, there would have been two plausible possibilities: the Tories would have turned not to her but to one or other of the 'Heath men' of the Shadow Cabinet as leader; or – despite all the discontent in the party – they might have decided to put off their decision until a more obvious leader emerged. In fact what happened was that for a couple of vital months Keith Joseph allowed the party to get used to the idea that they could be radical.

It did not make him popular with the collective leadership of the time – and one of the most interesting parts of the story is that he survived their disapproval for so long. After all, in Tory terms he had done the unmentionable – he had rocked the boat; and the Tory Party had always been good at dealing with boat-rockers, with a quiet word in the right places to destroy their chances of advancement. The party establishment would have been strong enough to do that with anyone else; but, in Joseph, they were confronted with something that threw them off balance. They could never quite get him in their sights. The special quality that had always made him an establishment figure, but never one hundred per cent in the establishment mould, was now a special strength. If he had not been so obviously a gentleman, things might have been different! Or if he had been a different kind of Jew. . . .

Of course there were serious criticisms of him after the Birmingham speech, but it was not really the critics who pushed him out of the leadership race. He pushed himself out of it.

Since Birmingham he had been increasingly tense, and some of those close to him sensed that what really worried him was actually the possibility of success; that he was less worried by the criticisms than by the evidence that people still wanted him to stand as a candidate. He still had not made up his mind: he could rationalise his hesitation by saying that the decision could be put off until Heath chose to stand down, or the party made its own arrangements for holding an election.

At the end of October, Heath was heartened by a poll showing that a majority of Tory constituency chairmen still wanted him to stay on. On 11 November an ORC poll showed that 54 per cent of Conservative voters also backed Heath. The Shadow Cabinet as a whole were warning the party against what Peter Walker in a speech on 3 November called 'hard-line economic policies'. They must beware, he said, of 'retreating into the bunkers and bolt-holes of narrow middle-class politics'. It was neither in the Shadow Cabinet nor in the party in the country, but among backbench Tory MPs that there was explicit demand for change. And they were all too conscious that the Tory tradition of loyalty to a leader militated against change. Somebody had to make a move, but Joseph still temporised.

Then one day at the Centre for Policy Studies – where the staff had a vested interest in the outcome of the leadership battle – there was an instinct that things might have reached a turning-point: the word went round the Wilfred Street office that a determined female voice had been overheard through an open door, saying: 'Well, if you won't stand, I will.'

Joseph remained a potential candidate until Thursday, 21 November – a date, as it happened, when all other events were swept into insignificance, before the day was out, by the worst of all the IRA atrocities, when a bomb went off in a Birmingham pub killing twenty-one people.

What happened earlier that day was recounted, in blow-by-blow terms, by Patrick Cosgrave, in a book he wrote before the 1979 election, *Margaret Thatcher: A Tory and Her Party*. After lunch that day, he records,

> she returned to her tiny, Spartan room on the so-called Shadow Cabinet corridor – one floor above the Chamber of the House and the room of the Leader of the Opposition. There Keith Joseph called on her a little later. He wanted to tell her that he was no longer a candidate for the leadership of the party. His was not the call of one relay runner to another, to whom he was about to pass the torch, but the act of a candidate for a job telling his best and most loyal supporter that he was no longer in the contest, and that he hoped she would not be upset or damaged by his decision to withdraw.

A major theme in the Cosgrave book is the ruthlessness of some of Heath's colleagues. After describing how Joseph told Mrs Thatcher that he had been greatly wounded by public and political reactions to the Birmingham speech, Cosgrave goes on:

> He had suddenly been given a bitter taste of what it was like being out in front in a political struggle, especially against a campaign team as hardened and ruthless as that supporting Heath and, after talking the matter over with his wife, had decided he wanted no part of it.

The following Monday, Mrs Thatcher gave a long interview to the *Daily Mail* in which the last point mentioned by Cosgrave was raised and she answered it thus:

> I don't think it was Keith or his wife who made it [the decision] – I should guess it was a family decision, made by them both. Privacy can be enormously important – and the publicity can have a dreadful impact on the harmony of one's family life. You don't have much of a private life in politics – and it does bring the children into the limelight. But my two children are now 21 and are mature enough to stand up to it.

This revealed more about Thatcher, perhaps, than it did about Joseph. She was now a committed – not just a potential – candidate, and aware of the need to show her confidence in her own resilience. Cosgrave, who was close to her campaign, quotes her as remarking at a private lunch shortly afterwards: 'I saw how they broke Keith, but they won't break me.'

Certainly there was a great deal of nastiness in and around the Conservative Party that autumn, as there tends to be when the sniff of revolution is in the air: on the one hand, the defensive aggression of all old guards, outraged at being challenged; on the other, the arrogance of all revolutionaries convinced that the world starts with them and that all that has gone before is invalid. In one sense Joseph, although very much part of the revolution, was outside and above the unpleasantness. Rationalising years later, he attributed the decision to withdraw from the race not to the thinness of his skin but to his realisation, after the Birmingham speech, that, whatever the wisdom of his ideas, he lacked the politician's sense of tactics. 'You see,' he said, 'there's such a thing as instinct, and Mrs Thatcher has a lot of instinct and flair and I don't, and nobody who knows me would think I had. Willie Whitelaw has instincts. Margaret Thatcher to an enormous degree has instincts and flair. Seldom puts a foot wrong.'

Once his candidature was out of the way, it seemed clear to most observers that Joseph, far from being embarrassed or depressed, faced political life with a fresh spring in his step. But he was almost immediately flung into another agonising situation on a smaller scale. He had agreed, some time before, to take on the Home Affairs portfolio in the Shadow Cabinet. (The offer may have been an attempt to keep him out of mischief by giving him more work to do, but it was more probably a genuine attempt by Heath to emphasise that his team was drawn from all wings of the party.) As Home Affairs spokesman, Joseph pronounced on prison policy: he was in favour of shorter, 'bleaker' sentences. He also had to voice Conservative reaction to the Birmingham bombing.

A group of Irishmen travelling by train to make the crossing back to the Republic had been arrested shortly after the explosion. The Tories, divided on so much, were bound to emphasise that they were the party of law and order, and for many of them this meant demanding a return of the death penalty.

Joseph was himself an abolitionist. He was also persuaded by the argument that hanging IRA men simply added martyrs to the already over-long Irish calendar of martyrdom. When the House debated the issue in the fraught post-Birmingham atmosphere (and with the Irishmen awaiting trial) he argued that, while the death penalty for murder was probably not a deterrent in a general way, and while it would not be useful in Northern Ireland, there was a case for executing those convicted of acts of terrorism committed on the mainland.

It was not one of his most impressive performances. Barbara Castle, whose opinion of him had not been raised by the Birmingham speech on birth control, listened to his death penalty speech from the government front bench and noted in her diary that it had been 'a contribution of marvellous tortuousness and circumlocution. At one point it looked as if he had convinced himself about the contradictions of his own case; then he swung back to his new tough (and popular with the right wing) anti-abolitionist line.' At the end, he had actually seemed to be inviting the Home Secretary to persuade him that he was wrong. Mrs Castle added the comment: 'He certainly seems a tortured personality. . . . I believe he is consumed with ambition as well as self-doubt.'

His speech, which effectively argued that the men arrested after the Birmingham bomb deserved to be hanged, was to look even more unsatisfactory in retrospect: years later, arguments were still going on about the validity of the evidence that convicted the men arrested in the train.

Mrs Thatcher's performance on the front bench at this time was more spectacular. She had now been appointed number two Treasury spokesman. Again, Heath was probably not only recognising outstanding debating skill but also trying to indicate that he wanted to preside over a broad-based team. As events unfolded, he was denied any credit for putting her there; he was derided instead for not seeing that she was a challenge to him. In any event, she had a parliamentary triumph just before Christmas when it fell to her to attack Labour's proposal for a capital transfer tax. The Chancellor, Denis Healey, faced with the still relatively junior Mrs Thatcher, was not reluctant to add sexism to his other talents of political abuse. '*La Pasionaria* of Privilege,' he called her. Mrs Thatcher, predictably, showed all the expertise of a tax lawyer in mastering the detail of the proposal, sometimes more impressively than the Chancellor did. But she also, for the first time, showed that she could exchange punches in the heavyweight class: 'Some Chancellors are micro-economic. Some Chancellors are fiscal. This one is just plain cheap. . . . If this Chancellor can be Chancellor, anyone in the House of Commons can be Chancellor. . . .' It was not the kind of speech that Joseph would have made. After that debate in December 1974, the idea crystallised in a number of Tory minds that, if they were going to have Josephite philosophy, it was much more attractive to hear it from a woman like that.

Still, as the House broke up for Christmas there were few who saw Mrs Thatcher as having a rôle any greater than giving Ted Heath enough of a fright to open the way for a suitable successor to come forward. There was substantial support, for instance, for Christopher Soames as a candidate. Soames, who would not be available until the end of 1976 when his tour as an EEC Commissioner came to an end, could have given the party what many felt it needed: reassurance. There would have been a sense of continuity of the Churchill ethos: Soames was married to Mary Churchill, and had been close to the old man in his last days.

Soames supporters often found it convenient in later years to have gaps in their memory about that part of the story. It is worth mentioning because it underlines the point that the Tory Party, as it gratefully saw the back of that unhappy year, 1974, was not hell-bent on Thatcherism or Josephism: it simply wanted to register disapproval of the status quo as represented by Heath.

When Mrs Thatcher fought the leadership election, her debt to Joseph was acknowledged, but he took little part in the campaign. He had little skill in back-room manipulation. One Thatcher campaigner recalled, rather contemptuously, that 'Keith was floating around'. Neither his support nor even the effectiveness of her recent performance on the front bench was as important at this stage as two more mundane factors. One was the peculiar electoral procedure that had been decided on. The other was the skill of Airey Neave's tactics.

The procedure was designed specifically for the case where the existing leader's close colleagues were unwilling to stand against him. If the first ballot confirmed the existing leader in office, then there would be no embarrassment. But if he failed to achieve a clear majority on the first ballot his colleagues were free to put themselves forward at the second: it was a device dubbed by cynics as the 'cowards' charter'.

As expected, none of the big guns among Heath's colleagues stood on the first ballot, which was held on Tuesday, 4 February. There were two main candidates, Heath and Thatcher, plus a rather whimsical third, in the aristocratic traditional Tory Hugh Fraser. It was taken for granted that Heath would come top of the poll; the question was whether Thatcher would win enough votes to trigger off the second ballot – which would be, so to speak, the genuine election, with the other big guns moving in.

At this point, Airey Neave, with his efficient intelligence service, knew better than anyone precisely what the score was, and he knew that it was potentially good news for Mrs Thatcher. His tactic was to express confidence in his candidate, but not too much confidence. He put the word around that she was going to do well enough to force a second ballot, but meanwhile allowed Members to get the impression that he was not really as confident as he said. On the eve of the first ballot, the Thatcher campaign team were instructed to walk around the Palace of Westminster looking unhappy. The word among those less well informed than Neave was that Heath was going to win at a canter. Neave was aiming boldly at MPs whose instinct was to vote for Heath, but without enthusiasm, or to abstain and then reconsider the position on the second ballot. Neave's ploy worked with such Members: as they watched the doleful faces in the Thatcher camp that Monday evening, and it dawned on them that by tomorrow night Heath might be back with a thumping majority, they resolved to take the only step open to them to ensure that the thing would go to a second ballot. They voted for Thatcher.

The MPs put their voting papers into a ballot-box in Committee Room 14 between noon and 3.30 on the Tuesday. Shortly afterwards the result was announced by du Cann as chairman of the 1922:

Heath	119
Thatcher	130
Fraser	16

Mrs Thatcher had failed to get an overall majority; there had to be a second ballot. But the damage she had inflicted on Heath was far more than the shot across the bows that many of those who voted for her had intended. Heath resigned.

When Neave summoned a meeting of her closest supporters, the following day, they were exuberant. Joseph's part in getting the show thus far on the road was marked by the cheer when he entered the room.

The big guns of the Shadow Cabinet were now wheeled up – Willie Whitelaw, James Prior, Geoffrey Howe; and there was added the less well known figure, John Peyton. But Mrs Thatcher was too far ahead to beat. The figures at the second ballot, a week after the first, showed the traditional Conservative faith in the truism that nothing succeeds like success:

Thatcher	146
Whitelaw	79
Howe	19
Prior	19
Peyton	11

Of her three major opponents, Howe was to prove one of the ablest practitioners of 'Thatcherism' and Prior one of its most robust critics. Whitelaw was to be the bridge between the old Conservatism and the new, completely loyal to his leader but knowing that he was always suspect, if not to her, certainly to some of those around her. Neither Howe nor Whitelaw could oust Keith Joseph from his special place in Mrs Thatcher's affections. (Willie Whitelaw, years later, was to remark that 'Keith held her hand before events; I held it during and after'.)

Among the 146 votes for Thatcher were several from MPs who were later to be robust critics of Thatcherism. The Parliamentary Conservative Party had not been converted to Thatcherism.

CHAPTER THIRTEEN

THE CAMPUS CAMPAIGN

Now [in 1988] we have a record to point to; but at that time we just had beliefs, faith in what could be done. Keith made that faith into something that intelligent people were willing to share. And their acceptance spread the message through the press and other media to everybody. If Keith hadn't been doing all that work with the intellectuals, all the rest of our work would probably never have resulted in success.

Mrs Margaret Thatcher, 1988

In 1975, Mrs Thatcher had won the leadership battle but she had not won the argument. Her mastery of the Conservative Party took years to accomplish; and Keith Joseph was an indispensable part of the process, first of all, in a sense, by helping her to define what the argument was. The way she expressed it when questioned for the purposes of this book about his contribution during the period leading up to her arrival in Downing Street in 1979 was: 'It was Keith who really began to turn the intellectual tide back against socialism. He got our fundamental intellectual message across, to students, professors, journalists, the "intelligentsia" generally.'

The impetus of the speeches in Upminster, Preston and Birmingham carried on from 1975 to 1979. His zeal as a speaker became almost a standing joke. The joke passed into the canon at All Souls, which had invited him in 1972 to return as a Fellow, an honour which carried the right to attend the kind of event he could appreciate, dining with people of the highest intellectual calibre in an atmosphere of public-schoolboy jollification. He duly featured in one of the comic songs that Fellows invented for their after-dinner amusement. The IRA were still active in various English cities, and the verse (the work of Alan Tyson, musicologist and psychoanalyst) ran something like:

But behold it was not high explosive,
Only a weekend speech by Joseph. . . .

If some of his speeches could still cause media explosions, it was not actually true of the bulk of the speeches he made between 1975 and 1979. Mostly his speech-making was an old-fashioned stump around the country, speaking notably at the universities, often to remarkably large audiences. The strain on him was not dramatic, as it had been after Birmingham, but it was cumulative. After Preston and Birmingham he was a figure both famous and notorious. During this period, 1975–9, he reached fresh heights of nervous energy. He was an easier target than Mrs Thatcher (and he had a thinner skin). So, as well as 'getting our fundamental message across', as Mrs Thatcher put it, he was riding punches that should have been aimed at her. He became the lightning-conductor for Thatcherism.

They were testing years. It was during this period that his marriage ended in separation.

His first speech of 1975 took place on the first of January and was in a low key. He had been invited, as a speaker now guaranteed to win headlines, to open the Camping and Outdoor Life Exhibition at Olympia, on New Year's Day. Standing in front of a façade of mock woodland, he made what *The Times* the next day called a 'curious' speech: 'From the freedom to camp in Western Europe, Sir Keith jumped to the collectivism of the Russian farming system and issued a warning about nationalisation in Britain and what could come to pass under socialism.' *The Times* story had all the hallmarks of a reporter who knows that during the Christmas silly season newspapers have space for whimsy: ' "Who is Sir Keith Joseph?" asked a small boy. "He's one of the most able politicians there is," his father replies.'

He was probably least happy, at this time, when speaking in the Commons. He may have been the voice of the future, but he was still the man who in the Preston speech had blown the gaff on a Tory government, who had said that the economic mess was largely the Tories' fault. It made the Conservative backbenchers uneasy. One saw this for instance in the budget debate in April 1975. It was not long after Mrs Thatcher became leader, and the Tories were in attacking mood. Joseph's contribution scarcely reflected it. It was a thoughtful speech that leaned over to be fair about Labour's budget problems: he conceded that it was never easy for a chancellor to cut public expenditure; he conceded that, if *he* were a minister and was asked to cut back, he 'would probably resist'; he admitted that part of the present chancellor's problem of a swollen government pay-bill was attributable to 'my reform of the National Health Service'. It was all very civilised, and the Labour Chancellor, Denis Healey, was not the kind of debater who enjoyed a mere exchange of academic points across the dispatch-box.

Healey, now and later, could be merciless with Joseph. He satirised the tendency to apologise, and to rush into print with explanations:

It is difficult to believe that the obscurity in which he clouds his words is intended. Yet the fact is that nobody with such skill in the use of words is so often and regularly misunderstood. . . . Over the coming weeks every newspaper from the *News of the World* to the *Yachtsman's Journal* will be flooded with letters and articles by the right hon. gentleman explaining what he meant to say this afternoon but, once again, failed to get across.

This was one of the first major debates after Mrs Thatcher had become Leader of the Opposition, but it was to Joseph, not to Margaret Thatcher or her Shadow Chancellor, Geoffrey Howe, that Healey turned in his winding-up speech in the budget debate. He seemed the easiest target. The Tories, said Healey, had been accusing the Labour Party of harbouring wild men; but look at their wild man! Everyone in the House respected the Joseph intellect, but

the House and the country are getting a little tired of these portentous sermons which carefully avoid giving any hint of what action would follow if anybody were unwise enough to take the right hon. gentleman's advice. . . .

The fact is that when the right hon. gentleman started on his crusade he was seen by many as a Moses who would save this country. In twelve short months he has turned into a Malvolio.

In fact that Joseph speech, which disappointed Tories and was derided by Healey, had a main theme that stands up, years later, better than that of most speeches. He was setting out the case for the enterprise culture:

The private sector, the indispensable base on which all else is built, is under attack. Those who attack it are in danger of sawing off the branch on which all our people and services are sitting. . . . Yet we discourage those who make it work. . . . The worker on his own cannot create wealth. We need the wealth-creating, job-creating entrepreneur and the wealth-creating, job-creating manager. We treat them very badly.

A dozen years later, this was largely taken for granted, but in 1975 he was breaking unfamiliar ground.

Of course, he conceded, financial reward was not the only motivation of what he called 'the ulcer people', but:

The rewards for increased responsibility of managers get less. . . . They have insecurity and worry. They are meant to take risks. . . . They deserve a chance of reward. These are the ulcer people – talented, job-creating, potentially wealth-creating for the country.

If they are not treated reasonably, if they do not feel appreciated, they will quit either by way of the brain drain or by the internal brain drain which might be called switching off. There is a great deal of switching-off in this country.

It was partly because he found himself mocked for this sort of speech at Westminster that Joseph came to devote so much of his energy elsewhere during the next few years. There was something wrong, he became increasingly convinced, with the political education of the supposedly educated classes. So he turned to the process of what Mrs Thatcher called getting the 'fundamental intellectual message across, to students, professors, journalists, the "intelligentsia"'.

In a sense, he also had to get it across, in the early days, to Mrs Thatcher herself.

The internal debate which had begun in the Conservative Party in 1974 and continued in 1975 had a major focus in the Centre for Policy Studies. Logically, it might have been decided that the Centre had served its purpose once Mrs Thatcher was elected leader and could have been wound up. By the traditions of the Conservative Party, she could organise the party's resources as she chose, and in theory could have arranged for Central Office and the Conservative Research Department to carry out any of the functions that the CPS could carry out.

She did indeed impose her mark on Central Office. As she was entitled to do (although outrage was expressed in some quarters), she sacked the director-general of the party organisation, Michael Wolff, who was a Heath appointee. She replaced Willie Whitelaw as chairman of the party with Lord Thorneycroft, whose resignation as Chancellor back in 1958 had marked the beginning of the reaction against government reliance on state expenditure as the key to prosperity. He was still a formidable well-respected figure and he served Mrs Thatcher well, although, as eventually emerged, he was less than one hundred per cent in sympathy with her style.

The Shadow Cabinet was reconstructed much less drastically than some of the anti-Heathites would have liked. As her deputy she appointed her main rival in the leadership battle, Willie Whitelaw. After him came Joseph, specifically recognised as number three in the pecking order.

Whitelaw's rôle was vital. So long as he stood by her, she had a firm base in the solid undoctrinaire centre of the party. He brought a clearly defined 'constituency' with him. Joseph's 'constituency' was less clearly defined, but it emerged as an important one over the next few years. He was given overall responsibility for policy and research. In other words, the themes that the old party establishment had found disturbing in the Preston speech were given the imprimatur of the new leadership. On the other hand, most of the old guard were still there in the Shadow Cabinet, and even on the policy and research side she was more cautious than she might have been. The Conservative Research Department (CRD) was left in the hands of the brilliant young Christopher Patten, appointed to be its director only the previous year under the Heath régime and regarded as being on the leftish wing of the party.

Chris Patten's CRD and Alfred Sherman's CPS were thus poised to be rivals for the intellectual soul of the party as it prepared for the long haul up towards a return to office. Relations between the two men were less than cordial, and the irony that both owed allegiance, through different chains of command, to Margaret Thatcher and Keith Joseph made for added sharpness. Some of the people at the CPS – the New Conservatives – regarded the old Conservatives at the CRD frankly as the enemy. The CRD regarded much of what went on in the Centre in Wilfred Street as mad, bad or ludicrous. There was talk of 'mad scientists', and eventually Joseph became 'the mad monk'.

Understandably it was the CPS, not the CRD, that he chose as a more congenial base for operations. The CPS, far from being made redundant, took on a new lease of life. The rivalry between the old guard and the new was eventually paralleled in the complex of policy groups and committees that any party in opposition sets up to handle the long-term review of policy in readiness for the next general election campaign. In effect, although neither Mrs Thatcher nor Keith Joseph may originally have intended it, they had established a shadow to the Shadow Cabinet. The appearance of continuity symbolised by the old faces still on the Conservative front bench in the Commons was gradually undermined. Between 1975 and 1979, Mrs Thatcher drew her advice and moral support largely from outside the official Conservative organisation, much of it from people whose base, physically or spiritually, was in Wilfred Street.

The reaction of the old guard was often irritation, sometimes patronising amusement; and, as during the leadership struggle the previous year, they still did not seem to realise the speed with which the power was slipping out of their hands. Nor did they realise how the 'shadow' structure that evolved in 1975–9 would prefigure Mrs Thatcher's method of exercising her authority once she moved to Downing Street in 1979. The operations of the CPS helped to provide her with both the confidence and the rudiments of a personal staff which enabled her to rely less on her colleagues than they had a right to expect she would.

The Centre propagated the New Conservatism, within the party and beyond it. Directly or indirectly, the CPS was responsible for enlisting support for the Tory Party from a substantial number of individuals, and from whole groups, who had hitherto been hostile or apathetic towards the Tories, or who had felt excluded by them: this was all part of the Joseph 'constituency'.

Pamphlets flowed out from the CPS. So did articles for newspapers and magazines willing to accept them. It was also a speech-writing factory. The accepted wisdom, in the television age, was that old-fashioned speeches were largely irrelevant. Keith Joseph proved that this was not so, with hundreds of speeches made during the heyday of the CPS, often to small groups and mostly unreported, that had an unquantifiable but substantial effect on changing the climate of political and economic thinking and assumptions among influential people.

His major set-piece speech of 1975 was at the Blackpool party conference, the first Conservative conference under Mrs Thatcher. Thorneycroft, in setting the tone as chairman, dropped broad hints that strong ideological feelings ought not to lead to Tories firing into their own ranks; he quoted Churchill to make the point. But the younger New Conservatives were not always slow to criticise the old establishment.

Joseph was given the task of replying to a 'discussion' – it was considered important that there was no motion before this particular session – on 'The Conservative Party and the Future'. His speech, a CPS composite exercise, was really the definitive Thatcherite reply to the case being put forward a year earlier for 'national unity'. He accepted that for a party set on gaining and keeping office the 'middle way', and the 'middle ground', was always attractive. But 'the trouble with the middle ground is that we do not choose it. We do not shape it. It is shaped for us by the extremists. The more extreme the left, the more to the left is the middle ground. The middle ground is a will-o'-the-wisp.' What had happened during the years of consensus was that the socialists had operated a ratchet – this was a metaphor that was dear to Sherman's heart. Each time the Labour Party had been in office they had moved things farther to the left; then, when the Tories got back, the 'ratchet' effect made it that much harder to get back to where they had been before. That was why the 'middle ground' kept shifting to the left. Joseph went on:

I am going to suggest a change of one word, one word only, which I believe will reconcile the need for a national approach with both the realities and with the values which, whatever the differences of emphasis, unite us as a party. The nation's need is that the democratic parties find the maximum practicable *common* ground.

He claimed to see this happening already:

> Only a year ago I was denounced for asserting [in Preston] that inflation actually destroys jobs, halts growth and hurts the social services, and I was denounced with bell, book and candle. And yet what I said then is being said by Mr Wilson, by Mr Healey, by Mr Foot and by Mr Jack Jones today.

Events were 'increasingly going to be our allies'. And, after all,

> we are only trying to achieve by argument what many European social democrats have long understood – that you cannot make the mixed economy work at all effectively if you cripple the private sector and lose control of the public sector. . . . And look at the results in western Europe.

The notion of 'common ground' was in tune with Mrs Thatcher's outlook, as it developed. She was to find that she was in many ways a populist, expressing basic feelings taken for granted by ordinary people although sometimes shocking to the *bien-pensant* liberal opinion that formulated the rules for the 'middle ground'. In the 'common ground' speech, Joseph had articulated, once more, an idea that provided an intellectual underpinning for her instincts.

During the next three and a half years he made 150 speeches at universities and polytechnics. It was now that, on top of the various other reputations he had, he acquired one for sheer guts. In the middle and late seventies the student scene, in Britain as elsewhere, was quietening down after the great age of student protest that had peaked in 1968; but a speaking programme like this needed remarkable stamina, and not a little physical courage.

The campus speeches had a special place in Keith Joseph's own heart – as emerged during one of the conversations he engaged in with the author of this book. We were sitting with a pot of tea and a plate of biscuits between us. He had been recalling some of the agonies that came with the job of Secretary of State for Social Services; how he used to take home boxes, weekend after weekend, with inspectors' reports on conditions in geriatric hospitals – 'harrowing reading . . . harrowing!' Later there had been the same kind of agony, he went on, at the Department of Education with some of the inspectors' reports about what was going on in the schools. Harrowing reading! His face screwed up with the memory.

It seemed as good a moment as any to ask whether there had been any happy moments in his political life. The transformation was instantaneous. His face lit up. The most fulfilment in his career, he said, had come with the speeches to students. It was 'self-inflicted misery', of course, but 'It was *lovely*. (Of course it was horrible at the time.) Very large audiences – almost to a girl or boy convinced statists if not socialists.'

The campus speeches were not speech-writers' jobs. He used the same basis and improvised when he got to the hall. As he recalled it, every morning that he set off he dreaded what might be to come. And when he returned to the Centre he might groan about how the universities were failing by not maintaining the traditions of freedom of speech. He was always heckled – that, he recalled, was 'proper and legitimate'. Sometimes they tried to shout him down, and on occasions they threw things at him. On six occasions out of the 150 – he counted, and he remembered, grimly – he was prevented from speaking at all. But it had been worth it.

> I'm sure they had never heard the moral case for capitalism. I put it – materially and psychically and socially – in thirty to thirty-five minutes; then up to an hour of questions, and that was fun. You see, they didn't realise how relatively easy it was to answer questions.
>
>   What I always said was that it was a jolly imperfect world, and all I was saying was that capitalism was the least bad way yet invented – as Churchill said about democracy.

At the end of the question-and-answer sessions around the country he had liked to invite suggestions about which country ran its society better than Britain:

> The answers changed. At first – Cuba, China, Yugoslavia. At the end they'd run out, because by that time all those Utopias had been exposed. At one of the final meetings there was silence, then a very tentative suggestion from one of the strident hecklers: 'The Paris Commune.'

The Paris Commune, he noted with satisfaction, lasted only for a few months.

The most celebrated occasion when a speech was stopped was at the London School of Economics. There the circumstances were complex, and mixed up with the arcane processes of student politics. A resolution was passed to deny him a platform. This shocked the then Director of the LSE, Ralf Dahrendorf, who put the whole of his considerable prestige behind assuring a hearing if Joseph would be willing to come back on a date of his choice. In the classic way of things that are banned, the LSE speech achieved a *succès de scandale*.

The LSE version of the speech was printed in extended form in *The Times* under the title 'The tyranny hidden in the pursuit of equality'. It started with the concept of 'equality of respect', and moved on to equality before the law and equality of opportunity, and then to egalitarianism: 'But there is no way of assessing such intangibles as merit or effort without giving someone arbitrary and discretionary powers to decide who is worth how much. Who is to judge?' So egalitarianism inevitably meant coercion:

> Only consider who would equalise the equalisers! Only consider the gross disparity of power in these régimes, nominally dedicated to equality of outcome: consider the quangoes – the proliferating public sector boards on which sit large numbers of Government supporters and allies, each drawing pay and expenses – the perquisites of a new ruling class.

If equality was achieved, it would be at a very primitive level of standard of living, without the market skills and the enterprise that those who provide incentives can provide.

Before ending, he defended himself, as he commonly did, against the charge of *laisser-faire*:

> I am not defending a free-for-all. The State must act to make and enforce rules to ensure the security of human life, protection against force and fraud and protection of those values and standards – social, economic, ecological – which represent the accumulated and current aspirations of our community.

The texts of these speeches gave few grounds for anger, but their author had come to symbolise something dangerous. It is odd, one of his colleagues mused later, how it is always saintly characters who are accused of being devils.

He found 'fulfilment' in going around the universities, and one of the commonest comments about him by colleagues, expressed indulgently, was that he was really by nature a don rather than a politician. He did not think that himself. He had had the chance of an academic job after the war and had turned it down. His own insistence that he was a 'late developer' gave him some of the qualities, in his fifties and sixties, of a perpetual undergraduate, with the eagerness of an enquiring intelligent twenty-year-old. He was forever happening on some new idea in a way that sometimes impressed the academics with whom he was now regularly in touch through the Centre; at other times they were astonished that he was so impressed with something they took for granted. His reading was extensive, deep and conscientious – he was an avid student of *The Times Literary Supplement* – but he had come to political philosophy relatively late in life.

His friends and advisers the Letwins – Bill and Shirley, respectively a political scientist and a philosopher – admired his intellect but felt that one function they had to perform for him was to teach him the academic process of working out that A logically leads to B, which leads to C. (The Letwins thought it characteristic of Joseph that he was unable to see how Alfred Sherman's Marxist past could vitiate his academic credibility. This emerged at their first meeting, when Joseph brought him to their flat. They did not take to Sherman, then or later. The atmosphere grew heated, then there was a respite when Sherman left the room to wash his hands. Joseph sighed and remarked, as he often found himself doing, that they mustn't mind Alfred, he was the salt of the earth – or words to that effect. The Letwins exchanged glances, and then one of them remarked that there was no need to apologise: as university teachers they knew all about ex-Marxists. Joseph was taken aback. Who had told them about Sherman's past? In fact nobody had told them; they had each deduced it, independently, purely on the basis of the way the discussion had developed.)

If Joseph had moved into university teaching, he would no doubt have learned quickly; but he was not a university natural. An important part of the work at the CPS was to tap the brains and channel the energies of a range of academics, but the ambience was scarcely academic – in the way that its friendly rival the Institute of Economic Affairs had a quasi-university quality. It was operating on a different time-scale: it had to show results by the time of the next election, which could come at any moment. It was the time-scale of Madison Avenue, not of academia.

CHAPTER FOURTEEN

A NEW SONG'S MEASURE

We are the music makers,
   We are the dreamers of dreams,
Wandering by lone sea-breakers,
   And sitting by desolate streams. . . .

One man with a dream, at pleasure,
   Shall go forth and conquer a crown,
And three with a new song's measure
   Can trample a kingdom down.

Arthur William Edgar O'Shaughnessy

O'Shaughnessy's romantic verses suggest at least part of the atmosphere at the Centre for Policy Studies in the later 1970s. Joseph, as one 'man with a dream', drew comfort from them. His affection for O'Shaughnessy had been noticed during the election of October 1974 when he used to quote the poem at meetings of possibly baffled electors. Being out of sympathy, during that campaign, with much of the official party line, he felt his speeches needed a touch of obscurity. The poem at least had that merit. Meanwhile other dreamers of dreams, with ambitions to trample down various kingdoms, had been forming themselves into a team under his aegis at the CPS.

The dreamers and music-makers of Wilfred Street were a mixed bag, bringing different talents, and attached to the organisation with varying degrees of permanence. Politically their backgrounds covered all parties and none. What they had in common was lack of sympathy with the old ways of the Conservative Party; most of them had a passionate dislike of Heath. The tune to which most of them were making music was an anti-establishment tune. It was small wonder that so many Tories (and most other politicians) regarded their dreams as wildly unrealistic and dangerous, and their music-making as evilly seductive.

But the talents in Wilfred Street represented a wealth of brainpower: the Centre certainly laid itself open to the charge of that classic sin in Conservative terms of being 'too clever by half'. On the other hand, the average rank-and-file Conservative probably did not regard the CPS as either an evil conspiracy or an inspired 'think-tank' holding the key to the future: most of them scarcely knew of its existence.

The effectiveness of the CPS lay in carrying out what, in commerce, would be called a public relations exercise, and doing so at a time when such exercises were still regarded as vaguely un-British. Here, again, the character of Keith Joseph was important. He was the antithesis of the popular notion of a smooth public relations operator.

Under Joseph as chairman, Sherman was still the most prominent figure at the Centre. Less flamboyant were Gerald Frost and Martin Wassell. For a time an important consultant was Jock Bruce-Gardyne, who as an MP had been one of the early advocates of monetarism but had lost his seat; he was one of those revered by the chairman as having seen the light before he did.

Apart from the regulars, a large number of sympathisers – academics, journalists, publicists, businessmen – lent their services: bright young men, and bright older men.

The CPS carried out the textbook public relations function of identifying target groups and making contact with them. They wined them and dined them – people in powerful or influential walks of life: eating our way to victory, as Sherman put it.

Not least important of the target groups was the most obvious: backbench Tory MPs, most of whom remained to be converted to the philosophy of their new leader.

Funds were not unlimited. From the outset, the Centre had had to be careful not to seem to be poaching funds from the sources drawn on by the Conservative Party. The quarters in Wilfred Street were not plush, and the staff were encouraged not to become over-lavish, as in this office memorandum: 'Liqueurs or brandy will *not* be offered to luncheon guests. The one exception will be when Sir Keith is hosting the lunch and he – and he alone – decides that it is appropriate to extend this additional hospitality.' The staff, like PR executives, were under pressure to show results. 'We seem bent on disproving Milton Friedman's dictum that there is no such thing as a free lunch,' Gerald Frost wrote drily to Joseph in a memo intended to make the point that they must strive to get more, in terms of some kind of commitment, out of their guests.

Part of the wining and dining was designed to raise funds as well as spread the message. One criticism of Sherman was that, while his vigour in message-spreading could be overwhelming, he could have a counterproductive effect in fund-raising. There was a celebrated occasion when a captain of industry, who was also chairman of an insurance group, was invited to lunch, with the idea very much in mind that he might come up with a substantial cheque. Since insurance was one of the many subjects on which Sherman had strong views, it was hoped that he might be lunching elsewhere that day.

In fact he turned up. Conversation flowed smoothly, until the guest of honour, after expressing his enthusiasm for the free-market philosophy of the CPS, went on to remark that of course there had to be sensible limits to economic freedom. In the insurance market, for instance, if competition was allowed to be too free it could harm the customer. This was the kind of special pleading that was a red rag to the bull in Sherman. He turned on the captain of industry and lectured him on the amount of damage done to the British economy because men like him had behaved as if market economics didn't apply to them. At the head of the table, Joseph made pacifying noises.

The fact was that Joseph often found himself adding respectability to what was a radical, even a revolutionary, organisation. Drafts of speeches and articles sometimes had to be toned down. Here he is minuting Sherman:

KJ to AS
I would prefer to omit 'class bitterness' on page 2 and the reference to 'mufflered men' in insert A. . . .

Speech-writing and pamphleteering were to a large extent a composite exercise. The atmosphere had something of the 'creative' conferences in an advertising agency, with ideas being bounced across the table, and vigorous debate about what the public would stand for. Draft would follow draft before the final work was put before the public who were to be persuaded to buy the product.

It was all more like Madison Avenue than All Souls. As the pamphlets and speeches flowed out, words were weighed and phrases honed and rehoned as painstakingly as advertising slogans. Then came the feedback: they noted how the public were reacting. Here is one report from a member of Joseph's staff:

After his speech at the Haberdashers' Aske's School KJ was asked a tricky question along the following lines: 'You have had a hundred years in which to operate the market economy and you have failed. Can you explain why we should let you have another chance?' What is the best answer – could it make a speech?

If Joseph had to curb the zeal of his young turks, it was sometimes they who had to hang on to his coat-tails. In one draft of a speech, on the perennial topic of the importance of entrepreneurship, he had built up an image of the entrepreneur as an 'Aladdin' whose magical touch could bring untold wealth. A minute to the draft survives: 'Some "wag" in the journalistic profession will seize on the "magical" aspects – "the mad scientist" may become "the mad lamp-rubber".'

That comment came from Martin Bendelow, who has to be introduced at this stage of the story, although it was some years before his name became known to the wider public.

Bendelow was one of the ablest of the CPS's phrase-makers and one of its most colourful characters; it is fair to add that he could also have brought disaster to the Centre as he did to himself. The story of the rise and fall of Martin Bendelow is worth telling briefly if only to illustrate how dangerously the New Conservatism was living.

He had come to the Centre highly recommended. He was a young man who had clearly made money, and seemed to be himself a model of entrepreneurship. Bendelow also had immense, if raffish, charm, of a kind that Joseph found invigorating. He could be rude about the stuffier kind of Tory politician, but he was not alone among the CPS staff in that; and it had never been part of the Joseph case in favour of entrepreneurs that they had to be *nice* people.

Bendelow had a way with words. All in all, he was seen as one of the highest of the high-fliers among the bright young men in Wilfred Street, and he moved naturally on from there to become a parliamentary candidate in the 1979 election. It was not Joseph's way to promote protégés as candidates. (Another member of the CPS staff once approached him to ask for advice on getting into the House. Joseph said he was delighted and told him never to hesitate to ask if there should be anything that he, Joseph, could do to help; it did not seem to occur to him that the approach was being made precisely to get help in the first place.) But Bendelow had no difficulty in getting himself selected as a Tory candidate, with Joseph's endorsement. He stood in the 1979 general election at Huddersfield East, where he reduced a large Labour majority, producing one of the largest swings to the Conservatives in the North of England.

There was, however, a mystery, even in his early days at the CPS, about just how he had made his money. Joseph made enquiries and satisfied himself that Bendelow's fortune had begun with importing Asian coats, which had been fashionable since the Swinging Sixties, and then had been multiplied in the property boom of the early seventies. The 'Asian coats' connection fitted in with Bendelow's flamboyant past. A vicar's son, he had belonged to the sixties generation of dropouts, hitch-hiking to Asia, then turning up in Africa, before returning to study at the London School of Economics, where he was attracted by the right-wing economics of Professor Peter Bauer. He was no scholar, but he soon picked up the free-market ideas of the CPS and was adept at translating them into the pithy phrases in demand in Wilfred Street.

What was not known at the CPS was that Bendelow's name was in FBI files as a man who had connections with drug dealers. As a parliamentary candidate, he told the local paper in Huddersfield that 'I'll be in the Cabinet within five years'. But long before that he was in prison. A few months after the 1979 election British Customs officers investigating a drugs ring found their enquiries leading to Bendelow's home in Barnes. The house, when it was raided, was found to contain large quantities of cocaine.

The first and wholly characteristic reaction of Keith Joseph, who by that time was a member of Mrs Thatcher's cabinet, was to visit him in Brixton prison while he was on remand. He was dissuaded by his colleague, the ever practical Jock Bruce-Gardyne, who pointed out that it was really inappropriate for cabinet ministers to visit prisoners. Bruce-Gardyne himself visited Brixton, as did other CPS colleagues.

Bendelow's story was that a gang in Bolivia, where he claimed to have legitimate business interests, had threatened his family if he did not help them by smuggling drugs. But his story changed. He later claimed that his motive was to use the money from the drugs for helping political refugees to escape from Bolivia.

He pleaded guilty and in December 1981 was sentenced to six years' imprisonment, which was reduced on appeal to five years.

The damage to the CPS and to Keith Joseph, when the case came to court, was minimal. The rôle of the Centre had been overtaken by events. If it had broken earlier, things might have been different. Apart from anything else, there were those in the CPS orbit to whom the notion of legalising drugs had an intellectual appeal: some theoreticians of the New Right saw parallels between economic liberty and moral libertarianism.

That the CPS managed to steer a course through these dangerous waters was further evidence that the emergence of Thatcherism owed a lot to good luck.

Bendelow was not the only, or even the best, wordmonger at the CPS. The phrases that flowed out from Wilfred Street may not have entered into the popular vocabulary like copy-writers' television jingles, but they moved into the vocabulary of the opinion-formers and the academic world. It is always difficult to establish who invents a catchphrase as distinct from who popularises it. To Sherman went the credit of 'the ratchet' – very much a CPS word, to capture the image of how the onward march of statism is much easier to continue than to reverse – but the analogy to a ratchet wheel had been used earlier by a German economist to describe how during wars governments assume powers which they are then reluctant to give up. It was Sherman who applied it to the expansion of state activity in Britain during the Butskellite years after the war.

Another phrase that found its way into a Joseph speech was concerned with the preservation of jobs, which were not real jobs, in subsidised industries. Just as there was an Unknown Warrior, there ought to be a monument, Joseph said, to the 'unknown unemployed' who had lost their jobs because the economy had been distorted by well-meaning subsidies intended to create jobs elsewhere.

He was always happy to give Sherman the credit for phrases. With one or two he liked to claim complete credit for himself. One was 'What Britain needs is more millionaires and more bankrupts': the idea, although not yet the words, actually went back to his maiden speech. A phrase that he seems to have made his own was 'wealth creation' – simple and obvious, but one which he seems to have given a place in the politico-economic vocabulary.

CHAPTER FIFTEEN

RADICAL RETHINK

Among new men, strange faces, other minds.

Tennyson, 'The Passing of Arthur'

Ideas as well as words were being fashioned and refined at the Centre. There were theoretical discussions about the nature of entrepreneurship and how the enterprise society must take over from the managerial society: one participant recalled an abstruse discussion on whether a manager could also be an entrepreneur. Discussions occasionally had the character of medieval disputation on how many angels could dance on the head of a pin; while others concerned the *Realpolitik* of how quickly a Tory government could neutralise the trade unions.

Part, but only part, of the philosophy was monetarist economics, on which there was an interchange of ideas between the Centre and various institutions in America, where the work of Milton Friedman had increasing political impact. There were contacts with Ronald Reagan, who had recently finished his term as Governor of California. It was recognised as a watershed in politico-economics when Friedman was awarded the Nobel Prize for Economics in 1976, the two-hundredth anniversary of the year of publication of Adam Smith's *Wealth of Nations*. Part of the Centre's function was to encourage interest in classical texts of economic liberalism – they found that there was difficulty, for instance, in getting hold of the works of Hayek, who had been one of the great opponents of the postwar trend towards governmental intervention.

The next great set-piece Joseph speech was the Stockton Lecture of 1976, which was entitled – another phrase from Alfred – 'Monetarism Is Not Enough'. The lecture was largely concerned with the imbalance caused to an economy with an over-large public sector. It then demonstrated how in that situation it was no answer simply to cut the money-supply, because 'Monetary contraction in a mixed economy strangles the private sector unless the state sector contracts with it and reduces its take from the national income.' To say that 'monetarism is not enough' was in no sense to retreat from monetarism: it was to advance from monetarism. Unless

113

the State contracted, there would not be the confidence or the climate for entrepreneurship and risk-taking which could alone bring prosperity. But 'Cuts mean cuts. . . . Pseudo-cuts of programmes or future programmes will not be enough.'

In the intellectual tussles at the CPS, one of the angels left poised in mid-air over the head of the pin, so to speak, was whether the Centre was aiming at what could truly be called Conservatism (which of course Joseph said he had been converted to) or at nineteenth-century free-trade Liberalism. Samuel Brittan, who had undergone his own conversion from Keynesianism and whose *Financial Times* columns were now emerging as perhaps the best-known British economic commentary, recalled trying to persuade Joseph that economic liberalism, and the removal of restrictive practices, could have a profoundly *radical* effect on society, and that Joseph shied away from the notion of radicalism.

So if there was a philosophy at the CPS it was a patchwork philosophy. Part of the patchwork had been provided over the previous decade by Enoch Powell, still a hero with some CPS people who were sometimes attracted by his flaws as well as by his virtues. Powell's anti-Europeanism (which like his anti-immigration campaign gave him a formidable populist following) was reflected in some quarters around the CPS – if only because the European Community was so closely associated with Ted Heath.

Joseph was an instinctive European (which was one of the things that contrasted him with Mrs Thatcher). A Common Market meant the breaking down of artificial barriers to trade, which had always been central to his beliefs. A European bureaucracy did not frighten him in the way that it frightened some of his colleagues, any more than sophistication of company management had ever frightened him, although one of his main themes now was that managerial structures were inadequate without the dynamic of entrepreneurialism.

In the European Community he could see the dramatic possibilities – and was aware of the irony that they should appeal to a Jew – of a return to the spirit of the days of unified Christendom, when civilised people enjoyed common standards and aspirations that transcended national boundaries. 'Europe' appealed to the romantic in him.

If, as has been said, British history has been a balance between Cavaliers and Roundheads, there was maybe more Cavalier than Roundhead in Keith Joseph. But, if so, he was a Cavalier helping to put Roundheads in power. Margaret Thatcher was a Roundhead or she was nothing. (The same was true of Enoch Powell.)

The Cavalier strain showed in Joseph's instinct to be attracted to the

Harold Macmillans rather than to the Rab Butlers and the Iain Macleods of the Tory Party. It showed in the way he had taken naturally to the rôle of the paternalist in government. And his moralism was not puritanism. He was often portrayed as an austere man, the man who wouldn't have a television set in the house, but he was no ascetic. He enjoyed his food, provided the menu suited his stomach. He loved abstract ideas, but the more so if there were colourful personalities to discuss them with. He enjoyed people who were good company. He was enlivened by the conversation of lively women. He disliked being bored, and even the famous courtesy did not always stop this coming across when he was confronted with boring people.

Enoch Powell was quick to make fun of the Cavalier in Joseph. During the mid-seventies he would have been less than human not to resent how Joseph was getting the credit for telling the country what he had been telling it for years. 'Keith Joseph?' Enoch would say when he was in roguish mood. Ah, yes: 'Like a gorgeous butterfly, with a coat of many colours, alighting first on this flower, then on that. . . .'

If Keith Joseph was a dilettante, it fitted in with the rôle of the Cavalier. Powell was not the only one to accuse him of dilettantism. People would watch him on one of his great fact-finding missions, forever asking questions and filling notebook after notebook with what people told him; some of them wondered how much of what went into the notebooks came out again in constructive form.

For his part, Joseph's attitude to Powell was characteristic. He would have liked to devise some formula during the late seventies to harness Powell's skills into the Thatcherite campaign. He could see real gold there, beneath the dross of the rhetoric on Europe and immigration. (Mrs Thatcher's own instinct on Powell was more down-to-earth: she saw things in simple terms of loyalty, and since Enoch had advised people to vote Labour there was no place for him in the Conservative Party.)

Equally characteristically, Powell would point to his own virtue during the years of the 'Barber boom', while Joseph and Thatcher sat in the Heath cabinet: 'There is something distasteful', Powell said, 'about the spectacle of men who followed him [Heath] through briar and thicket turning on him now as if that had never happened.'

The new fashion in 'Roundhead' standards reflected the high moral tone in the upbringing of Margaret Thatcher in Grantham, and it was often pointed out that it was a moral tone which in turn had a great deal in common with the spirit of the early Labour Party – more influenced by Methodism than by Marx, as the saying went. So New Conservatism appealed to Old Labour. An outstanding case of a Roundhead ex-socialist

Thatcherite was Dr Rhodes Boyson. Boyson, a comprehensive-school head, had once thought of Labour as the best hope for equality of opportunity and became disillusioned with a modern Labour Party apparently determined to destroy educational values. He became a zealous Tory and a zealous Thatcherite (but one who was immune to the butterfly charms of Joseph – a fact that was to cause problems when the two of them became colleagues at the Department of Education in the eighties).

Boyson was a pre-Thatcher recruit to Conservatism: his conversion from socialism pre-dated Joseph's conversion by about a decade. It was the period following Mrs Thatcher's election as Conservative leader that saw a succession of other more or less prominent ex-socialists coming over. Partly it was because the intellectual excitement of which the CPS was a focus was attractive, as the Fabian Society had been attractive to an earlier generation of high-minded, highly educated people. The best-known among ex-socialist journalists who moved over – but he was only one of many – was Paul Johnson, one-time editor of the *New Statesman*.

The same movement could be seen among academics. Here an interesting case was Hugh Thomas, the future Lord Thomas of Swynnerton, who eventually succeeded Joseph as chairman of the CPS. Sherman thought that Thomas, best-known for his work on the Spanish Civil War, would be useful on the foreign affairs side. (There was irony here: when Thomas took over as chairman, Sherman soon found that it was the end of the road at the Centre for him.)

As with other academics and writers who switched at this time from left to right, an important consideration in Hugh Thomas's case was a reaction against 'the establishment': it had once meant supporting the Labour Party in protest against the Tories; it now meant joining the Thatcherites in protest against traditionalist 'Butskellite' Conservatism.

Back in 1959, Thomas had actually edited a symposium entitled simply *The Establishment* (in which he argued, among other things, that Britain would not be free of the establishment frame of mind 'until the public schools are completely swept away, at whatever cost to the temporary peace of the country'.) It concluded: 'To those who desire to see the resources and talents of Britain fully developed and extended, there is no doubt that the fusty Establishment, with its Victorian views and standards of judgment, must be destroyed.' That was fairly orthodox left-wing thinking in 1959. Twenty years later it was the sort of thing the new CPS-style Tories were writing about the people who had been running the Conservative Party for the past generation or two. Mrs Thatcher, and the intellectual base that was being built up on her behalf at the CPS, appealed to people who wanted to sweep away 'fustiness'.

Egged on by Sherman, Joseph conscientiously wooed potentially important converts from the left. He lunched them or dined them and in appropriate cases passed them on to Mrs Thatcher. One specifically socialist recruit was Woodrow Wyatt. As a Labour MP he may not have been noted for his ability to win friends at the Commons but he had a powerful populist voice. He wrote a successful newspaper column. When he received his invitation to meet the new party leader in her home in Flood Street he recorded simply: 'She won me over.'

Keith Joseph was not always in tune with the ex-socialists. His 'conversion', after all, had been to 'Conservatism', not to anti-establishment radicalism. Other recruits were closer to his style, among them two or three, notably John Hoskyns, who were soon to move to the centre of things at Downing Street in the Thatcher team after 1979.

The process of trolling for talent was separate from the process of keeping in touch with representatives of all strands of opinion. Like all leaders of the Opposition, Mrs Thatcher made it her duty to see representatives of a range of interest groups. With Joseph she met, for instance, the officers of Amnesty (of which, as it happened, one of Joseph's cousins was a founder). Amnesty's then chairman, Canon Paul Oestreicher, recorded later how

> She did not readily grasp the universal structure of Amnesty's task in holding every administration, without exception, accountable for the treatment of its citizens. . . . Margaret Thatcher showed deep concern for the victims of communist persecution, but beyond that her sympathy appeared to wane. It was her friend and colleague, Sir Keith Joseph, who had to remind her that selective indignation is not a prerogative of the left.

There may be few valid comparisons between Margaret Thatcher and Winston Churchill, but in one respect the years leading up to 1979, when she came to power, had a similarity to the years leading up to 1939. Like Churchill in the 1930s, Mrs Thatcher in the 1970s was regarded with suspicion by the Tory Party grandees. Both showed what they thought of the grandees by getting rid of most of them and bringing in their own teams, including a substantial leavening of people from outside politics. Churchill did it quickly; Thatcher cautiously but eventually more ruthlessly.

John Hoskyns, who played a pivotal rôle in the couple of years before and the couple of years after Mrs Thatcher came to power, was yet another Sherman discovery. He was in his late forties, a former regular soldier who had gone into computers and built up his own highly successful company. He had also developed his own ideas about 'the British disease', and was articulate enough to put them on paper. An article he wrote came to the attention of Sherman, who introduced him to Joseph.

Hoskyns was a man of great personal charm and friendliness, but not disposed to be over-respectful to politicians, and his prejudices were confirmed when he got to know more of them. He found himself, as a mere businessman, being treated by the politicians as someone from an inferior world. It was an example, he deduced, of a typically British two-culture gap which had to be bridged. But Joseph, he decided, was different. There was a meeting of minds. In Joseph he observed something all too rare in politicians – an intellectual confidence demonstrated in his willingness to admit, when he met somebody from the business world: 'I do not understand your business but I should like to; if you will explain, I shall listen.' Joseph did listen, and was not frightened by the unfamiliarity of new concepts.

The other thing Hoskyns found refreshing was that, in a world where getting to the top of the greasy pole was everything, Joseph had shown no rancour when he slid off the pole by giving up the fight for the leadership.

Joseph, for his part, was fascinated with Hoskyns's mind, and how a computer man applied a systems-analysis approach to politics. He arranged for him to meet Mrs Thatcher.

Hoskyns's first meeting with Thatcher was successful; the second had him in despair at her naïve self-confidence in her ability to impose her plans in Whitehall once she got to Downing Street. She seemed to Hoskyns to be saying that she would sit down for an afternoon with the officials and then they would understand what it was they had to do. Hoskyns, if only because of his military training, saw the task of reversing the tide of socialism as a long-term operation that needed careful planning.

She proved much less interested than Joseph was in the systems-analysis approach. She became impatient with what Joseph called 'John's boxes': he would draw a neat square, and write the objective of the operation in it, at the top of an A3 sheet of paper. To get there, he would explain, you first had to do so-and-so, and he would draw another box, and so on until the boxes disappeared off the bottom of the page. This was an attempt to get home to her the realities of the time-scale that would be involved. It was not an approach that appealed to the future prime minister's instincts. Nevertheless, Hoskyns, with Joseph in the background, did educate Mrs Thatcher over the next few years.

The arrival of Hoskyns in the Thatcherite camp was to prove important enough. But a range of other businessmen who were essentially non-political animals, and who had looked on Conservative politicians as largely irrelevant to their culture, came to see the party with new eyes as a result of the Centre's activities, even if they did not become active politicians.

And beyond that there was a knock-on effect, among people who had never heard of the Centre, which led to interest in Mrs Thatcher's kind of Conservatism where there had been a contempt or an apathy about politics.

A class of citizens, outside traditional Conservative territory, who were attracted to the Conservative Party in the 1970s consisted of Jewish businessmen. Of individuals, the most notable, in the longer term, was possibly the future Lord Young, whose story fits better in a later chapter. Another important individual was Norman Strauss, who worked with John Hoskyns in the run-up to the 1979 election and then, on secondment from Unilever, in Downing Street. Yet another was David Wolfson (nephew of the founder of Great Universal Stores), who also went to Number 10, as Mrs Thatcher's chief of staff.

When Keith Joseph entered the Commons in 1956, he was one of only two Jewish Conservative Members. It was Labour, the party of the oppressed, the outsiders' party, that had always had a strong Jewish presence. By 1974 there were a dozen Jewish Tories. But it was really in the decade after that that there was a notably more accepting atmosphere at the top in Conservative politics – and Mrs Thatcher's rapport with Jews was much commented on. By the eighties a significant proportion of the Conservative cabinet was Jewish. All this was part of the political sea-change.

The relationship between the Tory Party and middle-class Jews was thrown into focus in a by-election which occurred early in 1978, at Ilford North, a constituency with a significantly large Jewish vote. It was caused by the death of the (Jewish) Labour Member who had won the seat from the Conservatives in October 1974. Mrs Thatcher needed to win the seat back to demonstrate that she was on the way to victory. But she had a special problem in that the defeated Conservative of 1974, the strongly individualistic Tom Iremonger, had now quarrelled with his party and was standing as an Independent.

The next complication was that the race question raised its head. The National Front planned a march during the campaign. Ilford, with its racial pattern, was a suburb of north-east London with a collective memory still conscious of marches by the Mosleyites through Jewish districts of the East End before the war. The Police Commissioner banned the Ilford march.

The National Front was attempting to exploit the fact that immigration had recently resurfaced as a live issue on the national scene. Mrs Thatcher had chosen, not long before, to pick it up in the course of a television interview, upsetting some of the Shadow Cabinet in doing so; this was only one of many instances, around this time, of her 'making policy on the hoof' – pronouncing on controversial topics without talking them through with colleagues. Britain, she told her television viewers, could not ignore the dangers of having too many incomers who lacked 'fundamental British characteristics'.

Tory campaign managers in the by-election were alarmed. Observations about 'fundamental British characteristics' were not normally made, at least openly, in polite conversation in Ilford middle-class society. There was much talk about losing the 'Jewish vote'.

Against this delicate background, Keith Joseph was invited to speak in Ilford. Sherman drafted the speech.

Sherman had sharp and well-known views on immigration. He saw no inconsistency in arguing that a country which had once admitted Jewish refugees might, subsequently, properly impose restrictions on other immigrants: too many of the later waves of immigrants, in contrast to most of the Jews, were shiftless and, Sherman would assert, all too willing to impose burdens on the State.

The speech that Joseph made to the Ilford electors included this passage:

> There is a limit to the number of people from different cultures that this country can digest. We ignore this at our peril, everyone's peril. Therefore I say that the electors of Ilford North, including the Jews – who are just like everyone else, as the saying goes, only more so – have good reason for supporting Margaret Thatcher and the Conservative Party on immigration.

The 'only more so' was a characteristically sardonic flourish from Alfred's pen.

The speech caused a fuss in the Jewish establishment. The President of the Board of Deputies, Lord Fisher of Camden, wrote:

> Sir Keith's outburst is not helpful and I say again, and so do all my colleagues – and so does the Jewish community – that there is *no* 'Jewish vote' as such. To continue to suggest this is not true and only gives comfort to our detractors.

Back at Wilfred Street there was more wringing of hands over another speech that had got Joseph into trouble, but Sherman, in political terms, seemed to have pulled it off. The episode was recounted in Geoffrey Alderman's book *The Jewish Community in British Politics* (1983): 'It was the first time, in over fifty years, that a leading Conservative politician, more or less officially, had appealed to Jewish voters to support the party on a major policy issue and secured a positive response.' The Conservatives won back the seat with a swing of 6.9 per cent, and Alderman cites figures showing that the swing among Jewish voters was larger – 11.2 per cent. Alderman added:

> For better or worse, Mrs Thatcher had correctly judged the mood of the country and Sir Keith had correctly judged the mood of the Jewish electors of Ilford. . . . During the 1970s Jewish voters had become increasingly alarmed at the spectacle of a renewed growth of racist and Nazi parties in Britain, feeding on the prejudice of the host population towards New Commonwealth immigrants. Mrs Thatcher's policy on this question seemed to offer the best hope of containing both the immigrants and the National Front.

CHAPTER SIXTEEN

THE RIGHT APPROACH

> We used to think you could just spend your way out of a recession and increase employment by cutting taxes and boosting government spending. I tell you, in all candour, that the option no longer exists, and that in so far as it ever did exist, it only worked on each occasion since the war by injecting a bigger dose of inflation into the economy, followed by a higher level of unemployment as the next step.
>
> James Callaghan, as Prime Minister, addressing the Trades Union Congress, 1976

The Labour government to which the Conservatives provided the opposition in the 1970s were by no means the full-blooded socialist régime they might have been. If they had been more full-blooded, the Tories' path might have been smoother. Some monetarists, indeed, remarked that Labour acted more responsibly than the Heath government had done. An essay by John Biffen, 'The Conservatism of Labour', pointed out that in the autumn of 1973 the money-supply had been increasing at 27 per cent per annum; in 1977 the figure was down to 8 per cent. Virtue was imposed on Labour to some extent by the International Monetary Fund when they got into trouble. Their ability to push through socialist legislation was limited, moreover, when their majority diminished as the Parliament progressed and they were dependent on support from the Liberals and Nationalists.

In seeking to contain inflation, Labour relied largely on the 'Social Contract', their answer to the conundrum of prices and incomes policy: the unions were expected to restrain their pay demands; in return, the powers of government were used to restrict prices – and as a reward for wage restraint the unions were accorded considerable new privileges. One result was to make it easier for unions to impose a closed shop. All this represented a political philosophy light-years away from the market economics being talked about at the CPS.

Nevertheless, the Labour cabinets of 1974–9 (with Callaghan taking over from Wilson in 1976) did have a greater sense of commercial discipline than was acceptable to their left-wing supporters. The Government's first Secretary of State for Industry, Tony Benn, had been keen on fostering workers' co-operatives in lame-duck industries. Significantly, Benn was soon moved on, to be replaced by Eric Varley, a survivor of the older, more pragmatic school of Labour politician.

To a degree, the Industry Department under Varley continued what had been started by his predecessor in the Heath government, Peter Walker, whose managerial approach to industry gave a significant rôle to government. 'I endeavoured,' Walker wrote later (in *The Ascent of Britain*), 'to create new relationships between the Department and industry.' He encouraged, for instance, contacts between his officials and the banks. 'I sent them a list of the key officials in the hope that they would try to establish close acquaintances. This did begin to happen and the civil servants soon came to realise the advantage, not least that of having rather better lunches!'

The character of the Department of Industry as it evolved under Varley as Secretary of State and Sir Peter Carey as Permanent Secretary forms an important part of the Keith Joseph story because it was an item of the luggage which the Thatcherites had to take aboard when they came to power in 1979, and with which Joseph was presented as his first responsibility in Mrs Thatcher's cabinet.

By the late 1970s the Department was acting not so much as an instrument of socialist policy in the sense that Tony Benn might have liked, but rather like a merchant bank – a merchant bank prepared to wait a long time before seeing a return on its money. Firms which constituted a substantial proportion of British manufacturing industry – notably the Austin–Morris–Leyland car-manufacturing group and the ill-fated Rolls-Royce – were its clients. The Department monitored their potential profitability and exercised power over them to put them out of business. It was a relationship which could be equally offensive to both extreme socialists and *laisser-faire* Conservatives.

If the Labour government were less extreme than it might have been, it was equally true that the Conservative opposition appeared to be conducting itself in a more traditional manner than the radicals in Wilfred Street would have wished. Reviewing the period leading up to the 1979 election, Butler and Kavanagh, in *The British General Election of 1979*, concluded that: 'Sir Keith Joseph failed to wield the expected influence on policies although he had a major part in shaping the intellectual atmosphere.' The first major Conservative policy statement during the opposition years, *The Right Approach*, which appeared in 1976, was largely the work of Chris

Patten. (The proofs were cleared with Ted Heath, to avoid problems with a public denunciation.) It was followed by *The Right Approach to the Economy*. Both documents, in the words of Butler and Kavanagh, 'conveyed the style of R. A. Butler': this was a reference to the Tory 'Industrial Charter' after the war which carried the message that the Conservative Party did not seek confrontation with organised labour. Now – after coming to grief at the hands of the miners in the winter of 1973–4 – the party was again nervous about upsetting the unions.

Tory labour policy was in the hands of Jim Prior, and he was reasonably happy that the party was still following the 'middle way', avoiding the doctrinaire excesses represented by Joseph and the CPS. He wrote later: 'In Shadow Cabinet we devoted considerable time and effort to debating our economic policy. The zeal of the monetarists was tempered by the rest of us.' The point very much in the minds of 'the rest of us' as they listened to the Joseph arguments was that they had been here before, in the late sixties; in 1970 they had gone into office with high hopes based on purity of economic doctrine, and then been forced by harsh facts to abandon what Prior called 'a load of philosophical baggage'. He and his friends were convinced that they had conveyed the need for realism to their new leader, and that the wild men of Wilfred Street could be discounted: 'During her first couple of years as leader,' Prior wrote, 'Margaret did not appear to be the convinced monetarist she became by 1979.'

The Right Approach to the Economy, when it appeared in 1977, was signed by Geoffrey Howe, Keith Joseph, David Howell and Prior, with Angus Maude as editor. Much was made of the point that if Prior and Joseph could put their names to the same document the party was well on the way to adapting the 'middle way' to the Thatcherite ethos, and vice versa.

It was not as simple as that. Mrs Thatcher was less than happy with *The Right Approach to the Economy*. It was published but not recognised as a Shadow Cabinet paper. She was meanwhile developing her own policy-making machinery. The Shadow Cabinet had less influence than its members may have thought. If some of them were patronising about the wild men trying to get the leader's ear, the lack of respect was mutual. About this time, Joseph, who usually tried to look on the bright side when talking about personalities, remarked sadly to a friend, talking of the Shadow Cabinet: 'We're very much a second eleven, you know.'

Mrs Thatcher would not have quarrelled with that judgement, and she was casting around for first-eleven advisers. Early on in the course of preparing for the election of 1979, she brought in John Hoskyns. As we have seen, Hoskyns, who exemplified the most intelligent kind of ex-soldier and the most effective kind of businessman, was not wholly in tune with Mrs Thatcher. If there was a military analogy, he thought she was inclined to behave like one of the agitators in the Second World War who would shout 'Second Front Now' without realising what a second front involved. Nevertheless he became a great Thatcherite, and there was mutual respect.

When Hoskyns was taken aboard Mrs Thatcher's planning staff, he represented a threat to the Tory establishment, not least to Chris Patten, who could have assumed that he would have the central rôle in drafting strategy papers. And, if Hoskyns was a threat, there was worse to come in the shape of his colleague Norman Strauss, who also emerged from the ambience of the CPS – and who had the same effect on some people as Alfred Sherman. In Hoskyns's words, Strauss 'scared the pants off the Tories'.

Strauss and Hoskyns were co-opted on to what was called the Steering Committee of the Shadow Cabinet, which otherwise consisted of Whitelaw, Joseph and Howe, apart from Thatcher herself when available. Whitelaw was the chairman, but in fact the arrangements were sufficiently flexible for him sometimes to find that he was left out. Much of the planning took the form of exchanges of ideas between Hoskyns and Strauss on the one hand and the politicians whom they dubbed (after characters in a strip cartoon then fashionable in trendy circles) 'the Silent Three': Thatcher, Joseph and Howe. The word *silent* indicates how, whether deliberately or not, the nature of the strategy of the future Thatcher government was not being blazoned forth to the party or the public.

Patten was minutes secretary of the committee but was replaced as the election drew nearer, on the grounds that he was going to be a candidate and had to devote more time to nursing his constituency. The job was given to David Wolfson.

The fruit of the Steering Committee's work was a document called – the title was Joseph's – 'Stepping Stones', designed to satisfy Mrs Thatcher's aims of changing the state of the economy and of British society but showing her how it had to be done in realistic stages. 'Stepping Stones' covered the changes in taxation, reduction in government expenditure, and especially the curbing of the unions. It was set out in a form which showed how success on one stepping stone would give the stability needed to move to the next. Mrs Thatcher was impatient of much of the paper that crossed her desk from the party's hundred and one planning groups – and Hoskyns's 'boxes' were too elaborate for her – but her eyes lit up when the draft of 'Stepping Stones' was shown to her.

All the parties were prepared for an election by the spring of 1978, although the Parliament elected in October 1974 in fact drifted on for a year after that. It was in March 1978 that Sir Keith and Lady Joseph issued their single-sentence statement to the press that they had 'decided to live separately'.

It had been a strange Parliament, even leaving aside an Opposition in the throes of transition. There had been the resignation, for reasons never fully explained, of a prime minister in good health and apparently reasonably in command of his party. There had been the removal, for reasons explained at great length, of the leader of the Liberal Party, Jeremy Thorpe, who had briefly played such an important rôle before Heath left office in March 1974. It was also an unusual Parliament because the Government, kept going by a 'Lib–Lab' pact, was always teetering on the edge of losing its majority.

Again, a factor alien to British political tradition had appeared with the referendums in Wales and Scotland on the question of devolved government. Meanwhile there had been the referendum on whether Britain should remain in the European Community.

Devolution on the one hand and the EEC on the other revealed internal strains in both main parties. The EEC referendum campaign found pro-Europe Tories on the same platform as pro-Europe Labour MPs. It all tended to keep alive hopes of the traditional party structure breaking down. This was important because it coloured the enthusiasm of many senior Tories as they watched the way Mrs Thatcher was taking her party. Her self-confidence seemed unrealistic. For the next few years, well into the Thatcher administration, there was always at the back of Tory minds the feeling that the Thatcher–Joseph theories would be swallowed up into some new version of the middle ground.

Joseph was still more active outside the House than in it, but we have a picture of him as a parliamentary performer at this time from the then doyen of Commons sketch-writers, Frank Johnson:

> Over the despatch box he crouches – festooned with his own copious notes and with such additional artillery as cuttings from the City pages, pamphlets from various right-wing institutes and study groups, the bulky report of some American Mid-Western university seminar on *Was Keynes a Monetarist?* As he speaks, the veins are prominent on the forehead, the brows are coiled, the eyes are half-closed with concentration. The whole head comes to resemble an over-wound-up alarm clock about to go off or burst its springs.
>
> He will either be speaking once more about the efficacy of free enterprise, before the glazed or baffled stares of Shadow Cabinet colleagues. Or he will be rebutting some inane intervention about Chile from a Tribunite while he is saying that capitalism is crucial to political

freedom. He will treat the questioner – no matter how nihilistic, mean-minded or uninterested in genuine discussion he or she may be – as an earnest seeker after truth, just like himself. Courteously, he will explain that capitalism is a necessary, but not a sufficient, condition of freedom. After which the world will go on its way with everyone believing what they did before.

The 'glazed or baffled stares' of his colleagues could turn into something angrier. As the pre-election run-up period extended, there was scope for policy differences to emerge, not least over relations with the unions. By this time Mrs Thatcher was highly sceptical about the rôle of pay policy in controlling inflation, and indeed about the prospect of any useful understanding with organised labour, whereas the general feeling in the Shadow Cabinet was that over-emphasis on monetary control was provocative to the unions.

Jim Prior, as the authority on union affairs, was offended when Joseph made speeches condemning the closed shop. As the member of Shadow Cabinet with the overall 'policy' brief, Joseph could argue that the closed shop was the most natural topic in the world for him. Moreover, since 1977 he had also acquired the Shadow portfolio on Industry, which made it all the more legitimate to tread into Prior's area.

Prior kept trying to keep channels of communication open between the Shadow Cabinet and trade union leaders; after at least one meeting with Shadow ministers the trade unionists reported how they had sat back and watched Prior and Joseph engage in verbal fisticuffs.

Shortly before the Brighton party conference in October 1978, Ted Heath entered the act. The Labour government had announced a 5 per cent 'pay guideline', and Heath called for all-party support for it: *The Right Approach to the Economy*, he pointed out, had emphasised that both incomes policy and monetary policy had a part to play in handling the economy. When Joseph came to the rostrum at Brighton, to deliver what *The Times* called 'a brilliant speech', it was feared he would stir things up. In fact he confined himself to broad policy – but afterwards went on television with remarks almost calculated to upset the carefully balanced Prior case.

He was 'nervous', he told viewers, that if governments set out what average pay increases the country could afford the 'average' would become the norm. And where did averages leave the case for differentials? 'It will be natural for people working for Ford to do better than people working for British Leyland.' He was specifically asked to comment on the 'incomes policy' passage in *The Right Approach to the Economy*, which read:

Yet in framing its monetary and other policies, the Government must come to *some* conclusions about the likely scope for pay increases if excess public expenditure or large-scale unemployment is to be avoided; and this estimate cannot be concealed from the representatives of employers and unions whom it is consulting.

That, he insisted on television, applied only to the public sector.

The Brighton episode left the Conservative Party with an exposed flank on the whole area of incomes policy and unemployment. If they had been able to resolve their differences then, they might possibly have avoided some of the difficulties of the first couple of years of the Thatcher government. But meanwhile their problems became insignificant beside those which developed for the Government at the end of 1978, with the onset of the 'winter of discontent' when wage disputes in the public sector brought chaos to public services. The sight of rubbish piling up in the streets and gravediggers refusing to carry out burials made the trade union movement even less popular than it had been, and contributed to the Labour Party's defeat in the general election of May 1979.

Nevertheless, several of those closest to Joseph were convinced of how worried he was that the Tories might be going to lose. At no previous election had he carried so much responsibility for Conservative policy. Among colleagues at the CPS, as the date grew nearer, any feelings of achievement were tempered with nervousness and irritation. Some of the blue-eyed boys were coming to realise that, even assuming the party won, and however much Mrs Thatcher appreciated their efforts, she was not going to give them the power that some of them thought they were entitled to. They were in something of the position of the able young executive who has worked his way up in the rat-race of office politics and then finds that the top job he covets is going to go, after all, to the boss's son. They saw the old-guard Tories still with too much influence.

To some extent this was the influence of Mrs Thatcher's choice of Lord Thorneycroft as party chairman. He was certainly on her side on economics, but he was also an old pro who believed that when you are about to fight an election you draw all strands and traditions of the party together. This was carried to what some saw as an absurd length when he tried, to Mrs Thatcher's alarm, to involve Ted Heath in the general election campaign.

The CPS, run on a shoestring, was still in a sense a poor relation. There was a sad note from Sherman during 1979:

AS to KJ

I have been working in a cellar without natural light for five years, during which I have – in your own unsolicited opinion – exerted considerable influence for good on the British political scene and the Conservative Party.

In the last year before the 1979 election Sherman saw part of his duty as being to offset efforts by the 'middle-ground' Tories to pre-empt election issues. By this time he had direct access to Mrs Thatcher, and had come to the conclusion that she had a toughness, which Joseph lacked, to put policies into action. In July 1978 he had written urging her to counter 'misbriefing of the press' by 'hostile' senior Conservatives. As the pre-election heat built up he returned to the theme:

Alfred Sherman to Mrs Thatcher   March 19, 1979

I read with horror in the Sunday papers that the Conservatives are proposing to promise a £1000 present of public money to every first-time home-buyer. . . .

A message came back assuring him that everything was under control. But Sherman was not one to give up – just as he was convinced that the middle-grounders would not give up. On 5 April he was chasing up the story about first-time buyers again. It was increasingly hard to get the leader's ear as the election approached, but he approached Richard Ryder, who ran her private office:

I was told there was nothing in it. However, the Briefing Note [from the Conservative Research Department] of March 22nd 1979 (enclosed) carried the same promise in rather attenuated form. . . . Margaret will be very busy. You would know whether you bring it to her attention or not.

By this time, what Sherman wanted, of course, was not only decisive influence in party policy for the election, but also power in Whitehall once the party was in office. He was not the only one. There is no doubt that many of the new breed of high-powered people, some of them academics, some of them businessmen, who had been attracted by the New Conservatism would have liked to take a very personal part in the revolution that they hoped to see sweep away the old guard in every area of British life. They looked at the system in America, where the winning party takes with it to Washington a vast range of high- and middle-ranking officials, politically committed, to see that party policy is effectively put into practice.

Sherman, with characteristic panache, had been drawing up plans for what he called a 'territorial army' of advisers who would be available to march into the departments with the victorious Tory ministers to ensure that radical policies would not be watered down by civil servants with an instinct to play safe. He could not see why his political masters seemed less enthusiastic than he was. There was a hurt minute from him to Mrs Thatcher on 20 November 1978:

Reserve Army of Advisers
KJ advised me that he would be dealing with this matter and that I should withdraw.

Joseph, in so far as he had addressed himself to the question of getting radical policies past the civil servants, was probably convinced that it could be achieved by rational persuasion and argument. And Mrs Thatcher, in the event, allowed her ministers to take into Whitehall only a very small number of political advisers. One reason was quite simply that to bring in more of them – even in numbers more modest than a 'reserve army' – would have looked bad for a government committed to cutting the Whitehall salary bill.

In any case, in the run-up to the election, to set up 'reserve armies' of zealots could have had a negative effect on the Tories' electoral prospects. To Sherman it seemed that Joseph was nervous about *any* undue manifestations of zeal. If the vote did go against the Tories, the CPS would have a lot to answer for.

The 1979 election campaign got off to a tragic start when, once again, Irish terrorism provided a twist to the British political wheel. On 30 March a car bomb killed Airey Neave as he left the House of Commons carpark. Neave had been close to Mrs Thatcher ever since he ran her leadership campaign. It was assumed he would have become Northern Ireland Secretary in her cabinet, and that he would have been one of those she particularly leaned on as prime minister. To compare his supportive function with that of Joseph (or Whitelaw) was not to compare like with like, but certainly Neave's death affected the balance of power at Number 10 when she eventually got there.

The importance Joseph would assume during the Thatcher régime was not reflected in his rôle during the campaign. One of the standing jokes of the election was that both parties had agreed to keep their wild men under wraps: Labour tried to keep Tony Benn from saying anything in front of the television cameras, and the Tories, it was said, tried to do the same with Joseph. The currency of such jokes indicated how, even weeks before the new régime began, it was widely assumed that the economic policies Joseph stood for were not something that really had to be taken seriously.

During the campaign he carried out his usual punishing round of speaking engagements, but by the time the election came he was tired and perhaps bored; he never enjoyed elections. A colleague who travelled with him was astonished on arriving at the station to start one leg of the tour to find Joseph sitting in his compartment reading, not the customary pamphlet or academic book, but a novel, by Stendhal. He still seemed to suspect that the Tories might not win.

As always, he found it hard to say no to an invitation to a meeting. While campaigning in Scotland, for instance, he made a quick trip south to a CPS reception for people who had switched parties, which was arguably a less than cost-effective way to use his time during an election.

There was a trip to Huddersfield to support Bendelow.

On 3 May 1979 the country voted emphatically for the Tories, and Mrs Thatcher formed her first government. As with her choice of Shadow Cabinet, her first list of ministerial appointments did not seem to match the strength of her determination to cut off from the past. From a fairly early stage in the Thatcher government, ministers were to be classified as 'Wet' or 'Dry', the Wets those the Prime Minister perceived as lacking the moral fibre to carry out her plans, the Dries those who understood her message and were able and willing to push it through.

In retrospect, the Dries in her first team of ministers were in a minority. There were more Wets, some of them in the most senior positions, and there were even more ministers who were hard to put in one classification or the other. But the key economic jobs significantly went to the Dries. Geoffrey Howe became Chancellor and Joseph Secretary of State for Industry.

The way the Prime Minister's mind was working was indicated in a story recounted in *A Balance of Power* by Jim Prior, who, Wet though he was, was appointed Employment Secretary. Mrs Thatcher took more interest than most incoming prime ministers in ministerial appointments at the lower level, and there was some difficulty over the junior ministers at Employment. It was made clear to Prior that he must take the deputy that Number 10 offered. The Prime Minister came on the phone personally to make the point: 'Then came her punch line: "I'm determined to have *someone* with backbone in your department."'

CHAPTER SEVENTEEN

UNSWERVING LOYALTY

> . . . the understandable suspicion that increased productivity
> might mean unemployment. I think we would agree that one
> of our main concerns must be to exorcise that nightmare,
> because I believe that it is a totally unjustified fear. We live in
> an expanding age. . . .

Sir Keith Joseph, maiden speech, 9 May 1956

The first two years of the Thatcher government were gruesome ones for
British industry. The unemployment rate rose from 5½ per cent to over 11
per cent; output fell by about 6 per cent. Firms were fighting for their
lives by shedding staff, and the fine words of the Joseph maiden speech
looked to be a sick joke. The nightmare of unemployment, so far from
being exorcised, became a reality for several million citizens. The message
of Preston, five years before, had been that the cure for the British sickness
would be painful, but the Preston speech had scarcely warned that it would
be as painful as this or that the cure would take so long.

Part of the trouble was the price of success: the financial capitals of the
world approved of Mrs Thatcher and what she represented, and their faith
in her was manifested in a soaring exchange rate for the pound, which
embarrassed exporting industries. To aggravate the problem, there was a
world recession. But part of the blame lay with the Government's mishand-
ling of the monetary strategy which was at the heart of their policy. As
emerged within a couple of years, the principle may have been right but
the Government got the arithmetic wrong. Moreover, as Joseph knew
better than anyone, 'monetarism was not enough', and the Thatcher
government was guilty of a mistake that he had specifically warned against
in the Stockton Lecture in January 1976 when he said that restriction of
the money-supply – unless state expenditure was cut at the same time –
would 'strangle' the private sector.

During the first two years of the Thatcher government, Keith Joseph played a large rôle in the management of the British economy. He was widely seen not only by the Opposition but also by some of those Conservatives who had doubts about Thatcherite economics as a sort of Svengali in the background in Downing Street. He deserves blame for what went wrong and credit for the way the Government kept its eyes on the distant horizon of a more competitive economy, and therefore for whatever the long-term achievement of the Thatcher years was to be. At least one of his colleagues was forever grateful. Looking back on the first years of her administration, Mrs Thatcher expressed it to me thus:

> His particular contribution was his absolutely unswerving loyalty to the fundamental economic beliefs that he had been advancing before 1979, and on which we had won the election. In the country and around the Cabinet table, Keith went on supporting the very tough policies that we had to adopt to turn the country round.
>
> It is difficult to remember now [this was in early 1988] just how much talk there was at that time about 'U-turns'. With rising unemployment (instead of the falls we are seeing now), a tottering economy (instead of the boom we have now), and rip-roaring inflation (instead of the controlled growth we have now), most people believed that we would not be able to stick with our policies for more than a few months. Keith never lost heart, and never wavered.

Joseph's responsibility in the economic sphere was twofold. He was Secretary of State for Industry. He was also part of the Downing Street team – as he had never been in the Heath government – at the centre of economic decision-making. As soon became well known, the new prime minister had no intention of submitting her general economic policy to a free debate in the Cabinet. She kept the economic reins very much in her own hands, working through the Chancellor, Geoffrey Howe, and in so far as she felt she required further ministerial advice she turned to the Dry colleagues she could trust. One of Mrs Thatcher's biographers, Kenneth Harris, noted that 'The economic policy that was pursued was thus kept firmly on the rigid monetarist lines envisaged by the Treasury Ministers (the Prime Minister is also First Lord of the Treasury) and Sir Keith Joseph.' The tone of economic strategy was determined not by full cabinet but by 'E' Committee. 'E''s membership included a notable Wet, Jim Prior, now Employment Secretary, but the Dries were emphatically in a majority: Geoffrey Howe, Keith Joseph, John Nott (Trade Secretary) and John Biffen (Chief Secretary to the Treasury, in charge of the vetting of government expenditure). Joseph was chairman of the cabinet subcommittee ('EEA') dealing with public-sector pay.

The exclusion of the Wets was emphasised when the Prime Minister, as she realised the problems of reaching unanimity, took to inviting the Dry members of 'E' to meet discreetly for discussions over breakfast at Number 10: 'morning prayer meetings' intended to give Thatcherite moral uplift to everything else that happened in Whitehall during the week. Joseph loved these breakfasts – it was precisely the kind of atmosphere where he blossomed. An '8.30 a.m. love-in', one of them called it. The discussions stiffened the hearts of the faint-hearted as the unemployment figures mounted. Sometimes this included hardening the heart of Mrs Thatcher, who was rather more pragmatic and less doctrinaire than her critics made out. Part of the Joseph contribution was to bring policy back to basic principles: such-and-such an issue, he would tell the Prime Minister, required 'fundamental thought'.

Mrs Thatcher had entered Downing Street with the words of St Francis of Assisi (chosen for her by her occasional speech-writer, the playwright Ronald Millar) on her lips:

> Where there is discord, may we bring harmony.
> Where there is error, may we bring truth.
> Where there is doubt, may we bring faith.
> Where there is despair, may we bring hope.

Among those who pondered what this might signify for their future were the officials of Whitehall. Stories abounded over the next couple of years of how this radical new government had outraged, offended or trampled over the civil servants. Certainly there were zealots in the Prime Minister's entourage convinced that the job could not be done without trampling the civil service into the ground. Years later, once the Thatcher revolution was more or less taken for granted, civil servants who had been in sensitive positions in Whitehall in 1979 tended to emphasise how they had had no difficulty in adjusting to the new Thatcherite ideas; after all, they implied, they were by definition educated people, knew about Adam Smith as well as about Keynes, and they had made a point of keeping themselves informed on the intellectual development of the Tory Party in the 1970s. In any case it was their job to adapt quickly to the new political climate whenever a different administration took over.

But they might have been excused for being confused about what that political climate was in the summer of 1979: some incoming ministers were confused. Jim Prior indicated in his memoirs, *A Balance of Power*, how little the cabinet of which he was a senior member was thinking with one mind:

It was really an enormous shock to me that the Budget which Geoffrey produced the month after the election of 1979 was so extreme. It was then that I realised that Margaret, Geoffrey and Keith really had got the bit between their teeth and were not going to pay attention to the rest of us at all if they could possibly help it.

The civil servants at the Department of Industry, who had the arch-Thatcherite, Keith Joseph, as their master, were in a particularly interesting position. A contemporary observer, Hugh Stephenson, in *Mrs Thatcher's First Year*, set out the widely accepted perception of what happened: 'The atmosphere in the Department during May was distinctly edgy. This was not helped by the traditional first meeting between the Minister and his senior officials on the day of his appointment.' When they produced files on British Leyland, British Steel and other client organisations of the Department to place before Joseph, 'he told them as a tutor to his students to go away and read, or read again, certain works which would make it clear how he wanted them to approach industrial policy. . . . It was an unnerving start, but it was not to last long. By the middle of June his senior civil servants were confident that they had got the guru under control.' This was a telescoped account of Joseph's arrival at the DoI. He certainly never accused his officials of subverting his principles. The story of the civil servants being handed a 'reading-list', which provided laughs in Whitehall, Westminster and Fleet Street during the early weeks of the Thatcher administration, arose from an unguarded conversation by a civil servant in a Turkish bath, and as circulated the story was that the new Secretary of State had handed out a list on his first day. In fact he prepared it only at the Department's request.

At the initial meetings with officials he did indeed turn the talk to broad economic policy – you do realise, he told them, that the problems are all on the *supply* side? But what emerged was not his desire to impose a theoretical basis: on the contrary, he specifically declined to define a government 'industrial strategy'. After all, the logic of the philosophy he had evolved over the past five years was that a Department of Industry ought not to exist at all. Later he agreed to make a speech on DoI policy, but only in circumstances – it was made to the Bow Group – where he was sure it would not be reported.

His cabinet colleague Francis Pym found the same difficulty as the civil servants when he moved into a job where he was expected to have some general oversight of presentation of policy. Pym recorded in his memoirs, *The Politics of Consent*: 'When I became Leader of the House in January 1981 I asked Keith Joseph for a brief on his industrial strategy and was told there was none. I suppose this was at least a step forward from his original strategy, which was to abolish his own Ministry, but it was still a disarming reply.'

The famous reading-list has therefore to be seen against that reluctance to issue a policy statement. There were twenty-nine titles on the list. (A working copy presented to the author of the present volume – complete with departmental tea stain – was annotated to show that only two of the twenty-nine were already available in the office. As if to underline the fact that it was an informal document, it had three or four spelling mistakes in the names of books or authors.)

Most of the publications on the list were no more than pamphlets. Eight of the titles were by Joseph himself. Two others, on Upper Clyde Shipbuilders and the Meriden motor-cycle co-operative, were case-studies of Government-financed enterprise that had gone wrong. The authors' names, if not all familiar to typists, were well known at the Centre for Policy Studies or Institute of Economic Affairs, or both, as pioneers of the New Conservatism or the new radicalism. There were also the obvious classic titles. In alphabetical order by author, the list read:

Peter Bauer: *Class on the Brain: The Cost of a British Obsession*
Samuel Brittan: (1) *Second Thoughts on Full Employment*
                    (2) *Government and Market Economy*
Frank Broadway: *Upper Clyde Shipbuilders*
Jock Bruce-Gardyne: *Meriden: Odyssey of a Lame Duck*
John Burton: *The Job Support Machine*
S. N. S. Cheung: *The Myth of Social Cost*
Colin Clark: *The Political Economy of a Christian Society* (published by
                    P. F. Swarbrick, 52 Moorcroft Crescent, Ribbleton, Preston)
Jane Jacobs: *The Economy of Cities*
Peter Jay: *Employment, Inflation and Politics*
John Jewkes: *Delusions of Dominance*
Sir Keith Joseph: (1) *Why Britain Needs a Social Market Economy*
                    (2) *Reversing the Trend*
                    (3) *Stranded on the Middle Ground*
                    (4) (with Jonathan Sumption) *Equality*
                    (5) *Conditions for Fuller Employment*
                    (6) *Monetarism Is Not Enough*
                    (7) *Solving the Union Problem Is the Key to Britain's
                    Recovery*
                    (8) *Bibliography of Freedom*
Frank Knight: *Risk, Uncertainty and Profit*
S. C. Littlechild: *The Fallacy of the Mixed Economy*

Frank McFadzean: *The Economics of John Kenneth Galbraith*
James Martin: *The Wired Society* [on freeing telecommunications]
Lord Robbins: *Liberty and Equality*
J. A. Schumpeter: *Capitalism, Socialism and Democracy*
Adam Smith: (1) *Wealth of Nations*
            (2) *Theory of Moral Sentiments*
Alexis de Tocqueville: *Democracy in America*
W. Niskanen: *Bureaucracy: Servant or Master*

(Joseph always made the point that Adam Smith was a two-book, not a one-book, man. As he put it to me: 'The two really complement each other. . . . The propensity of people to truck, barter and exchange one thing for another – and yet to be loved!')

One of the first indications by the new government that they really believed in the doctrines of Adam Smith was a decision to abolish the Prices Commission. The Prime Minister also decided, although it was not announced, effectively to have nothing to do with incomes policies; the Tories, after a generation of such devices, were going to rely on market forces.

But there remained the question whether the Government had to have an incomes policy of some sort – the point mentioned by Joseph in his controversial television interview the previous autumn – on pay in the vast public sector. The Callaghan government during the winter of discontent had bought time by appointing a 'pay comparability' commission, under Professor Hugh Clegg, to make recommendations when public-sector pay claims came forward, and during the election campaign Mrs Thatcher had agreed, to the dismay of some colleagues, that the Tories would honour the Clegg decisions. Politically, there was seen to be no option; the public sector covered a large part of the population, and the Tory campaign managers' instinct was that unless they stood by Clegg they could damage themselves with the public-service white-collar workers who were largely natural Tory voters and blue-collar workers who were potential Tory voters.

The consequences of Clegg became a Joseph responsibility when he was put in the chair of the Cabinet subcommittee dealing with public-sector pay. A fellow-member was Jim Prior, who remembered how, as applications came in from various ministers regarding pay increases for which they were responsible, 'The monetarists didn't really care too much about Clegg at first. I used to sit in amazemeht as increases were sanctioned, not because they were acceptable, but because the new theory stated there would be no pay policy, since control of the money supply would force

down the level of settlements.' The Clegg awards, according to the Chancellor when he presented his budget in March 1980, added £2 billion to the
public-sector wage-bill. He called it a post-dated cheque the Labour
government had left behind.

The logic of the monetarist position, as described by Prior, had assumed
a level of commitment from two groups of people who did not yet fully
grasp it: on the one hand the unions, and on the other most of the ministers
responsible for State-sector employees. Most ministers did not take the
point that higher pay-levels logically meant employing fewer people; the
unions did not grasp that under monetarism they could preserve more jobs
on lower pay-scales and/or higher productivity.

But Joseph applied this logic in one area – the nationalised steel industry
– where he had responsibility. Steel was the scene of the first major
industrial confrontation of the Thatcher years, and it was Keith Joseph
who had to hold the line for Thatcherite principles.

The State-sector steelworkers were at that time each effectively costing
the taxpayer £1,800 per year. Their pay demand, which could be met by
the loss-making British Steel Corporation only if there were substantial
further subventions, led to a long and bitter strike. The steelworkers'
leader, Bill Sirs, was by no means an extremist. The accepted wisdom in
high places was to give in, and ministers watched Joseph's intransigence
uneasily.

In contrast to the attitude of so many previous governments during con-
frontations with nationalised industries, however, Mrs Thatcher took the
strict constitutional line that the dispute was the responsibility of the Steel
Corporation; and in so far as the Government were involved, as the
Corporation's bankers, decisions lay with Sir Keith Joseph, not with her.
'The hon. gentleman cannot know about relationships between nationalised
industries and Prime Ministers,' she retorted to one questioner in the
Commons. 'In a properly run government, the matter does not come to
the Prime Minister.' There was no question of bringing the parties together
over beer and sandwiches at Number 10, although at one stage one civil
servant close to the top sensed that the Prime Minister would have liked
to knock together some heads in unions and management. When the Prime
Minister did agree to meet Bill Sirs – on the understanding that the meeting
was not to be regarded as part of the negotiating procedure – he got the
impression that she had not troubled to grasp the detail of the dispute.

The culture shock for the trade union establishment was considerable.
'Talking to you', the TUC general secretary, Len Murray, was reported
to have told Joseph, 'is like trying to tèach Chinese to a deaf mute.'

The steel strike during the early months of 1980 was in its own way as
fierce as the coal strike five years later. At that time Mrs Thatcher

(who *was* closely involved in that strike) defeated Arthur Scargill in a confrontation which was compared, in terms of her resolution, with her performance over the Falklands. It was Keith Joseph who showed the resolution during the steel strike of 1980, before the Falklands had provided the benchmark in such matters: much of the official advice reaching him (and the Prime Minister) in 1980 was that it was impossible to hold out against the steel strikers.

His courage was, predictably, physical as well as moral. He met the steelworkers themselves on the picket-lines and set himself the thankless task of trying to persuade them with academic logic that it was not he or the Government who were to blame, that their plight was to do with the state of world steel markets. In Ebbw Vale his car was damaged. In Swansea there were tomatoes and eggs. The abuse he suffered was worse than anything the students had done to him.

The strike ended, after three tough months, in a way that had some superficial resemblance to the settlement of disputes in the days of beer and sandwiches: there was an independent inquiry which recommended a settlement that did in the short term increase the burden on the taxpayer. What was different from the old days was that the strike was followed with an insistence that the industry must pay its way in future, and the pay increases were accompanied by removal of restrictive practices and massive reductions in staff.

CHAPTER EIGHTEEN

LAME DUCKS AND RED ROBBOES

Everybody is always in favour of general economy and particular expenditure.

Anthony Eden, 1956

Meanwhile the logic of Conservative policy was being implemented by running down the activities of the Department of Industry. The initial programme had inevitably looked piecemeal to those who believed that the civil servants had 'got the guru under control'. There was a £233 million cut in industrial aid; the Secretary of State refused to waive the £1.2 million repayment due from the Meriden motor-cycle co-operative which had been a model case of state investment under the Benn régime; the National Enterprise Board, the organisation set up to hold the Government's stake in 'lame duck' companies like Rolls-Royce, was told to sell off £100 million of its assets – but was not abolished, as would have been logical. Overall, even if he failed to satisfy the fire-eaters on the Tory backbenches, there were enough cutbacks to enhance Joseph's reputation on the Labour benches as a wild axeman; *any* cutbacks in DoI expenditure, it has to be remembered, were seen as insupportable, in neo-Keynesian terms, at a time of high unemployment.

Joseph's first months at the Department had been filled with the usual frenzy of activity, inside the office and in the country. He liked to see for himself or, rather, to listen for himself: the visual displays of gadgets and widgets that factories lay on for VIPs could bore him. It was people and ideas that caught his interest. The *Financial Times* accompanied him on a tour and reported that 'Sir Keith's intense inquiring style when conducting meetings quite often pulls people out of their prepared speeches and into some acceptance of his ideas.' His 'ideas' – about the merit of market forces, however painful in the short term – were not only anathema to Labour but also disagreeable to the left of his own party. After six months, his colleague Sir Ian Gilmour, Lord Privy Seal and arch-Wet in the Cabinet, made a speech in which this passage was assumed to refer fairly directly to Joseph:

> Lectures on the ultimate beneficence of competition and the dangers of interfering with market forces will not satisfy people who are in trouble.
>
> Economic liberalism *à la* Professor Hayek, because of its starkness and its failure to create a sense of community, is not a safeguard of political freedom but a threat to it.

But meanwhile, on the right, he was accused of pussyfooting. (There was an explosion, indeed, early on at Number 10 when Joseph proposed spending *extra* money on a scheme to help with technology training. The Downing Street staff, with difficulty, persuaded the Prime Minister that he had not 'gone native' at the DoI, but was transferring funds, on a modest scale, to a legitimate DoI activity.)

He himself was conscious that his axe was not sharp enough, if they really believed the theme of his lecture 'Monetarism Is Not Enough': the cutback in public expenditure had to be massive unless the private sector was to suffer disproportionately. In the autumn of 1980 he admitted publicly that the Government had 'lost the first year'. But, if he was less than ruthless at the DoI, it had to be seen in the context of what was happening in the economy overall. To use a medical analogy, the Government felt they were in the position of a surgeon who knows that the patient is so ill that he needs drastic surgery, not just treatment of the symptoms; but if the symptoms become much worse he may not be able to carry out the drastic surgery. Ministers were taken aback by several things: the way that unions failed to recognise economic facts; the pattern of the world economy; and the pattern of exchange rates.

Joseph did not make his own task easier by having to justify his decisions against first principles and against the main thrust of government strategy. One of the few times he was seen to be angry with an official came during an intellectually rigorous meeting after he had observed that such-and-such a course would be out of keeping with 'the moral basis of Conservatism': the unfortunate official remarked that he wasn't sure what that was, and his tone indicated that he didn't greatly care.

Joseph took it for granted – and claimed to be more than satisfied – that his civil servants, once they knew what the ministerial line was, would be supportive. He worked with the team he was given. This applied to the junior ministers at the DoI. In 1979 he chose not to put in requests for particular colleagues to form the ministerial team – an indulgence of which one colleague, the future Lord Bruce-Gardyne, wrote (in *Ministers and Mandarins: Inside the Whitehall Village*): 'This was considered eccentric – indeed downright foolish.'

After a short time as Secretary of State he confided to his Permanent Secretary that it would be useful to have somebody outside the normal hierarchy with whom he could talk through issues. He needed, he said, an *advocatus diaboli*. Sir Peter Carey, after thinking about it, suggested not an *advocatus* but an *advocata* instead. The woman he had in mind was a bright young economist not long in the Department. This was Colette Bowe (who a few years later, as Head of Information at what had then become the Department of Trade and Industry, had the misfortune to have a central rôle imposed on her in what was possibly the biggest political crisis of the Thatcher government, the Westland affair).

To fill a similar rôle he also brought in Professor Harold Rose from the London Graduate School of Business Studies.

Some of the soul-searching involved in reconciling theory with political reality was explored in the long interview with Joseph which appeared in 1987 in the *Contemporary Record*, journal of the Institute of Contemporary British History. He was asked:

> Did you find difficulties at Industry in having to be more statist than you would have liked? Why did that happen, because you had such a clear grasp of the philosophy of anti-statism as applied to economics and industry and yet if one looks dispassionately at your period you were as much of a statist as the rest?

He began his reply by saying he was not sure that he would 'accept the full indictment'. He admitted the 'half-heartedness' of his policy regarding the massive losses of British Leyland. On the other hand, he went on:

> I do have to say in areas of less difficulty, such as British Aerospace, British Steel, British Telecommunications, the Post Office and Cable & Wireless, I was able to move more in line with my own previous analysis and policy recommendations. Nevertheless, British Leyland may wipe out all of those.

The Joseph period at the DoI did in fact see the first steps towards what became known as privatisation, which was later hailed as a great political success. He sold the government stake in British Aerospace and Cable and Wireless. And the British Telecom share sale, which ushered in the age of popular capital-owning after Joseph had moved on from Industry, had its inception early on. In 1979, the British telecommunications system was part of the Post Office, which was one of the many elements of the corporate state that came under the DoI. Keith Joseph, as it happened, always had a deep suspicion of the Post Office, for reasons which seemed to be instinctive rather than logical. (His officials once organised a visit for him behind a post-office counter, to let him see the strain under which the counter staff worked, and the amount of cash each worker had to account for.) However, leaving aside any ministerial prejudice, there were several grounds why the Post Office offended against the new political outlook. It held important monopolies, for the delivery of letters on the one hand and on the other for telecommunications, including the telephone service and the other forms of telecommunications which were clearly going to form one of the big growth sectors of the 1980s.

Keith Joseph separated the postal service from telecommunications. This seemed a modest enough move, which had been on the cards for some time, but it was done with a clear sense of how it could be the first step towards taking these activities out of the public sector. More significantly, and to the surprise of his officials, the new Secretary of State pushed ahead with highly practical steps which involved important liberalisation of trade and increased choice for the user. It became slightly easier for independent carriers to compete with the Royal Mail monopoly. More important, private enterprise could enter the telephone business. The telephone user no longer had to buy his equipment from the Post Office. He also had the choice in due course of using the rival Mercury system. And the phone system could be used by suppliers of 'value added' services providing information and entertainment.

The reins of control in the state sector were complicated by the existence of the National Enterprise Board, consisting of businessmen intended to provide expertise, as a middle tier between firms like Rolls-Royce and their government backers. Its chairman was Sir Leslie Murphy, a banker (former deputy chairman of Schroders) but a banker whose sympathies had lain largely with Labour – he was shortly to become a founder of the SDP – and who had a vision of joint ventures between state and private capital which did not fit in with the Joseph vision of the entrepreneurial future of British industry. The contrast between the two men was indicated in a lecture given by Murphy early in 1981:

> Exhortations alone are not enough: we shall fail to cure the deep-seated problems that afflict our society – unemployment, decrease in living standards, falling behind in the technological race – unless we develop an effective industrial strategy.

The notion of 'industrial strategy' was a measure of how the NEB under Murphy was unlikely to work well with the DoI under Joseph. Murphy represented much of the consensus approach of the sixties.

While not abolishing the NEB, Joseph announced that it was to concentrate in four main areas: it could provide loans to small businesses; it would encourage regional development in England (Scotland and Wales having their own development corporations); it would continue to have a rôle in firms where it was already involved; and it could help companies engaged in development of advanced technologies.

This was all a far cry from a total hands-off policy and it upset the Tory Right on the backbenches. Tony Benn, when the NEB announcement was made in the House, sardonically congratulated Joseph on recognising the State's rôle in the development of new technology.

But the NEB's financial resources were greatly reduced. Sir Leslie Murphy, who was soon to resign, argued that this did not stop money going into supporting lame ducks: huge new commitments were entered into on an ad-hoc basis. 'This,' said Murphy in 1981, 'was stupid. Sir Keith now has to go back to Parliament to increase them back to where they were before: how humiliating.' What brought the uneasy relationship between the DoI and the NEB to a head was Rolls-Royce. Rolls-Royce's chairman, Sir Kenneth Keith, did not find himself in sympathy with Murphy. The Secretary of State eventually decided to make Rolls-Royce answerable to him directly, not to the NEB, who regarded this, with reason, as proof of his lack of sympathy with their 'industrial strategy' concept.

The resignation of the chairman of the NEB, when it came, would have been an added worry for a troubled Secretary of State but one he could have lived with. He became much more anxious, however, when told that the whole Board – representing a fairly impressive array of business talent – were threatening to resign, too; in a sense it was to be a demonstration of doubt among the business establishment about the Government's lack of an industrial strategy. But, if the threat of mass resignation was a classic establishment ploy, there was a classic establishment counter to it. Sir Peter Carey reacted with all the resource of a practised Whitehall mandarin. He told the Secretary of State not to worry, then got on the phone to some of his contacts. When the Board carried out the threat and resigned *en masse*, Carey had a list of substitutes lined up to take over.

On the technology front, the case that earned most prominence was Inmos, a high-tech venture planned for Bristol, if government backing could be provided. The pros and cons of funding for Inmos ebbed and flowed through the DoI, and eventually the decision was to fund it – but in unemployment-ridden South Wales, not in prosperous Bristol: it could be regarded as a regional development case rather than a high-tech case.

Inmos was an instance where the Secretary of State was accused of vacillation. There were far fewer such instances in fact than there were in the Whitehall folklore that built up about Keith Joseph at Industry. His decisions may not always have been what his critics, on one side or the other, would have wished, but he did make decisions, and the evidence from the Department seems to be that he seldom changed them. What happened from time to time was that interested parties, the parties who had lost their case, would try to keep the file open by encouraging speculation that he was still dithering.

There was, however, one spectacular instance of him changing his mind, but it was a very special case, that of Leyland.

Like Rolls-Royce, British Leyland had a name rich in symbolism. The company was all too British in having a record that was the record of much of British industry: low productivity, overmanning, restrictive practices, poor management, inability to meet foreign competition, and unsuccessful attempts to solve management problems by becoming bigger and bigger. It also symbolised the constant and often pathetic conviction of the British that their industry, if only it could be given a fair chance, was basically a world-beater. BL's appalling labour troubles filled the headlines. (There was a spectacular shop-steward in 1979 called 'Red Robbo'.) The defects of some of BL models were a man-in-the-street talking-point. So the company's future, subsidised by the taxpayer, was no mere academic exercise for political economists. Apart from anything else, many thousands of people's livelihoods were at stake, directly or indirectly, in a huge industrial complex. Another consideration was the British car industry's importance to the balance of payments.

Leyland was now being pulled round by its new chief executive, Michael Edwardes, whose ambitions for the resuscitation of BL paralleled those of the Government for the whole British economy. In the background, as a powerful advocate of efficiency, was BL's deputy chairman Ian MacGregor, who was soon to move into the foreground of the Joseph story. There was enough good news at BL to dispose Keith Joseph in its favour. But it was obvious that apart from dynamic management the company in its present state required enormous further injections of capital. The logic of the Conservatives' pre-election stance was that if BL came looking for further capital from the State the answer would be dusty.

This, indeed, had emerged months before, at a dinner when Edwardes invited Mrs Thatcher, Keith Joseph and Jim Prior to meet his board for an exchange of views on what might happen at BL if the Tories won the 1979 election: Edwardes planned the *placement* at the dinner-table carefully, putting Mrs Thatcher in the position where she would feel least awkward at a table of men; he discovered quickly that the lady was hard to embarrass and fully confident in explaining why BL should not expect any more money.

Various writers from the Centre for Policy Studies stable were meanwhile setting out the case for putting the company into receivership. A theme that emerged was that at BL, and other ailing companies, too, the receiver – far from being like an undertaker or a debt-collector – could have a constructive rôle, picking up the pieces after a financial disaster: other companies would be willing to buy those components of BL that were viable; at the same time, so the argument ran, the loss-making components which went to the wall would represent a vast net saving to the taxpayer and hence the release of extra funds for reinvestment in more promising ventures.

After the 1979 election BL was struggling with its labour problems and making valiant efforts to improve efficiency but also, unsurprisingly, came back for more state money. The case for calling in the receiver was pressed vigorously on Joseph by Tory backbenchers, but certainly not by all the Tories. The range of Conservative attitudes was set out shrewdly by Michael Edwardes in his memoirs of the period (*Back from the Brink*, 1983):

> Conservative MPs with constituencies around BL's main manufacturing locations, such as Birmingham, Coventry and Oxford, were strong supporters of the company's battle for survival – even to the extent of being genuinely concerned, and perhaps alarmed, by our alleged brinkmanship in industrial disputes.

He commended the 'refreshing lack of attachment to political dogma' shown by those MPs, and also by a second school of Conservative thought, which

> saw BL as an engine of industrial recovery for the rest of Britain. They hoped that our plant closures, removal of restrictive practices, low pay settlements and the firm line we took with the militants would set an example elsewhere in industry, and thus help to restore Britain's industrial competitiveness.

Next, moving a little further to the right, Edwardes noted another group of Conservatives who would not have been too unhappy if union intransigence had indeed forced BL to the wall: it would have been an awful warning to the whole British trade union movement:

> A catastrophic closure of the company would, in their view, have had short-term political advantages and perhaps long-term economic and social benefits if it were demonstrably the fault of militant shop stewards, combined with poor trades union leadership. The future of BL itself was less important to them than the shock-wave effects throughout the economy.

Finally, in Michael Edwardes's analysis of the Conservative Party's dilemma over his company's future, was an even more extreme view that

> the short-term impact on regions such as the West Midlands and on the balance of payments might soon be offset by the beneficial effect of the shock of closure on trades union and employee attitudes across the country. Restrictive practices would be swept away, pay increases would be held down and more rapid improvement in Britain's competitiveness would thus be achieved through the closure of BL than by any other means available to the Government! . . .

The 'shockwave' theory weighed heavily with Keith Joseph as he considered BL's financial demands. But there were so many other considerations, giving him ample scope for enhancing his reputation as a politician who saw too many sides of every problem to be a decisive minister.

When he met the motor industry unions in October 1979 he told them that he saw his rôle as 'to look after the electorate, not the motor industry'. Of course the two were not mutually exclusive. BL was the source of work for a large number of small businesses, and the accepted wisdom of the Thatcher government was that the revival of the country's fortunes was less likely to lie in the hands of the British Leylands and the Rolls-Royces than in the little businesses that would be spurred into being by the new enterprise culture.

Again, there was a party-political dimension to the BL issue. Joseph on his own had no difficulty in seeing beyond it, but the political dimension exercised his colleagues: the country where BL was centred in the Midlands was important to hold electorally.

Then there was the balance-of-payments factor: if Edwardes could turn BL round, it would be an important earner of foreign currency; if he failed, the consequent increase in car imports could threaten the pound. Joseph was not an ardent balance-of-payments man – he inclined to the view that, if the world was genuinely one market, national advantages would tend to cancel each other out – but the importance of the balance of payments was pushed hard on him by the DoI.

Meanwhile BL was one of many companies suffering from the effect of the high pound on exports. An argument had now begun among economists about how much the pound was affected by Britain's new rôle as an oil-producer. 'If the Cabinet do not have the wit and imagination to reconcile our industrial needs with the fact of North Sea oil,' Michael Edwardes remarked in a much quoted aphorism, 'they would do better to leave the bloody stuff in the ground.'

Edwardes's relations with the Thatcher government were a mixture of impatience and mutual admiration. His summing up (in *Back from the Brink*) of his dealings with the Secretary of State for Industry was:

> Many people have an impression of Sir Keith Joseph which is way off the mark. There is, of course, Sir Keith the politician and there is Keith Joseph the man, but both personalities have one thing in common: integrity. He may change his mind (and I can bear witness to the fact that he can and that this can be very disconcerting!) but I'm prepared to argue that he will only do so if he is persuaded by the intellectual case put to him. . . . I have to say that he was easy to work with. . . . He is one of those people who is always 'a pleasure to do business with'. In a nutshell, I trust him.

Each year BL was required to detail how it saw its next twelve months as a step to a return to profitability. In the autum of 1979, Edwardes submitted a request to Joseph for a further £300 million to carry them through 1980, and waited to see which strand of the arguments over the company's future would predominate in government thinking. One day, he was called off the squash court at the Lansdowne Club, around the corner from his office, to sign a letter, the terms of which Joseph wanted to announce to the House that afternoon, agreeing that if the company's rationalisation plans were thrown off course by labour troubles the company would be closed. On that basis a £300 million injection was announced just before Christmas – 'the most begrudged Christmas present ever shoved into a laddered stocking', *The Economist* observed.

Part of the BL plan involved international collaboration, and eventually it was decided that the best partner would be Honda. Joseph held Edwardes's hand while the idea went to Cabinet committee. The critical negotiations took place just before Christmas. Keen to see the deal go through, Joseph urged Edwardes to fly to Tokyo, to be on the spot to clinch it immediately the Cabinet gave the go-ahead. Edwardes felt this was over-dramatic. In the event the go-ahead came on Christmas Eve, and Edwardes flew to Tokyo on Christmas Day.

High drama tended to surround everything connected with BL: in its high-profile management; at the government level; in the perennial strikes and disputes; in the lobbying that went on at Westminster by the various Conservative factions and by the Opposition; and in the crisis atmosphere of the Midlands, which since the war had been the scene of everything that was bright in the British economy and was now plunged into gloom, even without the prospect of BL going out of business.

The arguments about BL went on throughout 1980. Productivity was increasing, but nobody imagined that the £300 million was enough to make the company viable. Collectively the Conservative Party had not made up their mind. They wanted to see the Government out of car-making, but saw no immediate solution. Some favoured the 'receivership' approach, with the profitable elements sold off. Some would have liked to aim for flotation. In the later phases of privatisation by the Thatcher government the technique was to be to make a nationalised industry profitable and then to float it – but this was possible because the nationalised industries were monopolies that could put their prices up. BL had no monopoly and, indeed, was steadily losing custom to overseas suppliers.

When the end of another year approached, and there had to be another reappraisal, Joseph was warned that the next demand for capital, to cover the two years 1981–2, would be of the billion-pound order. Edwardes had few grounds to be confident that he would get the money, and he was rather surprised, during the negotiations in the autumn of 1980, to be asked informally by Joseph whether he was willing to stay on at BL – his secondment was due to end in March 1981. Joseph appeared to be thinking in terms of a medium-term future for the company under government auspices.

In contrast to some other issues of the time, BL's fate was never a simple argument between the Dries and the Wets. Years later, Keith Joseph described how he felt he was 'responding to the realities of the time'. In the end:

> I didn't have the guts to desubsidise Leyland. I could have said I would desubsidise it and would resign if my colleagues didn't support me. I myself flinched from the recommendations of my own analysis. Whatever the Prime Minister wanted, I could have crystallised the issue, but instead I temporised.

Apart from anything else, he was not confident that the entrepreneurs, and the capital, would have been forthcoming to fill the gap if the thousands of jobs at BL ceased to exist. And on the question of the salutary shockwaves that might have transformed the national psychology if BL had been 'desubsidised' he was aware that even the fear, without the actuality, of closure was bringing realism to the BL workforce. As he put it sardonically:

> He [Edwardes] was able to brandish as part of his change of culture at Leyland that the men really couldn't bank on that madman at the DoI or that mad woman at No. 10. To that extent my reputation was a help. But that's as far as it went – being a convenient madman.

Shortly before Christmas 1980 a meeting with the BL team was held in Keith Joseph's office. On the ministerial side of the table were three Dries and a Wet: Joseph, Biffen, Nott and Prior. Only Nott at this stage seems to have felt that enough was enough, and a paper was drawn up for Cabinet recommending that BL should get the money; the sum required was now put at £990 million.

But a final decision was put off till after Christmas. Over the holiday, Joseph rearranged his thoughts. A major factor in his mind in agreeing to the paper going forward appears to have been the balance-of-payments argument. Then he had a conversation with the Chancellor, Geoffrey Howe, which persuaded him that this was no longer relevant; in fact the Chancellor had meanwhile come to accept that BL should have the money, but not for that reason.

The next stage was a meeting of ministers presided over by Mrs Thatcher. The agreed paper, recommending without enthusiasm that BL should get the money, came forward, and Joseph was invited to speak on it. He did so, by speaking against his own paper. He was now in a minority, more Thatcherite than Mrs Thatcher, and presumably calculated that the only way he could possibly have tried to impose his new view on her was to offer to resign unless he got his way. In fact he did not do so. Of Mrs Thatcher's part, Jim Prior has written in *A Balance of Power*:

> Margaret's behaviour was fascinating. She was in favour of saving BL, and other interventions by Government to aid industry. But Margaret knew that these decisions did not fit her rhetoric and her image, nor did they reflect what many of her true and fervent supporters wanted. She would therefore conduct a very penetrating cross-examination in Cabinet and Cabinet committee: poor Keith used to have sweat all over his face as he contorted himself and his conscience.

Prior had his own reasons for putting that gloss on the episode, but there was certainly some ambivalence about the way the BL situation was conveyed to Michael Edwardes. He was summoned to a meeting on 20 January 1981 at 11 Downing Street with Joseph and the Chancellor and was apparently asked if he could give a guarantee, if he got the money, that the company would be sold off as soon as possible. The announcement was to be made the following Monday, 26 January. The days beforehand were occupied with drafting and redrafting of the various statements to be issued, and they appeared to be complete on Friday, the 23rd. Then the Prime Minister took over the redrafting herself over the weekend: there was to be a Thatcherite message contained in an un-Thatcherite decision.

After all of which it was Joseph who had to read the announcement on Monday afternoon. It was another of his less happy Commons performances.

Mrs Thatcher, questioned on television a few days later about the decision, defended herself by saying it was a question of choosing the right time for the State to rid itself of BL. Was this really, she demanded, the time to say: 'No, I'm going to chop you off at the stocking-tops?' There had been an enormous increase in productivity, and a new spirit in the industry, she said, and a new car, the Metro, was about to come on the market. But, she told the interviewer, 'I never want to take on another British Leyland'.

CHAPTER NINETEEN

ALL THE TALENTS

Who, whom?
Lenin

Initially the main contribution of the Centre for Policy Studies to the staffing of the Thatcher régime consisted of John Hoskyns and Norman Strauss in Downing Street. At the DoI, Keith Joseph brought in one 'industrial adviser' from the CPS stable – David Young, who was given the status (unpaid) of a civil servant at the principal grade. It was an unlikely toehold from which the future Lord Young eventually established himself as one of the most powerful members of the Thatcher retinue.

Young was a successful businessman, largely in property, who was yet another anti-Conservative who had developed political ambitions during the disillusioning days of the end of the Heath administration. He had become attracted when he visited the United States by the American political practice of employing 'dollar-a-year' businessmen, and academics, in jobs in government and decided that there must be something he could do to instil businesslike procedures into British government. In the early days of the CPS he made himself known to Joseph at a lunch connected with the Jewish charity ORT (Organisation for Rehabilitation by Training), concerned with helping refugees in Third World countries, of which Young was chairman. Subsequently he asked Joseph how he could help, expecting to be snapped up as a valuable asset. In fact Joseph's immediate response was: 'But you don't believe.' Young suggested that they should try him. He joined the CPS, raising money for it, and contributing to a range of policy papers for the Opposition.

As the 1979 election approached, he sold out his business interests, and on the first day Joseph was installed at the DoI he was summoned to serve, in rather more austere surroundings than he had been used to in the property business. Initially his work at the DoI was largely on the property side, concerned with industrial estates, but he gradually took on other responsibilities and was promoted from 'industrial adviser' to 'special adviser'.

His rôle did not cause the fuss that other special advisers might have caused if they had arrived from outside. The importance of his time at the DoI was not in the direct impact he had on it but in the experience he was gaining of the ways and byways of Whitehall. It also gave him the opportunity to make himself known in Downing Street. Without the experience of Whitehall he could scarcely have progressed as rapidly as he did when he was himself appointed a minister without the normal political apprenticeship. Not since Churchill's wartime cabinet had there been a case of a minister brought in by the back door assuming real power with such confidence.

If David Young arrived in the commanding heights almost unnoticed, the same could not be said, however, of the man that Joseph brought in in 1980.

The appointment of Ian MacGregor as chairman of the British Steel Corporation was very much a Joseph responsibility. Like the steel strike which preceded it, the appointment showed his courage in the face of vilification, courage that in any other minister might have been dismissed as foolhardiness. The appointment also exemplified two of his beliefs about the needs of British industry. He had always, from his maiden speech on, argued for paying large rewards to get the right man. He also believed that managerial meritocracy is international. He had little patience with chauvinism.

MacGregor was an American, albeit born and brought up in Scotland. After taking a First in metallurgy at Glasgow University he had gone to the United States, where he built up the metal group Amax Inc., expanding it into coal, oil and gas. Then, at the age when most men are thinking of retiring, he moved into merchant banking and was now a partner in Lazard Frères. His success was of the kind that appealed to Thatcherite economic philosophy. 'The world', he liked to say, 'is not forgiving towards those who are uncompetitive.' Mrs Thatcher was said to have described him later as the only man she knew who was her equal.

In particular, although this point was scarcely mentioned during the nine days' political wonder of the announcement, he was an outstanding salesman, which in the world conditions of the early 1980s was what the British steel industry needed. The British Steel Corporation also needed, like British Leyland, a powerful man to restructure it.

That said, there were plenty of political arguments against what Joseph did in appointing MacGregor. The financial arrangements startled MPs, Tory as well as Labour, when Joseph announced them, less than a month after the ending of the steel strike, on 1 May 1980. The Opposition front-bench spokesman called it 'the most staggering statement that this

House has heard in a long time'. MacGregor's firm, Lazard Frères, was to be paid what was instantly dubbed a 'transfer fee' – of up to £1,825,000 – linked to the performance of BSC under his chairmanship. *The Times* observed sternly that it was

> quite extraordinary that the British Government should have agreed to this further substantial payment to be calculated on the basis of events that have nothing to do with any loss that Lazard Frères may have suffered by the departure of Mr MacGregor. . . . There ought to be an element of public service in such employment. To deny it entirely is the sort of mistake a Conservative government should not make.

What Joseph was doing, quite consciously, was dragging the British public sector, kicking and screaming, into the top levels of the international market in managerial talent. For good or ill, he was also consciously turning his back on vague arguments about 'elements of public service'. And it was another farewell to the accepted wisdom of the 1950s, 1960s and 1970s that it was necessary to apologise for high rewards for the top people while telling the rank and file – as the steelworkers were being told – that they were pricing themselves out of the market.

Ultimately, the MacGregor episode enhanced Joseph's parliamentary reputation. After a sticky beginning, he saw off the Commons critics in one of his ablest debating performances. When the original announcement was made in the House, the reaction took a predictable course: the mad monk had finally gone over the top. One Labour Member interrupted the statement to ask whether the right hon. gentleman was feeling all right. The Employment Secretary, Jim Prior, who had become much involved in British Steel matters during the strike, was unable to be present on the day of the announcement but has recorded how he phoned the Chief Whip to ask how things had gone. '"Disastrous," was the reply. "I don't think we shall get away with it, there was no support at all."'

Both Houses of Parliament formally debated the appointment a couple of weeks later, by which time another twist to the story had been uncovered. A large fee was being paid to a firm of 'head-hunters' who had acted as intermediaries between MacGregor and the government. This seemed odd to many people. It was not as if MacGregor needed to be discovered. He was well known in Whitehall. The Labour government had brought him in as a deputy chairman of British Leyland in 1977. Moreover, only a few weeks before, his name had been specifically suggested to Joseph by Jim Prior, who was personally acquainted with MacGregor: his son, David Prior, was working for him in New York, and Prior has recorded that he knew MacGregor was interested in the job.

All this made the Tories nervous as the two MacGregor debates approached. The Lords debate came first. There the argument put forward by Joseph's deputy, Viscount Trenchard, must rank as one of the more curious defences ever put forward by one minister of another:

> Let me say this – and I have not consulted my right hon. friend [Joseph] on these words – that he has characteristically apologised for the way he presented this appointment. I have learned in the time that I have worked with him that with his very quick mind he sometimes follows a complicated path with very great clarity, and it sometimes takes time for the rest of us to absorb the process of his actions and his reasoning; so we fail, initially at least, to understand his correct conclusions, and they are very often correct.

After which introduction, Lord Trenchard got around to the kernel of the argument:

> In this case our minds were perhaps too encrusted in the framework of Britain, and perhaps in the perennial sickness of some of our nationalised industries. Perhaps we were too unimaginative to grasp the world dimension in which his [Joseph's] mind has been working for some time in order to try to solve a very difficult British problem of already far too long a standing.

When the Commons held their debate the following day, Joseph was more robust than that. It was one of the great parliamentary set-pieces of the first year of the Thatcher administration, but only a half-day debate, starting at half-past seven, opened by the Opposition and closed from the government front bench. Everything would stand or fall on the closing speech, which Joseph chose to make himself. He made it a sharp political debating speech. As the Opposition attack mounted, messages had passed to and fro between the front bench and the civil servants in the Official Box to produce the appropriate debating-points. The civil servants were told to go off and dig out, for instance, more details about Labour's record in appointing chairmen of nationalised industries. As he rattled out the answers in the fourteen minutes that were all the time he had for his reply, it became clear that this was the kind of performance the Tories wanted. The MacGregor episode ended as a plus for the Government.

Throughout 1980, Mrs Thatcher's economic policy came under withering fire from her foes and from supposed friends. By the autumn the Director-General of the Confederation of British Industry, Sir Terence Beckett, was calling for 'a bare-knuckled fight' with government policy. (ICI, pacemaker of British capitalism, had just declared, for the first time in its history, a loss.) It had never, of course, been any part of the Thatcherite strategy that their policies would be painless. William Keegan, describing this period a couple of years later, in *Mrs Thatcher's Economic Experiment*, quoted a 'ministerial source' as saying:

> 'The monetarists' real problem was that they could not make up their minds whether the squeals from British industry were a good thing or not. They wanted to weed the inefficient out. And even when ICI reported a quarterly loss, some of them thought: "Oh ICI – they're just as bureaucratic as the Civil Service."'

At the 1980 budget, as part of government policy to encourage small businesses to take up some of the slack, 'enterprise zones' – a particular enthusiasm of Geoffrey Howe's – had been promised. They would create an environment where new businesses would not have to worry overmuch about planning and other restrictions, and the Industry Secretary was enthusiastic about the fillip the enterprise zones and associated measures would provide. *The Times* reported:

> He was clearly elated. 'This country has for too long discouraged existing small businesses and the creation of new businesses,' he declared. . . . There is, according to Sir Keith, an 'untapped source of entrepreneurs', many small businesses just waiting to be started, and cohorts of business-men queueing up to find premises in which to start firms employing maybe only half a dozen people.

By the end of the decade the truth of this was beginning to be seen, but in the spring of 1980 it was largely a matter of faith. At the DoI, as the news came in of businesses closing down, there was a ritual where the Secretary of State asked his Permanent Secretary sadly whether there was any sign yet of the little green shoots. No, Sir Peter Carey would report, no green shoots yet – only snow and frost on the ground.

The industrial news continued bad through the summer of 1980. Mrs Thatcher, at the Conservative Party Conference that October, made her famous retort to the Wets who wanted a U-turn, or at least a moderate turn, in economic policy: 'You turn if you want to. The lady's not for turning.'

But it was not only the Wets who were worried about the direction of government policy. Among the worried Dries was Alfred Sherman, who comes back into the story.

The Centre for Policy Studies had continued in existence after its founders moved into government. Under the new régime in Wilfred Street, Sherman gradually lost the power he had once had, and eventually his job. He had lost also his influence on Joseph when he entered the Cabinet.

Joseph had not made any determined effort to get him a job in government, beyond arranging for him to have an interview with Sir Peter Carey, who asked Sherman what he would do with the Department of Industry. 'Abolish it,' said Sherman. It was not a fruitful interview.

The Sherman–Joseph axis was irremediably fractured. Each man was aware of the other's limitations. No man is a hero to his speech-writer, Sherman liked to say. By the summer of 1980, Sherman was convinced that at Industry Joseph – 'a lion in opposition, a lamb in government', as Sherman summed him up – had fallen all too predictably into the hands of the civil servants.

Sherman was still, however, on amicable terms with the Prime Minister. Indeed, at a certain level, she had more in common with the ex-Marxist than Joseph had ever had. She used him as a speech-writer and treated him as a sort of privileged court jester, allowed to say outrageous things: he put into words – and they could be scarifying words – many of her feelings of contempt for her Wet colleagues.

After the Government had been in office for a year, Sherman felt especially angry that the taxpayer was still supporting British Leyland. He gave vent to his feelings about his old patron in a note to Mrs Thatcher, composed with his usual flair for mixing virulence with imaginative imagery. It put the seal on the break-up of a notable political partnership:

Alfred Sherman to Prime Minister 14.9.80

HIGHLY CONFIDENTIAL: FOR YOUR EYES ONLY

I fear that KJ and his Ministry have not engaged in the basic thinking which is a precondition for denationalisation.

Sherman went on to recall how he had seen all this before; how Joseph, back at the time of Selsdon Park, had come to be regarded as one of the great radicals of the Tory Party – before taking office in the Heath government:

Within months of his return to office in 1970, the Ministry [the DHSS] swallowed him up so completely that I virtually came to regard meeting him as a waste of time, till the collapse in early 1974, when defeat again shocked him into radicalism. You know the rest.

Now, I fear, history is repeating itself. Months have passed since I last saw him; and, even then, there was no meeting of minds. . . .

I wonder whether I should continue to lend intellectual respectability to an enterprise which diametrically contravenes our aspirations. Do you remember the music-hall song: 'Turn Albert's face to t'wall mother!'? That expresses my feelings.

*

There is no doubt that Keith Joseph, by not producing more dramatic results in dismantling the corporate state between 1979 and 1981, disappointed many of his allies on the radical right. It did not look like that to the Prime Minister, certainly not in retrospect. Moreover it is fair to judge his political impact in the critical first years of the Thatcher administration by the same standards as his impact between 1975 and 1978: by his influence, behind the scenes, on the attitudes of the opinion-forming classes. Then, part of the evidence of his influence had to be looked for in what he was doing in the universities. Between 1979 and 1981, his record at Industry consists of more than the sum of the decisions he took as a Secretary of State, or his contributions in Cabinet and Cabinet committees; it has to take account of his effect on the thought processes of the Whitehall village.

In his relations with civil servants he started in 1979 with an advantage over almost all his colleagues in having a special rapport with the mandarin mind. And he was well aware that the mandarin mind had become adapted to administering a certain kind of remedy for the ailing British economy.

For one civil servant, that pattern, and the way in which Sir Keith Joseph broke it, was summed up by what happened right at the start of the Joseph régime in one of the cliché phrases of Whitehall in the 1970s. The phrase was 'When's the meeting?' The 'meeting' had become a hallowed part of the process of industrial rescue. When a business was threatened with closure, the company on the one hand and relevant trade unions on the other would make representations to the local Member of Parliament. The MP would approach the appropriate Department. The next stage was 'When's the meeting?', a meeting that might not please everybody but usually led to some measure of government intervention, some measure of financial involvement by the taxpayer, and would save at least some of the jobs at risk. In the view of this particular civil servant, a major sea-change began on day one of the new régime when it was made clear that there would be *no* meetings of that kind in Whitehall, at least not under the auspices of the Secretary of State for Industry.

There was also a sea-change implicit, when industrial lifebelt operations were being discussed, in the care with which Joseph would try to impose a norm on the wording of all discussion: it was not 'the Government' but the taxpayer who put up the money. There was more than quirkiness here. The detail of the language Keith Joseph used throughout his ministerial career, even in quite casual exchanges, always repaid study by anyone able to read nuances. Emphasis on the point about the taxpayer, from anyone else, might have been no more than the small change of the conversation of the New Right. But coming from *this* minister it could carry vibrations throughout a sensitive, intelligent community like the Whitehall village, where words were weighed and nuances studied.

Then there was his aphorism, 'Jobs occur if allowed', which summed up the argument against the interventionism of the 1960s and 1970s. Keith Joseph threw himself passionately into trying to impress on civil servants not just that private enterprise was more efficient than the Government in creating jobs, but that government action was positively harmful, by interfering with the benevolent effect of the interaction of a multitude of decision-making economic organisms.

From the standpoint of even a few years later than this, when 'Thatcherism' had begun to generate its own momentum, such matters of semantics would seem trivial. In 1979, in a sense, the Thatcherite momentum was almost non-existent. As we have seen, some senior ministers were finding it difficult to adapt mentally to the implications of what Mrs Thatcher and the small group around her were trying to do. The same was true of civil servants. Their loyalty may have been impeccable, and their intellectual integrity unquestionable. But there was a background of assumptions which, from the point of view of the incoming government, had to be overturned. Margaret Thatcher had her own remarkable techniques for overturning things, but her techniques often lacked intellectual coherence and consistency. Keith Joseph filled the gap, and through the Whitehall network and his seniority in the hierarchy, he exerted a powerful educational influence.

It extended to the Whitehall methods of accounting. In the DoI, and in so far as he was involved elsewhere, he was zealous that costs should not be in 'funny money': one of the assumptions that had grown up was to take inflation for granted in financial projections, in a way that he saw as encouraging self-fulfilment of prophecies.

His Whitehall educational rôle went largely unnoticed. There was so much else to be noticed. The Secretary of State had an unenviably high profile whenever fresh evidence came to the surface of industrial disaster. And among the New Right zealots, not just Sherman, there was the tendency to note what he was not doing, rather than what he was.

Sherman was busy seeking to influence general economic policy, particularly on management of monetary policy. Specifically he was in touch with Alan Walters, who had been in at the start of the whole monetarist controversy but who had gone off to America because he thought Britain, under its succession of spendthrift governments, was finished. Joseph (who would have liked to have him working for him when he joined the Heath government back in 1970) would also have liked to be able to persuade Walters to come back to a central position in Whitehall in 1979. That had not happened, but now arrangements were being made for Walters to join the Downing Street staff as the Prime Minister's personal economic adviser.

He did so at the start of 1981; but before that, in October 1980, he had dinner with Sherman and John Hoskyns of the Number 10 Policy Unit. These three men, only one of whom had any official position, took a decision, backed by the Centre for Policy Studies, which had far-reaching impact on the next stage of the Thatcher administration.

There were common-sense reasons for concluding that Mrs Thatcher's monetary policy was too restrictive. (William Keegan quotes a Bank of England official as commenting: 'In the summer of 1980 you only had to look out of the window to see that monetary policy was too tight.') Monetary measurement was a hideously complex subject, involving the definitions of 'wide' versus 'narrow' money, and how far 'Sterling M3' was the appropriate measure on which to base Treasury policy.

Mrs Thatcher had been arguing about it, often angrily, with the Bank of England throughout the summer. Relations between her and the then Governor of the Bank, Gordon Richardson (who was to be replaced in 1983), were not smooth. (One problem, according to a joke of the time, was that 'he was feline, she was canine'.) In any case, monetary policy was bound to be an explosive subject, painfully near the heart of the whole Wet–Dry controversy.

By the time of the dinner in October, Walters had come to the conclusion that over-reliance on 'M3' could have meant that the monetary screws were too tight. One of the many complications was how far North Sea oil was creating problems by keeping up the value of the pound. To Sherman, the obvious way to get answers to this kind of dilemma was to bring in an expert, a hand-picked expert known to have his political heart in the right place. He asked Walters for names, and Walters came up with that of Jurg Niehans of the University of Berne. Niehans was duly commissioned by the CPS, and his report confirmed the view of other, by no means Wet, economists that the monetary screws in Britain were indeed too tight. Not all economists agreed with Niehans, but his report was influential as having something of the air of an independent arbitration. Not least significant was that it knocked down the argument that everything was the fault of North Sea oil.

Mrs Thatcher was not inclined to see changes in monetary policy. She complained, using one of her favourite words, that the City were a lot of whingers when they went on about the rise in the value of sterling. Nevertheless she had agreed by the autumn to take the point and, quietly, the Government relaxed the screws slightly when, within a few weeks of the 'lady's not for turning' speech, interest rates were brought down by two points. Apart from anything else, while Mrs Thatcher the economic supremo could see the logic of high interest rates, Mrs Thatcher the politician wanted to see lower house-mortgage rates.

It was not a U-turn. However, from now on, less was heard about M3, and more of the PSBR, the Public Sector Borrowing Requirement. It was *public* borrowing that was to be squeezed. The autumn of 1980 thus saw a re-emphasis on the message that 'monetarism was not enough': unless accompanied by reductions in public expenditure, monetary restraint simply hurt private industry.

So the Whitehall departments were told that the cuts already made in their budgets were not enough. The Wets of the Cabinet were no happier with the shift in emphasis, and the end of 1980 saw the Wets making their most determined bid yet to moderate the Thatcher policy. Jim Prior records:

> Amongst the proposed savings was a plan to remove that year's indexation of state pensions – in other words, the basic old age pension would not even have been increased in line with prices. But I went to Cabinet equipped – as was Patrick Jenkin, the Social Services Secretary – with copies of Geoffrey Howe's and Keith Joseph's own personal election addresses in their constituencies in the 1979 election, in which they had specifically pledged to protect pensioners against inflation. So that idea was soon thrown out – Margaret was too good a politician to allow that to happen.

But Margaret was also a good politician in knowing that what could not be achieved through the front door might be achieved through the back. We saw how, before the election, when the Conservative establishment was not producing the kind of policy documents that suited her, she had brought in outsiders who spoke her language. The strengthening of the Downing Street team by bringing in Alan Walters as her own economic adviser can be seen in the same light.

There was, however, a logistical problem before Walters could be taken aboard. He was now accustomed to transatlantic earnings. The principle of paying the rate for the job having been established in the case of Ian MacGregor, it was decided that Walters should receive about double the going rate on the Whitehall salary scale: the balance would be met not from public funds but by the CPS. (Contributors to the Centre's funds were given an assurance that the money had been specially raised and was not coming out of ordinary subscription income.)

This amateurish arrangement for paying a man who was to hold a substantial share of the responsibility for the nation's economic welfare was a nice footnote to the history of the CPS: the dichotomy that the CPS symbolised between the thinking of the old Conservatism and the new was alive and well in Downing Street.

The scene was now set for Geoffrey Howe's third budget, in March 1981, often regarded as the turning-point of the Thatcherite experiment – and the effective humiliation of the Wets.

The British tradition is that the budget is the responsibility of the Chancellor, not of the Cabinet, who are informed of the budget's content only a matter of hours before the Chancellor introduces it to the Commons. The Prime Minister, First Lord of the Treasury, is a special case. Keith Joseph, although not a Treasury minister, also proved to be something of a special case in 1981.

The planning of the 1981 budget had specifically been kept well away from the cabinet Wets. But the ex-CPS team at Downing Street were greatly involved. According to Kenneth Harris in *Thatcher*:

> It was a Budget that was uniquely shaped by Mrs Thatcher. The Treasury drew up a list of proposals for cuts in the PSBR, feeling that really radical changes would not be called for. Sir Geoffrey Howe and Sir Douglas Wass, the head of the Treasury, were, however, summoned to No. 10 Downing Street to be confronted by Mrs Thatcher, Alan Walters, David Wolfson (Mrs Thatcher's political secretary) and Sir John Hoskyns. The Prime Minister told them that the Treasury's list of proposals was unacceptable.

The Treasury view, initially, was that public expenditure was under control. Walters, meanwhile, had calculated in the light of the Niehans report that to bring interest rates down safely, keeping the PSBR under control, £6 billion had to be taken out of the economy. He was pessimistic about the chances of it happening. Sir Douglas Wass told him that he agreed intellectually, but politically . . .

The people involved in planning the budget were disparate individuals each with strong views about the shape the budget should take: Treasury ministers, Treasury officials, the Prime Minister's official staff at Number 10, and her advisers who in a sense had no *locus standi*. On the other hand there were the non-Treasury ministers, at least some of whom took it for granted, given the level of unemployment, that the Chancellor would take the opportunity to pump spending power *into* the economy, not take it out; that had been the conventional wisdom in the old days. The most articulate of the academic economists were saying the same. And there were the official spokesmen of industry, like the CBI with their 'bare-knuckles' threat.

Everybody agreed that British industry was at a turning-point. To some, including Joseph, the Thatcher experiment was at a turning-point, too. He was persuaded by Walters that, unless the PSBR was reduced drastically, there would be a financial crisis by the summer, and it could be the end of Mrs Thatcher.

It was one of the most important occasions when he used his right of privileged access to the Prime Minister as senior keeper of the Thatcherite conscience. His relations with the Prime Minister's staff were proper – the convention was that non-Treasury ministers did not know what the budget was going to be – but he knew enough of the nature of the debate going on between 10 and 11 Downing Street to be able to pick his time for going to her to argue that the 1981 budget was not just about M3 and PSBR but about the survival of principles he and she believed in.

The budget presented on 10 March 1981 reduced the PSBR from £13.5 billion to £10.5 billion. The hostile and horrified reaction included the memorable protest by 364 economists that 'present policies will deepen the depression, erode the industrial base of our economy and threaten its social and political stability'. As it happened, it was about the time of the budget that output began to rise in the economy.

Keith Joseph claimed that the number of times he had serious influence in helping the Prime Minister choose among options was quite small. It was in *tête-à-tête* conversations with her that he tended to fill this rôle, the rôle of reminding her of first principles. He would call in sometimes late in the evening at Number 10, or drop into her room at the Commons. At the end of ministerial meetings, he might be the one to stay behind to chat. One of Mrs Thatcher's ministers said she treated him as the ayatollah who had pointed her, back in 1974, towards the Promised Land. Another said simply: 'She trusted him, totally.'

Little of the relationship of trust from the Prime Minister was visible at cabinet meetings. Several colleagues have recorded, indeed, being shocked or embarrassed at how harshly she could treat him in front of colleagues – no worse than she treated others, perhaps, but there was something about his manner that made him seem almost to invite bullying. (Some visitors to the various departments where he was a minister observed that he could lay himself open to what looked like bullying from civil servants.)

He did not regard himself as a great cabinet performer: he was much more effective in smaller ministerial groups. He was a more prominent speaker in Mrs Thatcher's cabinet than he had been in Ted Heath's, when, as he had so often explained, he had kept his eyes largely down on his departmental brief. The two cabinets, although both under strong-minded prime ministers, had of course very different modes of operation. In a famous remark shortly before the election she had explained that 'As Prime

Minister I couldn't waste time having any internal arguments'. She could be as impatient with Keith Joseph as with the others when she felt they were going on too long. Sometimes he seemed unable to take the hint, and would keep coming back – 'I really must insist, Prime Minister. . . .' On one remarkable occasion when he kept on, and she continually interrupted him, she was pulled up by Nigel Lawson, telling her to give the man a chance; according to the recollection of one of those present, the words were actually 'Shut up, Prime Minister'; whatever the wording, that was the effect for several minutes.

By the summer of 1981, the Cabinet was ripe for change. Mrs Thatcher was now confident enough to get rid of some important Wets who had seemed important to include a couple of years earlier.

The Wets had sealed their own fate when they had failed to act over the 1981 budget. They had expressed shock, privately and semi-privately, they had grumbled and they had held discreet confabulations. But none of them was prepared to carry protest to the point of resignation. Throughout the summer the Prime Minister considered how to reshuffle her cabinet to make it more clearly an instrument for what she hoped to do next, and in September she struck.

So far as the Department of Industry was concerned, her inclination was that Joseph had had enough; but she would probably not have asked him to move if he had wanted to stay. Asked, for the purposes of this book, about his contribution at Industry, she summed it up thus: 'He began the liberalisation of the telecommunications industry; he began to get some of our worst nationalised industries back on to their feet; he paved the way for the massive privatisation programme we now have.' (So much for Sherman's dismissal of his contribution to privatisation.) The question of promotion to the Exchequer appears not to have arisen this time, as it had in 1970 and possibly in 1979. An obvious move would have been to a non-departmental job. But Joseph had made his own assessment of the reshuffle. He knew that one of the people Mrs Thatcher intended to get rid of was the Education Secretary, Mark Carlisle, and he went to the Prime Minister to ask if he could replace him.

She may have been surprised; she may indeed have found it hard to imagine why anyone could want to go to Education – she had been there herself and bore the scars to prove it. For him, it would be a move sideways rather than promotion, but at this stage in his career that was not something that would upset him. Moving to Education at the age of sixty-three was a natural culmination; education, in the broadest sense, was what his whole career had been about.

As the Prime Minister worked her way down the list of possible cabinet changes, the Thatcherites among her entourage in Downing Street worried whether she would be as bold as they felt she ought to be. John Hoskyns went off on holiday to Italy leaving elaborate arrangements to hear the news as soon as she made up her mind. He had a chart made out with possible names along one axis and the cabinet jobs along the other; the coded message that would be telephoned to him would be like a chess game: P–Q5, and so on. When the message came through, it was obvious that the lady had gone far to checkmate the Wets.

Jim Prior had not been sacked but had been moved, in humiliating circumstances, from the Department of Employment to the Northern Ireland Office. Publicly he made much of the fact that he remained a member of 'E' Committee – but his presence there had scarcely been an insuperable obstacle to the Prime Minister in getting her own way in the past.

Two other major figures were simply told that they were out. One was Lord Soames, minister responsible for the civil service, who had been considered too soft in handling a civil service dispute that dragged on for months. His departure meant the severing of the last direct link with the party of his father-in-law, Churchill. The fact that the carrier of the Churchill mantle, talked of only six years earlier as a possible prime minister, could be dismissed without the heavens falling in showed how far the Thatcherite revolution had gone.

The other major Tory to go was Sir Ian Gilmour, major intellectual of the old Conservatism and author in the mid-seventies of the best-known summing-up of the 'Wet' case, *Inside Right*. Since 1979 he had become the master of the 'coded' speech, coming as near as any minister has ever done to repudiating the policies of the cabinet he served in: 'coded' politics was one of the features of the Conservative Party during the 1980s.

Gilmour's reaction to dismissal was characteristically languid: 'It does no harm to throw the occasional man overboard, but it does not do much good if you are steering full speed ahead for the rocks.' This was the orthodox Wet view of the time. Unemployment was heading for the 3 million mark. The summer of 1981 had seen inner-city riots in Toxteth, Brixton and Moss Side which seemed to show that the Thatcher revolution had now fostered another kind of revolution. And electorally the Conservatives seemed in deep trouble: later in the autumn the new Social Democratic Party, with Shirley Williams as their candidate, overturned a 19,000 Tory majority in Crosby.

But if the Government was heading for the rocks there was now a markedly more united crew occupying the bridge and the engine room. The Prime Minister's most radical backers had high hopes that they might really be on the way to Thatcherite radicalism. Not least, some of them hoped, the new Secretary of State for Education might use his analytical gifts to change the face of Britain's schools and universities.

Keith Joseph's last day as Secretary of State for Industry, the day when the cabinet changes were announced in time for the early-evening news, showed Joseph at his most characteristic. There had been plenty of rumours about who was in and who was out, but as the day passed normally at the DoI it was assumed that he must be staying there. At four o'clock there was a one-hour meeting about the future of Telecom. He presided with all the usual gusto. When it ended, he asked David Young to stay behind. For a while he worked at his papers; then, looking at the clock said: 'Now I can tell you.' He said he was going to Education and wanted Young to go with him. (In fact Young stayed at the DoI before going on to head the Manpower Services Commission, but in due course had an important indirect impact on education.)

It probably never occurred to Joseph to be other than meticulously discreet about the cabinet changes until the time of the formal announcement: he gave no hint to the Private Office or to the Permanent Secretary. It was an appropriate final flourish that summed up much of the rather strange relationship between him and the Department of Industry. They loved him – or most of them did – but he had never really fitted, and had never made them fit him. The abruptness of his departure irritated Sir Peter Carey, who had an evening engagement which it was too late to cancel, and who would otherwise have thrown himself immediately into the briefing of his new Secretary of State.

When the Conservatives met at their conference a few weeks later, the new Secretary of State, Patrick Jenkin, summarised the achievement of the DoI under Joseph:

> We had a grim inheritance. . . . [But] since January, our competitiveness as a nation has improved by around 10 per cent. Across the country, firms, large and small, have been dramatically increasing their efficiency. . . . Next year British Steel will break even. . . . British Leyland is following hard behind on the road to profitability. . . . British Shipbuilders too is on the road to solvency. British Airways has begun to set its house in order. . . . A whole new battery of incentives has been introduced to encourage the birth and growth of small businesses.

CHAPTER TWENTY

THE SECRET GARDEN

Children's as good as 'rithmetic to set you findin' out things.

Frances Hodgson Burnett, *The Secret Garden*

Around Westminster, when it was announced that he was moving from Industry to Education, much of the comment was along the lines that 'Keith would be happier there'; which told its own story – there cannot ever have been many politicians whose promotions, upwards or sideways, are discussed in terms of whether they are going to be happier. One ministerial colleague noted that Keith was able to 'work with the grain' at Education, whereas at Industry everything went against the grain, since fundamentally it was a department he wanted to see abolished.

At Industry he had spent two years resisting pressure to define an 'industrial strategy'. Now he threw himself with relish into education strategy. His long tenure of the job – nearly five years, the years that saw Mrs Thatcher's government fortified by victory in the Falklands and then victory in the general election of 1983 – ended with him prepared to claim modestly that he had 'put education at the top of the agenda'; in the face of the acknowledged ills of British education his achievement had been in diagnosis rather than in cure.

On the education of children, his diagnoses were clear and often inspired. On higher education his policies, by contrast, often seemed confused. In both the schools and the universities his scope for action was cruelly constrained by the Government's financial policies, to which he was pre-eminently loyal – more loyal, it was sometimes said, than was healthy in a minister in charge of a major spending department. The financial policy meant that for his whole period at Education he was in dispute in one way or another with the teachers' unions over pay and conditions. The never-ending conflict not only made it hard to implement reforms – although he was surprisingly practical in improving the content of the curriculum, the examination system and the education of the less able pupil, for instance – but also poisoned the atmosphere of the whole educational scene. Joseph was never able to operate at his best in an atmosphere of hatred. His failure to solve the teachers' pay dispute was a major failure in this period of the Thatcher administration, for which his colleagues must share some of the blame: there was a point where Keith Joseph perhaps needed to be saved from his own financial conscience.

Although he was able to 'work with the grain' at Education, there was nevertheless an ideological dilemma, as there had been in his last job. At the Department of Industry it had been the ideological case for abolishing the department altogether on the grounds that the State had no business to get involved in industry. The same argument was almost precisely replicated in the minds of many New Conservatives who thought the State had no business getting involved in the actual process of education: this was the case for financing education with vouchers and letting individual schools, funded with vouchers, get on with teaching the children. Like teachers' pay, the 'vouchers' issue hung over Keith Joseph's head in some form through his years at Education, and arguably, like teachers' pay, it absorbed a needless amount of intellectual and emotional energy. If he had been able to break through the teachers' pay issue (which he never did) and break through the vouchers issue (which took him a couple of years), his five years might have been as fruitful in cure as in diagnosis.

Vouchers were a shibboleth of the Thatcherite radicals, whose guru Joseph had been. He had disillusioned many of them by not being more radical at Industry; he disillusioned more of them when, reluctantly, he rejected education vouchers. Vouchers apart, education was in some ways one of the most obvious areas of divide between Thatcherite radicalism on the one hand and socialism and Wet Toryism on the other. Oversimplified, the radical Thatcherite view on education was that the changeover to comprehensive schools in the 1960s, fostered by Labour and Conservative local authorities alike, had been a disaster; and that the curriculum in Britain's schools had become largely woolly in content and sloppy in standards.

The radicals were especially contemptuous of a certain kind of Conservative who enjoyed serving on education authorities: most of those traditional Tory councillors, they would say (with some justification), knew very little about state education for the simple reason that they took care to have their own children educated safely outside the state system; so their supposedly Conservative education policies fell into the hands of educational 'experts' – at best trendy innovators, at worst social revolutionaries – who had played havoc with standards in schools. The radicals saw the voucher as almost a panacea to solve all those problems at a stroke.

Trying to be fair to the case for and the case against the voucher, in an interview in 1987, Joseph set out what he saw as its attraction for a Conservative Education Minister:

> One is always as a Minister looking for a single lever that would transform attitudes. I think that at Industry there were such levers. Denationalisation was a lever, provided there was competition. One looked for the same sort of lever at Education.

To the Tory radicals in 1983 the introduction of vouchers seemed to possess the same potential that denationalisation had in industry: it would dismantle a monster of an organisation that was out of touch with ordinary people: the 'voucher', provided by the taxpayer, would give every parent the purchasing power to pay for the kind of education he wanted for his children and to shop around among available schools. Being in a position to pay the piper, the parents would call the tune.

Vouchers seemed to the new Secretary of State to be a noble concept, and he never changed that view: they could be a lever to stimulate the motivation of parents, children and teachers which was indispensable to effective schooling. Eventually he came to the conclusion that the decision must depend on three issues:

(1) Would it be sensible to give vouchers to parents paying for private education? This would result in a deadweight cost, and preliminary thinking on the issue was hostile.

(2) Would it be sensible to turn all state schools into voucher schools on a given date or should there be a pilot scheme? He decided that, superficially, an imposed change with no pilot scheme first would appear as dictatorial as had the much criticised requirement by the Labour government which decreed that all secondary schools should become comprehensive. In fact the parallel, he argued, was false, because vouchers, in contrast to comprehensivisation, would not impose a single system; they would be allowing freedom for each school to choose. Nevertheless he hesitated to legislate for vouchers for all. And he came to the conclusion that *either* approach would be bitterly fought – in Parliament, in the Tory Party, by most local education authorities, by most teachers, and perhaps by the churches.

(3) The pilot scheme approach would, he also concluded, have raised its own difficulties. The necessary legislation would be long and complex as well as being bitterly fought, and would occasion widespread parental alarm. In the circumstances, would a pilot scheme give vouchers a fair trial? Might not the Tory Party, he wondered, be faced with years of conflict and hubbub – during the period of legislation, then years of preparation, and finally the years of the pilot scheme? Enquiries had revealed no local areas eager to be guinea-pigs. He foresaw the

possibility of perhaps ten years of intense controversy, producing at
the end only a mouse of results of the experiment.

His conclusion was to prefer other means of giving parents a better deal
for their children – means which certainly did not involve abolishing the
centralised educational system: the Department of Education, at the end
of his régime, emerged more powerful than it had ever been. In two years,
for instance, he doubled the proportion of educational funds at the disposal
of central government as distinct from local education authorities.

Keith Joseph arrived at the Department of Education and Science with
the benefit of his intellectual reputation and his reputation for integrity,
although his political philosophy made him anathema to the left. Over the
next few years, while antagonising some of the zealots on the right, he
made himself friends on the left, and gained the respect of education pro-
fessionals. This had to be set against his overall failure to reach a working
arrangement with the teachers' professional organisations. It said something about Britain's teachers that one of the more academically inclined
ministers they had ever dealt with was not in tune with them collectively.

A hint of the ideological problem emerged during his first appearance
wearing the Education hat at the Tory annual conference, just a few weeks
after he took over. The verbatim report records how he was interrupted
when he came to this apparently uncontentious point in his speech:

> So here we are, with over 85 per cent of secondary pupils in comprehen-
> sive schools. . . . If I may say so, to whomever interrupted, it is not
> 'wet' to recognise that that is where we are. For the sake of all the
> children in all those schools, or who are to go into them, we need to
> make the best of them enthusiastically.

He said he wished the country had not gone so fast towards comprehensivisation. Then he went on:

> Now I must speak personally for a moment. I have been intellectually
> attracted to the idea of seeing whether eventually a voucher might be a
> way of increasing parental choice even further (*Applause*) . . . let me
> finish please. It is not as easy as that. There are very great difficulties in
> making a voucher deliver, in a way that would commend itself to us,
> more choice than the 1980 Act will deliver. [The 1980 Education Act
> required schools to publish information about themselves to provide
> parents with an element of choice.]

A major problem in getting the voucher to 'deliver' – indeed, a major
problem in everything to do with the schools, including fixing teachers'

pay and terms of service – was that the schools were currently run not by the Department of Education but by the local authorities. A large proportion of the authorities were Labour-controlled. The others were often run by the 'Wet' Conservatives disliked by the zealots.

Joseph had already established working relations with the local authority representatives. The then chairman of the Association of Municipal Authorities, the socialist Mrs Nikki Harrison, always recalled their first meeting over tea, just before that Conservative conference. She came to the conclusion that this was something out of the ordinary in the way of Education ministers when he opened the conversation by remarking that as he was observing the Day of Atonement he had to be out of the office before the sun went down.

She and he quickly came to terms. Part of the rapport may well have been because each privately sympathised with the other for having to cope with colleagues who were much less intelligent than they were. 'We clicked,' Nikki Harrison recalled, and their rapport helped to make the conflict with the education world less fraught than it might have been.

Given Mrs Thatcher's own suspicions of the educational establishment as represented in the Department of Education, it was a department ripe, so to speak, for a Thatcherite takeover when Mark Carlisle was removed from it. There was already a junior minister keen to take part in the takeover if he got any encouragement. Rhodes Boyson had been made an Under-Secretary under Mark Carlisle in 1979 – a less than generous reward, many thought, for a man of his political record. He had helped to produce the 'Black Papers on Education', but his effectiveness as a campaigner went far beyond education. His platform style, patriotic, straight-from-the-shoulder speaking in bluff North Country accents, went down outstandingly well with Mrs Thatcher's new constituency of working-class Tories. In some important strata of society Boyson's political *persona* was better-known than Keith Joseph's.

He was among those with little time for the way schools had been run by Wet Tories, and it had seemed odd that when he was made a junior minister at Education in 1979 it was decided to keep him away from the schools side of the Department, which he was itching to get his hands on: his brief initially was higher education.

Now, in the 1981 reshuffle, he had been passed over for promotion. He and the new Secretary of State, although they subscribed to the same economic philosophy, were scarcely cut out for serving closely in the same team: it was the old Cavalier and Roundhead conflict.

Boyson had an important ally in the Department in the shape of an adviser brought in by Mark Carlisle: Stuart Sexton, formerly a businessman

(Shell International) and local councillor, who had come to the attention of Dry Conservatives by writing papers on how to restore traditional values in education.

The Joseph régime got off to a curious start which did nothing to offset the Secretary of State's reputation for being a soft touch for civil service mandarins. When he arrived, the suggestion apparently came from the officials that Sexton had served his purpose and could be dispensed with. The new Secretary of State did not demur, indicating that he was in favour of saving on the salary bill. It was only after representations from elsewhere that Sexton was reinstated, and then only as a half-timer. Then, after further representations, this time from Downing Street, he was restored to a full salary.

As at the Department of Industry two years before, the civil servants at the DES awaited the arrival of their new master with interest. At the first session between him and his senior officials he expressed one of his main anxieties with a remark that he was often to make: here was a nation which compelled its children to spend eleven years of their life in school; yet 50 per cent of them left school, as soon as the law allowed them to leave, with virtually no benefit to them, in character or in preparation for work, adult life or citizenship. The reaction, at least among some of his listeners, was urbane: 'Oh, don't say fifty per cent, Secretary of State,' said somebody, 'say *forty* per cent.'

Privately, Keith Joseph stuck to his guess of 50 per cent of pupils failed by the system, but the official DES line became that there was a neglected 40 per cent of the school population. The 'bottom forty per cent' became a slogan of the DES, as the 'cycle of deprivation' had been at the Department of Social Services ten years earlier.

In the first weeks at the DES there was no reading-list circulated, just one book, a book which had been commissioned by Joseph at the Centre for Policy Studies: *Lessons from Europe* by Max Wilkinson, then an education journalist. Wilkinson had put together damning evidence about how the British system lagged behind the Continent. Keith Joseph now decided to back this up officially by sending missions of Her Majesty's Inspectors to France and West Germany. The evidence of how those countries helped children at the lower end of the educational scale had considerable influence on the plans that emerged during the Joseph years at the DES.

The Sexton episode had not raised the spirits of the Tory radical zealots, who wanted to see vouchers as something more than 'intellectually attractive'. As it was, the intellectual content of the policy-making process was notably increased when the Secretary of State recruited another adviser to join Stuart Sexton: Oliver Letwin, a young political high-flier whom Joseph had come to know through his parents, Bill and Shirley Letwin, who had provided intellectual input at the CPS. (There was no salary problem with Letwin: he was unpaid, until, later, he moved to a similar job in Downing Street, where they were able to fit him into their budget.)

If intellect alone could have solved problems, the DES would have been rapidly problem-free. On the official side, an intellectual pacemaker was Walter Ulrich, deputy secretary, a Wykehamist who had been a famous figure at the Department since he moved to it, from the Cabinet Office, in 1977.

From 1981 until 1983 the DES was the setting for a sort of stately quadrille as Sexton and Letwin put the case for vouchers, and watched it being knocked down by what seemed to them an unending succession of officials. Vouchers were of course only one issue. The DES provided ample scope for administration by discussion and discussion paper – the favourite Joseph technique of 'Socratic government'.

It was a form of debate more suited to a university than to a department in a Thatcher government, although the concrete block where the DES was now installed could scarcely have been less like an ivory tower. Elizabeth House, facing the Shell Centre at Waterloo, has been dubbed the 'white man's grave south of the river'. Built with shops on the ground floor to maximise site value, it overlooks the station and the giant round-about leading to Waterloo Bridge. The ventilation was less than perfect and in summer the staff had either to perspire or open the windows and let in the noise of the trains and buses and lorries.

Sir Keith, Fellow of All Souls, would sit, with coat off, displaying his elegant braces, at the centre of his long table, on which landed the mass of paper generated by the Department and at which he presided over discussion after discussion with officials and outside experts. The gatherings were often large and the discussions long. Mr X would be encouraged to build up a case, then the Secretary of State would turn courteously to Mr Y at the other end of the table and invite him to shoot it down. Everyone usually agreed that it was stimulating; it was no way to run a revolution, which was what the zealots wanted.

Rhodes Boyson often found it more constructive to find other things to do when these meetings took place.

It was not just at the highest intellectual level that Joseph drew his inspiration. Visits to schools would include meetings, without anyone else present, with children to get their ideas. Both sides sometimes emerged baffled from these encounters.

He made use of the background notes supplied to him before visits. Before a meeting with some unemployed young people the briefing note read: 'Don't take any notice of their rather original hairstyles: some of them are bright, and some of them are very good children.' He could surprise headmasters by announcing when he arrived at a school that he would particularly like to meet Mr So-and-so – Mr So-and-so being the most outspoken union activist in the staff room.

Always there was the urgency of cutting government expenditure. School rolls were falling, so that expenditure per child would still be going up in real terms, but it was not an argument acceptable to the teachers' organisations during the depressing range of strikes, work-to-rules and other confrontations. Joseph was particularly outraged that the unions had found methods of disruption short of complete strikes, so that the teachers still drew their salaries. A different kind of politician might have found it easier to do a deal with the teachers' unions – and a different kind of politician did so, when Joseph eventually handed over to Kenneth Baker.

The negotiation procedures were determined by intricate arrangements that went back half a century. At the centre was the Burnham Committee which technically fixed the salaries, which then had to be paid by the taxpayer and the ratepayer. The traditional 'two sides of industry' were fragmented on both sides. The teachers were represented not by a single union but by contrasting organisations with different aims, philosophies and degrees of militancy. The employers, although most of the money had to come from central government, were the local authorities, who equally represented a variety of philosophies.

Joseph tried to work through these complexities according to a fairly simple set of principles. He believed that teachers should be well paid, although he regarded some of the demands as absurd; but what was more important was that good teachers should be paid more than the less good. This meant a career structure which would recognise merit; it meant some kind of assessment system; it also meant getting rid of poor teachers. All this was seen as common sense by the average voter, and indeed by the average teacher, but to get it accepted by the teachers' organisations proved to be beyond Keith Joseph's powers. His failure made his achievements in other parts of the education field the more remarkable.

He might have found it easier to settle with the unions if government philosophy had been more amenable to the idea of an incomes policy in the public sector. He would certainly have found it easier if he had been less highly principled on the financing of his department. To a degree perhaps unique among ministers, he declined to 'play the Whitehall game' against the Treasury. Other ministers might happily wear one hat in defending financial stringency in general, but another hat in arguing their own department's case. The Whitehall structure had been built to accommodate just such double standards, but they were alien to Joseph's nature, and playing the Whitehall game would have offended his personal sense of loyalty to this prime minister. Several times during his years at Education the Treasury were astonished when he accepted a *No* which other ministers would have regarded only as a first stage in a negotiating process. The Education budget lost out at a time when it perhaps ought to have fared better relatively than other departments.

By early 1983, the education debate took on an extra political dimension, as the time came when Mrs Thatcher had to decide when to go to the country. The next general election was, since the Falklands, something to which her party could look forward with more relish than had seemed likely only a year earlier.

Geoffrey Howe was given the job of co-ordinating policy for the election which eventually took place in June 1983.

Education, not least the notion of 'parental choice', fitted in very well with a broader theme which appealed very much to the Prime Minister. The fact that her thoughts were moving beyond the economic was perhaps symbolised by the arrival of a newcomer to head her Policy Unit. John Hoskyns had left. Joseph was given the task of trying to persuade him to stay in the government machine, by moving over to head the 'think-tank' at the Cabinet Office, but the proposal had foundered because there was no guarantee of freedom of action that Hoskyns would have wanted.

The Downing Street job was taken over by Ferdinand Mount. Mount's philosophy had been elegantly set out in his book *The Subversive Family*. The 'subversion' in the title tuned in with Mrs Thatcher's instinct that the family, in the sense of a solidly family-based culture, could stand up against a presumptuous State: part of the Thatcherite vision on the far horizon, as she looked forward to the 1983 election, was a Britain which had rejected socialism and in which the norm was that every family would care for its own, and for their material and spiritual welfare. Papers had been circulating in Whitehall setting out how, for instance, the National Health Service could be largely displaced by private insurance.

Education vouchers could have been an important part of this vision of the future. When Geoffrey Howe made a wide-ranging speech which was intended to demonstrate his mastery of the wider political scene beyond the economy, he commended vouchers. At the Department of Education, however, Joseph was increasingly aware of the practical problems. By the spring of 1983 he had satisfied himself that vouchers, despite their intellectual attractiveness, represented political risks he was not prepared to take, at least for the present.

When the election came, the Conservative manifesto, in its section on education, merely referred to 'increasing parental choice'. But during the campaign the hopes of the zealots among the party's policy-makers spilled out in the 'Daily Notes' that were sent out to brief campaign workers: 'We intend in the next Parliament to make schools more responsive to parental choice. One way of achieving this would be by the introduction of education "vouchers" or "credits".' The Secretary of State found himself in the rôle, so familiar to him, of explaining a misunderstanding. The commitment was not to vouchers, he said, but to parental choice. An easier system to implement might be 'open enrolment', as had been tried in the schools of Kent.

It was more than a playing with words. There was a real conflict behind the scenes over how radical the next stage of the Conservative programme could be or ought to be. In the event, the Tories scarcely required their theme on family responsibility to win them the 1983 election. The Labour Party, fighting one of its most disastrous campaigns, almost won it for them.

At one point the opinion polls, while showing the Conservatives comfortably ahead, showed the two Opposition groupings – Labour and the Liberal–SDP Alliance – running neck-and-neck. At Conservative Central Office there was momentary panic lest the thing they had greatly feared was about to happen: that the Alliance would become a credible Opposition. If that happened, then dissatisfied Tories might flock to join them, which they would never do so long as there was a danger of letting Labour in. Joseph upset some campaign managers when an offhand remark, presumably intended to be no more than realistic and slightly funny, was quoted in the media: 'These last days [of a campaign] are very nerve-racking. It could still crumble. Anything could happen, and probably will.' It was understandable that Central Office encouraged him to keep a low profile in terms of the national media. But he fought a vigorous campaign, and when he happened to find himself at the centre of an incident in which the Tories could have been seriously embarrassed he showed himself, it was widely agreed, at his best.

He had undertaken to go to support the Tory candidate at Stockton South. This was a seat where the Labour Member, Ian Wrigglesworth, had defected to the SDP, the old Labour vote was consequently split and the Tories were in with a chance.

On the morning that Joseph arrived in Stockton, the constituency found itself in the headlines: it had emerged that the Conservative candidate, Tom Finnegan, had in 1974 stood as a National Front candidate, and had failed to disclose this to those who had now picked him as a Tory. Joseph, as he was to explain next day, felt 'confused and embarrassed, not because of Mr Finnegan's former connection with the National Front, but because the party did not know about it until that morning'. He declined to accompany the candidate on the street campaigning that had been planned, but turned up at the hall where he had arranged to make a speech. By this time the media had descended in force on what had until then been an ordinary marginal constituency. Next morning, there were accounts in the papers of how the Secretary of State, when his turn came to speak, 'jumped off the platform' and delivered his speech from floor level, rather than speak from the same platform as a former National Front candidate. This was a needlessly dramatic interpretation of what was actually his normal practice. At smaller public meetings he liked to get physically close to his audiences. The technique had been documented long before (by Simon Hoggart) in one of the many newspaper profiles written about him over the years: 'At political meetings he will descend with microphone into the audience to ask them questions, like a cross between Socrates and Des O'Connor.' But leaping into the audience at Stockton did him no harm in the eyes of reporters sent to Stockton to look for a good story.

On polling day, Mr Finnegan failed to win the seat by 103 votes.

Overall, the Tories had a victory of landslide proportions, with a majority of 144 seats. The creation of the Social Democratic Party had harmed Labour far more than it had harmed the Conservatives.

With the general election out of the way, Joseph announced in July 1983 that vouchers were off the agenda for the time being. He was at pains to get the message across that parents must be involved in education. Invited by the *News of the World* to contribute a message for the end of the summer term, he wrote:

> Our decisions to give parents more choice – through the enactment of the "Parents' Charter" – and to tear away the veil of secrecy by publishing HM Inspectors' reports are already having an impact on standards and quality of our schools. . . .
>
> After allowing for higher costs, more is being spent now on each school child than ever before.

It was reminiscent of his pride in achievements when he had been at Housing or at Social Services.

From now on the emphasis was on what the Department could do to raise the quality of education. To use the metaphor that floated around in the educationists' world at this time, he began to push open the door to the 'secret garden' where every previous Education Minister had been reluctant to walk. The secret garden was the content of education: the tradition in British education had always been that the schools were the responsibility of local, not central government, and moreover that individual schools and individual teachers made their own decisions about what was taught and how it was taught. The Government was now laying powerful hands on the curriculum and on the examination system. After all the long-drawn-out discussions in Elizabeth House, the Secretary of State's decision, reluctant but resolute, was that standards would never rise without clear leadership from the centre. By early 1984 the President of the National Union of Teachers was talking of 'Government intervention on the grand scale; he [Joseph] has twisted and skewed a system that was based on partnership and consultation'. There had never, he added, been a Secretary of State who had done so much.

The NUT, with its fight over pay, and its suspicions of measures to weed out bad teachers, had its own reservations. But, for most workers in education, Keith Joseph's stock rose markedly during 1984. As always, he was able to disarm people with modesty: when he came to the job, he said, 'I underestimated the task which we face raising standards in schools. In particular, I did not at that time fully appreciate the problems of low-attainers and the special difficulties faced by teachers in many inner-city schools.'

As before, he heralded the new phase of his career with a speech. The 'Sheffield speech', as it was known when it entered education folklore, was delivered to the North of England Education Conference on 6 January 1984. After two years of reading inspectors' reports he had come to the conclusion, he said, that 'much of what many pupils are now asked to learn is clutter'. The speech set out minimum standards that ought to be achieved by 80–90 per cent of pupils. In English, this would include the ability to speak confidently, read and pass on information and state their views clearly. In history they should understand cause and consequence and be able to extract information from evidence. He set out similar basics in mathematics and craft, design and technology.

The reference to 80–90 per cent of pupils showed that he was shifting away from what was often called the élitist emphasis in British education and was a response to all the evidence that poor education at the lower end of the pupils in British schools had played a part in the country's industrial decline.

He was determined also to hasten the shift away from the false interpretation of what ought to be meant by a liberal education. He was much impressed by the arguments set out by Correlli Barnett about this time in his book *The Audit of War*, linking the decline in Britain's economic power with the failure to adapt the education system to the modern industrial world.

Greater respect for the scientist became a Keith Joseph theme. It was often remarked, however, that he seemed, paradoxically, to have a blind spot when it came to polytechnics.

The theme of the 'bottom forty per cent' led to the change in the examination system with the introduction of the General Certificate of Secondary Education, intended to give a more realistic qualification attainable by the less able pupil but without reducing standards to be attained at the top end of the scale. In January 1983 he had announced a £2 million scheme to assist thirteen selected local authorities to develop courses for non-academic children. (This was an example of the use of funds clawed back out of the education budget into the hands of central government, to use at its discretion.)

CHAPTER TWENTY-ONE

CLASS AND CULTURE

I'm afraid the fellows in Putney rather wish they had
The social ease and manners of a 'varsity undergrad,
For tho' they're awf'lly decent and up to a lark as a rule
You want to have the 'varsity touch after a public school.

John Betjeman

The year which had opened with Joseph moving confidently forward to carve out a brave new world for the schools ended in near-disaster with him offering his resignation. It was almost like the Birmingham birth-control story of 1974 all over again. In 1974 his misjudgement, according to the cynics, was to link the two topics on which the British are most hypocritical: sex and social class. This time the sex element was missing, but class was at the heart of the problem. Briefly, by threatening to deprive better-off parents of their subsidy for sending their children to university, he set himself on a collision course with the suburban middle class who were the power-base of the new Conservative Party.

His reconciliation with the educational establishment really applied only to schools, not to higher education. He never really reached a clear vision of what he thought British universities should be trying to do (still less what the polytechnics should be doing), or perhaps as always he saw too many sides to the problem. All his work over the years on the improvement in industrial skill and standards of management might have led him logically to want to see a much larger higher-education sector on the American pattern, with a far larger proportion of young men and women going on to some kind of college. His instincts seem to have been against that, although an acceptance of a larger higher-education sector would have paralleled the dream of helping the 'bottom forty per cent' in the schools.

The universities had been suffering their own kind of stringency under the Thatcher government. As Joseph put it, after twenty-five years of uninterrupted growth, they were having to 'adjust'. There had to be financial adjustment, but it is fair to say that there was also an ideological

180

dimension. The same anti-establishment instincts that had attracted the electorate to Mrs Thatcher also made them suspicious of much of what went on inside the universities.

Yet there was a paradox. The new upwardly mobile classes which had helped to put Mrs Thatcher into power formed part of the first middle-class generation in Britain which took university education as part of the norm for itself. Partly it was because they acknowledged that, for good or ill, a university degree was now a prerequisite for most good jobs. Moreover, although their inclination was probably to be antagonistic to 'students' as a class, and to what they knew of the modern ethos of the campus, so far as their own sons and daughters were concerned they saw three years at college as a desirable experience.

The precise way in which higher education should be organised and paid for was something – one of many things – that the new middle classes had not rationalised in their collective mind. If they had any twinge of conscience about the volume of taxpayers' money being spent on their offspring, it was easy enough for them to silence it by telling themselves that the middle classes still, even after reductions in income tax rates, paid large amounts of tax.

The Prime Minister herself had not thought through such matters. A periodic theme in her speeches was 'middle-class values'. She liked to praise what she saw as the middle-class ethos as represented by qualities like self-reliance, good housekeeping, prudent provision for the future, all of which fitted in with Thatcherite economic policy. But there was a paradox here, too, which irritated some of her colleagues, notably at the Treasury. Since she took it for granted that 'middle-class values' included buying a house on a mortgage, she had a notorious blind spot in regard to the tax privilege of mortgage tax relief, which blatantly contradicted the Thatcherite fiscal principles which her chancellors tried to follow.

Keith Joseph had a rather different interpretation of middle-class values. He liked to talk of *embourgeoisement*. Up to a point he and she were talking about the same thing, but there was a different connotation to *embourgeoisement*. It carried noble, if vague, suggestions of how the under-privileged, the bottom forty per cent, as they were educated for something better, would not only be able to earn enough to pay their mortgage but would also refine their tastes: pop music would give way to grand opera, fish and chips to *bœuf bourguignon*. Put another way, Keith Joseph lacked his leader's earthy links with the new suburban middle class.

When the 1984–5 parliamentary session got under way and he did his sums at the DES, he decided that more had to be found to pay for scientific research. To balance the books he decided that student grants – which had already been substantially reduced for the children of parents able to support them – should be further cut, and that better-off parents should contribute towards tuition fees.

The decision created perhaps the greatest upset to the Parliamentary Conservative Party since the Falklands War; and the way that money was extracted, literally overnight, from the Treasury to pacify rebellious backbenchers was described as the first U-turn of the Thatcher administration. That was overstating the case. There had been earlier less dramatic but more costly changes of policy. The interest of the storm over student grants – after five and a half years of government economies which never sparked off a revolt on this scale – was what it showed about the psychology, and the sociology, of the party.

Part of their anxiety arose because there was a by-election taking place the following week in a London suburb, in which student fees had become an issue. The climax came on 4 December at what was technically a meeting of the Conservative backbench education committee, to which the Education Secretary had been invited to explain the grants decision, but it turned effectively into a meeting of the bulk of the backbench party. More than 250 backbenchers turned up, and mostly they were, in the words of one of them, 'baying for blood'.

Before the meeting, Keith Joseph had to make a duty appearance elsewhere at a drinks-party. Obviously painfully aware of the ordeal awaiting him in Committee Room 14, he was accosted at the party by one of his left-wing acquaintances who told him what a mistake he was making by wanting to make parents pay more. 'How can you as a socialist,' he retorted, 'say it is wrong to make the well-off pay towards their children getting a university education?'

It was not an argument he could use at the Tory backbenchers' meeting. Thirty-three MPs spoke at the meeting. Thirty of them criticised him, some in very strong terms. Of the three who were not hostile, one, according to the *Guardian* report, 'secured a degree of embarrassed silence when he pointed out that it was difficult to defend attacks on pensioners and other disadvantaged members of society when the Conservative Party refused to contemplate charging more to the better-off members of the community'. The Secretary of State gave little away in his defence. He conceded, bleakly, that what he was proposing was going to disrupt some household budgets and the planning of family finances.

At least some of his ministerial colleagues, in the background, were sympathetic enough, even if they thought it was his political naïvety, and over-conscientious loyalty to the Chancellor's financial targets, that had got him into the mess. One member of the Cabinet commented later, on the events in Committee Room 14: 'The middle classes are the meanest, most griping people.' Other colleagues frankly considered that, whatever his great merits in the past, Keith was now expendable.

In any case, the cabinet consensus – Mrs Thatcher happened to be out of the country, in Dublin, and indicated later that she would have known how to sort things out if she had been in London – was that there would have to be a climbdown in the face of the backbenchers. The rumour in the corridors at Westminster that night was that Joseph would resign.

The following day he had indeed to announce a climbdown. It was only partial, but painful. The *Observer* the following Sunday commented:

> Watching him at the despatch box last Wednesday withdrawing the proposal to charge parents for university tuition fees, it was hard not to feel sorry for him. His head was bowed, and his hoarse voice held a familiar note of plangent regret, like a toff down on his luck asking the Bench for one last chance.

On one side of him on the front bench as he made the statement was the Chancellor, Nigel Lawson, and on the other the Prime Minister, now back from Dublin. He had, although this was discounted by Downing Street at the time, told her that he ought to resign because he had proved an embarrassment to her. She apparently told him not to be ridiculous.

There had been some hurried sums done since the meeting the previous evening. The cost of the concession would be £21 million in 1985–6. He had been able, he told the House, to find savings elsewhere in the education budget to provide £11 million of the concession.

Critics from the previous evening congratulated him on his courage in changing his mind. The Liberal leader, David Steel, remarked that it would not be lost on the House that the first successful Conservative backbench rebellion against Mrs Thatcher had been over the interests of the better-off constituents.

The Prime Minister made her first public comment in a newspaper interview a few months later in which she made it clear that she had not approved of the original decision. Things had moved too fast, 'and when I got back – I was away – and actually looked at details, it was too fast, particularly on a group of people who very much plan their budget'.

The relationship between the universities and the Thatcher government could never have been a smooth one. It was not a question of the higher-education community being inevitably and constitutionally hostile to a right-wing government, although there was obviously plenty of ideological hatred, in senior as well as junior common rooms, for what Mrs Thatcher stood for. The popular notion of universities as left-wing hotbeds has never been true and was not true in the early 1980s. There was much in the

Thatcherite philosophy to which the university establishment could say amen: Thatcherism represented a reaction against all that was sloppy and ill-considered in the thinking and the values of the sixties, and there was probably a majority in the university community willing to agree that there was a lot to react against. There was a widespread welcome for Thatcherite condemnation of the academically less respectable social scientists who had emerged in the new universities. The growth of the new university network which had followed the Robbins Report had never been universally welcomed: the traditionalist university view had been summed up in the epigram 'More means worse'.

As for Keith Joseph's contribution in the 1970s to things intellectual, there was recognition, albeit sometimes grudging, that the Centre for Policy Studies had encouraged useful questioning of the balance of some of the teaching that had been fashionable in the sixties in academic disciplines like politics, economics and history. But there was also, it must be said, irritation among many academics at the way the Centre had encouraged certain of their colleagues to venture across the boundary between scholarship and pamphleteering.

Overall, however, there was perhaps more willingness than most people imagined in 1979 for the academic community to give the Thatcher government a fair trial. But, from the start, in 1979, there was obviously going to be financial pressure. Few foresaw how much pressure. By 1985, *The Times Higher Education Supplement* was claiming that 'The gap between what universities need and what the present Government is prepared to provide is now virtually unbridgeable. It is not hundreds of thousands and millions, but tens of millions and even hundreds of millions of pounds wide.' This referred to a shortfall over and above that which worried the 'mean, griping' middle-class parents. The reductions in central-government funding of the universities meant that several thousand academics were made redundant over a few years, the cuts falling often in an arbitrary way.

Some university vice-chancellors became irritated, too, when they met the Secretary of State to discuss, as they thought, future patterns of finance, and found him leading off with a discussion of militant students who were still trying to deny platforms to political speakers they disapproved of. Keith Joseph's devotion to the liberal university ideal was undeniable, but the place he gave on the agenda to the issue of freedom of speech on the campus seemed, to some, to be little short of self-indulgent. There were indeed some disgraceful campus incidents. The Secretary of State condemned the culprits in heroic style in a letter to the president of the National Union of Students: 'They have forgotten that our protection of free speech is not designed merely to allow that which is popular to be said but also, far more important, that which is unpopular or wrong. . . . But the new barbarians are not interested in such discussions.'

The university cutback, which according to one calculation was equivalent to closing down five average-sized universities, had started before Joseph arrived at the DES. One of his early moves was to ameliorate the impact by introducing 'new blood' funds without which there would have been an effective total stop on the recruitment of young staff. He encouraged universities to look for funds elsewhere – for instance, by doing contract research for industry – and, as we saw, his motivation in trying to get more out of the middle-class parents had been to shift resources into research. But, even taking those extra funds into account, his policy seemed to assume a shrinkage of the higher education field, in which British spending, as a proportion of GNP, was already low by American and some European standards.

The same article in *The Times Higher Education Supplement* noted that ministers

deny that there is any serious threat to the excellence of Britain's universities. In evidence they call our impressive total of Nobel Prize winners – although *sotto voce* they may also hint that the universities produce too many science superstars and too few industrially minded technologists. But today's Nobel Prize winners are the result of yesterday's investment, the great expansion of the universities in the 30 years after the war.

In comparison with the policy for schools, where the universality of the need for sound formal education lay behind what he was trying to do, Keith Joseph could scarcely be said to have given a lead about the rôles that were to be played by the universities, the polytechnics and the other agencies educating young adults, nor how the whole was to be financed.

His Green Paper on higher education, published in May 1985, set out high standards that had to be met by the higher education institutions if the country was to retain its competitive position economically, but indicated that this had to be done on funds cut by 2 per cent a year in real terms. This was justified on the basis of declining numbers of young people in the relevant age-groups. Among critics was the Conservative MP Robert Rhodes James, to whom Mrs Thatcher had entrusted the task of trying to liaise between the party and the universities. He resigned the job, commenting that

The DES does not understand what universities are about. The Green Paper was not only illiterate but innumerate. . . . The brain drain from universities is not just anecdotal. Industry rather belatedly has discovered there are some very bright people in universities and polytechnics. Hatfield Polytechnic has lost virtually its entire computer staff to British Aerospace.

There was a certain irony in the fact that this movement of computer experts, represented as failure in Keith Joseph as an Education Minister, could also be represented as some kind of acknowledgement that everything he did as an Industry Minister had not been wrong.

In the spring of 1986, it became known that he would soon retire from Education. He was very tired. He was driving himself as hard as ever, and the behaviour of militant teachers distressed him in a way that militant students and militant steelworkers had not done. There was an occasion when, confronted with the customary protesters when he visited a school, he turned on them abusively, then recovered and explained, almost in tears, so it was reported, how he was only getting a couple of hours' sleep at nights.

He had now been in the front line of the political battle without respite since 1970. Apart from Mrs Thatcher, eight years his junior, there was perhaps no politician with the same kind of continuous service; the period in opposition, 1974–9, had been almost more strenuous than the years of office.

His last months at Elizabeth House saw another effort from the voucher lobby. Once again the idea had captured imaginations in Downing Street, where Oliver Letwin was now installed as an adviser, and where the Policy Unit was now under Professor Brian Griffiths, an economist noted for his dedication to the ideal of resolving economic issues in terms of moral values: Griffiths saw a large part of his task as to restore to the individual and the family the responsibilities taken away from them over the years by the State.

In fact the trend in 1986 at the DES, where Joseph had been joined by his old critic Chris Patten as Minister of State, was to move even further in the direction of central control. There was an analogy here with the Thatcher government's record on local government: that, in the cause of freedom of the individual, powers were transferred from the town hall to Whitehall. This was a major feature of the new Education Bill, which became law under his successor, Kenneth Baker.

The Baker Bill provided for schools to 'opt out' of the local authority system, and also aimed to encourage greater financial accountability in individual schools – both measures which could smooth the way towards a decision to go over to a voucher system in due course. But it was not the radical change in the system which the voucher enthusiasts thought could revitalise British education.

Why did Keith Joseph resist the 'intellectual attractions' of the voucher? Basically the reason he gave was that it would cause an enormous row, between the political parties and within the Conservative Party – Edward Heath had promised to lead a crusade against vouchers: the bitterness could be enough to counterbalance the benefits; the scheme would have to be imposed on unwilling local authorities and on unwilling teachers.

In the voucher lobby there was the feeling, however, that this was not the whole story, that in the subconscious of the Secretary of State there was a fundamental reluctance to take the plunge of applying free-market forces to parental power in education. A clue may be found in the 'One Nation' pamphlet *The Responsible Society*, for which Joseph had been partly responsible as a young MP back in March 1959. The pamphlet set out an early form of the philosophy of family responsibility which had become associated with Thatcherism; but it recognised more limitations than the Thatcherites would recognise. It approved of the notion that the individual should pay for his health care and for the education of his children. But it included this caveat:

> We could not, however, support the right that this implies for persons or parents to neglect their own or their families' health or education. Such neglect would be as much a wrong as positive ill-treatment.

There are different kinds of neglect. There was a part of Joseph which was always suspicious of whether parents knew what was best for their children. At the Department of Education he retained much of the character of the paternalistic Tory.

In May 1986, after four years and nine months as Secretary of State for Education and Science, he resigned. A few days before, he gave an interview to a teachers' union magazine, the organ of the Assistant Masters and Mistresses Association. As reported, it was an interview in the classic Joseph style:

> I asked Sir Keith if he looked back over his period at Elizabeth House with a sense of achievement.
> 'No,' he replied.
> 'Not at all?'
> 'Even my worst critic would admit that education is now at the top of the agenda. . . . I welcome it but I don't think it's due to me.'
> Sir Keith's Press Officer, silent up to that point, weighed in. . . . Sir Keith would have none of it.

To another interviewer he summed up his achievement at Education like this:

> I have put in place the building bricks from which a change in effectiveness may emerge. . . . What would I like to be remembered for? Drawing attention to the 40 per cent who get little benefit from education, perhaps? I don't know.

POSTSCRIPT

Lord Joseph's career has to be judged, unfair though this may be, in terms of what is called Thatcherism. He helped to make it possible, he helped to define and refine it intellectually, he helped to defend and sustain it through dark days, and his own unique contribution provides, so to speak, a pair of spectacles through which the phenomenon of Thatcherism may be examined more clearly.

Phenomenon it has been, rather than readily defined political philosophy. If we consider some of the characteristics that the public seem to associate with Mrs Thatcher, and which seem to make her electorally popular –

(1) faith in sound money, incorporating not only doctrines of the Chicago School but the ethos of the grocer's shop in Grantham;

(2) simple patriotism, verging sometimes into chauvinism;

(3) a preference for taking decisions rather than fudging them, for conviction politics rather than consensus, and for confrontation rather than compromise;

(4) a moral code that implies working with the grain of human nature rather than appealing to unrealistic idealism;

(5) deep suspicion of all individuals, and groups, claiming a stake in resources, or a right to privileges, which have not been earned;

(6) indignation at any suggestion to take away privileges and perquisites which *have* been earned;

(7) and, underlying most Thatcherite policies, a sense of anger that ordinary British people had been cheated out of their just rewards by the political leaders of the past half-century, including those leaders of society known as the establishment

– when we consider those features of Thatcherism, it is hard to imagine Keith Joseph endorsing it as a cohesive whole, without elaborate and carefully considered qualifications and caveats. Put another way, it is hard to associate him with a woman whose political dominance has often taken the form of what in popular parlance is called going over the top. It is significant that much of the criticism of Mrs Thatcher's government from the Wet side of her party has settled down into attacks, not on specifics of policy, but on her 'style'.

Yet part of the success of Thatcherism seems to have been that much of her policy as well as her style has sometimes 'gone over the top'. In the recently published symposium *Thatcherism*, Professor Patrick Minford, writing from an economic viewpoint sympathetic to Mrs Thatcher, describes how her government won its victory over inflation almost inadvertently, through the mistake made in the way of calculating the money-supply. It was less a matter of pure economics than of winning a psychological battle in a society where governments had largely lost credibility. As Minford puts it:

> It is rather like a general who announces he will crush the enemy with the gradual pressure of an infantry attack. The enemy does not believe he will attack at all. He does, but his commands are misinterpreted and activate the tanks and heavy shelling. The effects are devastating: the battle is won, but the casualties are high. How much better if we could rewrite it: he threatens the tanks, the enemy believes the threat and, when the tanks duly appear, surrenders – a victory with no casualties. But I hasten to add that the analogy is also correct in suggesting that gradualism was unlikely to succeed, just as an infantry attack would be too feeble against a stubborn enemy.

If the economic battlefield in 1979 was bloodier than it might have been, Keith Joseph must be numbered high in the ranks of those urging that there should be no retreat. His own hesitations at the Department of Industry have to be set in the context of his actions over, for instance, British Steel and British Leyland, when he could prove tougher than the Prime Minister.

In so far as this meant that he believed in extreme policies, it seems to contradict his famous capacity for seeing all sides to every question – until we remember that this was the man who approached the challenges of first the Ministry of Housing and then the Department of Social Services with a single-mindedness that seemed to cut him off from awareness of what was going on in other parts of government policy; or, indeed, we remember that this is the same highly ambitious young man who got into trouble for working too hard on a building site.

The ability to oversimplify, to identify a mainstream and remain with it, is part of the technique of politics, and Keith Joseph has been far more of a politician's politician than the public – or, indeed, most of his political colleagues – have recognised. All the stories of infelicities on television or in press interviews, of choosing words which could be reported to make him look like a political novice, make it all too easy to ignore a long record as a powerfully effective platform performer in a tradition that pre-dates television. He is adept, as one ministerial colleague recalls, at 'working an audience'. The fact that he could be in agonies before speeches does not gainsay the fact that he is a confident, professional – indeed, calculating – public speaker: pre-speech nerves were a sign of respect for, rather than fear of, his audience; for the same reason, Churchill could be nervous behind the scenes before a speech to the Commons.

Those seemingly innocent questions – back to first principles – that form part of the small change of the Keith Joseph technique in discussion with smaller groups have often brought groans from world-weary colleagues, but he is not so innocent as not to know that innocence can be a sophisticated political weapon. Equally, the formal, sometimes archaic or mannered language that recalls a bygone world can be more incisively relevant to current issues than the slick clichés of the 1980s.

Keith Joseph, more than once, has got away with flouting the party line in ways which, in a less highly respected politician, would have meant being packed off to the wilderness. Like all practised politicians, he knows how to exploit his assets. His astuteness as well as the more widely recognised qualities have proved of formidable value, time and again, to Mrs Thatcher in her ascent to power since 1975.

The paradoxes and puzzles remain, and they are worth noting for more than biographical reasons. They tend to point to paradoxes and puzzles in the Conservative Party as it approaches the 1990s, and in the whole British political pattern as it has evolved during the Thatcher years.

Some apparent paradoxes are easily disposed of, like the simplistic criticism of Joseph that, having devoted himself to ameliorating the plight of the underprivileged, in housing and social services, he suddenly switched to launching economic policies that caused misery and unhappiness. He had always been, more or less, an economic Dry, however Wet on social policy. A consistent theme through his political career was the need for industrial efficiency to produce the resources to pay for social betterment. His vision – the dream of security and an enriched life for ordinary people on a scale once available only to the privileged few – is considerably broader than that of what may be called the typical Thatcherite politician. Indeed, it was that breadth of vision which got him into trouble with his colleagues when he was Education Secretary.

His rôle as a one-time Wet brings us to the famous 'conversion'. It was not a case of being converted overnight to 'sound' economics; he had always been more aware than the average Tory of the rôle of the 'entrepreneur' and of the case, as he expressed it, for having 'more millionaires and more bankrupts'. Nor was he converted in 1974 away from the priorities of social needs. It is certainly true that he became more sceptical about how far the State could provide for those needs, but it was a scepticism based on experience rather than on political theory. And he became more acutely aware of the dangers of fostering a 'dependency culture'.

What seems to have struck him like a blinding light in the spring of 1974 was the nature of the peculiar process, during the period of the postwar governments of both parties, which had not only shackled the British economy but at the same time closed the eyes of governments to the obvious way to free it from those shackles. There was nothing new in all this – people had been talking about the 'British disease' for years – but it is a familiar phenomenon in public affairs that a new voice can have a dramatic impact when it uses the right words at the right time to utter old truths. Successive governments had rendered themselves impotent with a corrupt interpretation of the concept of 'full employment' which in fact militated in the opposite direction by reducing the very standards of productivity which are a prerequisite of all material advancement. As Professor Robert Skidelsky expresses it in his introduction to the essays in *Thatcherism*, the importance of the Preston speech in September 1974 was how Keith Joseph

> identified the full employment commitment as the error from which the whole drift towards ungovernability flowed. Breaking this commitment was a necessary precondition for a more viable philosophy of government. . . . With public spending robbed of any macro-economic function, the way was cleared for its reduction as a percentage of GNP, making possible tax cuts which would improve the 'supply side' of the economy.

There had been, so to speak, an unintentional collective conspiracy to prevent economic progress along lines which had been taken for granted since 1945 in the rest of Europe, in America and in the Far East. The fact that it had the effect of a conspiracy perhaps explains why Alfred Sherman could play such an important rôle in analysing the situation: Alfred Sherman is a great man for sniffing out conspiracies.

It would certainly not be true to say that Joseph and Sherman were pushing at an open door, let alone that they were pushing at it alone. But the times were ripe for what they were doing. There were plenty of approving nods when they put into words what many people were thinking or feeling. Churchill once said that it was the British people who had the lion's heart: he had the privilege of being able to provide the roar. Keith Joseph found a more modest version of the metaphor in 1986. He had been invited to write an introduction to a fresh edition of *Self-Help* by Samuel Smiles, and he was delighted to happen on a word new to him, from the pen of a critic who once described Smiles's achievements as having been to catch 'a culture's hum and buzz of implications'. Keith Joseph likes to think that in the mid-seventies he caught the 'hum' of the implications of the British culture of the time.

He had the advantage over Mrs Thatcher of being more sensitive to the way that the culture of a nation is a complex of lesser cultures, and simultaneously a part of other greater world cultures. Institutions, it has been said, are anathema to Mrs Thatcher: show her an institution and her instinct is to take a swipe with her handbag. Part of Keith Joseph's contribution to her cause has been to work through, not against, the institutions. He sees the evolution of society not in terms of a simplistic individualism but in interrelationships. An interesting illustration is one of his retirement interests: the launching (as part of a team also including his old Permanent Secretary from the DoI, Sir Peter Carey, and Lord Sieff of Marks & Spencer) of a movement called Partnership Sourcing. The concept is that businessmen and their suppliers form long-term commitments to 'tackle the supply of goods or services as partners not adversaries'; an application, in the words of the organisers of the movement, 'of a total business philosophy dedicated to the long-term development of excellence, and better value for money'. Perfectly in tune with the enterprise culture, but not the kind of thing to excite the libertarian wing of the new Conservative Party.

Another of his retirement tasks is setting up a panel of speakers, not only Conservatives, to continue to take the free-enterprise message around the universities and polytechnics, and also sixth forms.

If Margaret Thatcher has, as is often said, a strong populist streak to her politics, Keith Joseph provided added respectability to that populism with his theme of the 'common ground'. He is well aware, though, of how the 'common ground' argument can be used to back up what are to him repugnant traits of human nature – an urge to 'string 'em up', 'send 'em home' and so forth. His own equivalent of populism would be *embourgeoisement* (his theme for his maiden speech in the House of Lords).

A fair criticism of Lord Joseph might be that he has been less robust than he ought to have been in distancing himself from the less attractive manifestations of Tory populism.

A greater criticism – and it points to a possible major criticism of the modern Conservative Party generally – concerns his approach to the great issues of poverty and deprivation which started him off in politics. It might be fair to say that Lord Joseph, given his prestige, could have been doing more to turn the eyes of the new Conservative Party to the challenge of how some of the wealth created by the Thatcherite enterprise culture ought to find its way to the underprivileged. Mrs Thatcher's party has not yet really addressed itself to the question of whether it wants to improve or to abolish the Welfare State.

It has to be said, of course, that Lord Joseph did throw himself powerfully into the cause of helping the underprivileged as an Education Secretary – and bears the scars, inflicted collectively by the teachers among others. But his work there possibly provides a marker for his party when it tries to work out a social philosophy.

And the Conservative Party looked, at the time Lord Joseph left government, to be the only party in a position ever to implement any kind of policy: he had played his part in destroying the pretensions of the Labour Party; and his work in expanding the Tory constituency among non-Tories had an influence in balking the emergence of a powerful third party. Lord Joseph is a Conservative – he always was one, and after conversion insisted that it was to Conservatism, not to Victorian Liberalism, that he had been converted. But his story raises interesting questions about how far the Conservative Party is now Conservative, whatever that means, and how the party structure will settle down, whatever settling down means, after Mrs Thatcher.

These are not distinctions that have concerned her overmuch. When the present author asked the Prime Minister in 1988 how much Keith Joseph had been responsible for creating a new Conservative Party, her reply was:

> It wasn't really a question of creating a new Conservative Party. It was more a question of bringing the old Conservative Party (and the country) back to life. It was a question of restating fundamental principles that would have seemed absolutely obvious to our ancestors: principles like self-determination, pride, ownership, prudent housekeeping, things that any nineteenth-century Tory would have taken for granted. They had to be brought out of the grave, and given back their vitality.
>
> That was what Keith really did for us. He gave us back our intellectual self-confidence.

SELECT BIBLIOGRAPHY

Arnold, Bruce, *Margaret Thatcher: A Study in Power* (Hamish Hamilton, 1984)

Bacon, R. & Eltis, W. A., *Britain's Economic Problem: Too Few Producers* (Macmillan, 1978)

Barnett, Correlli, *The Audit of War: The Illusion and Reality of Britain as a Great Power* (Macmillan, 1986)

Bartram, Peter, *David Steel: His Life and Politics* (W. H. Allen, 1981)

Beer, Samuel H., *Britain against Itself: The Political Contradictions of Collectivism* (W. W. Norton, 1983)

Blake, Robert, *The Conservative Party from Peel to Thatcher* (Methuen, 1985)

Bosanquet, Nick, *After the New Right* (Heinemann, 1983)

Brittan, Samuel, *Capitalism and the Permissive Society* (Macmillan, 1973)
 Economic Consequences of Democracy (Wildwood House, 1988)
 Left or Right: The Bogus Dilemma (Secker & Warburg, 1968)
 The Treasury under the Tories (Penguin, 1964)

Bruce-Gardyne, Jock, *Ministers and Mandarins: Inside the Whitehall Village* (Sidgwick & Jackson, 1986)
 Mrs Thatcher's First Administration (Macmillan, 1984)

Butler, David and Kavanagh, Dennis, *The British General Election of February 1974* (Macmillan, 1974)
 The British General Election of October 1974 (Macmillan, 1974)
 The British General Election of 1979 (Macmillan, 1980)

Castle, Barbara, *The Castle Diaries, 1974–76* (Weidenfeld & Nicolson, 1980)

Childs, David, *Britain since 1945* (Methuen, 1986)

Cole, John, *The Thatcher Years* (BBC Books, 1987)

Conservative Party Conference reports

Contemporary Record (journal of the Institute of Contemporary British History), vol. 1, no. 1 (Spring 1987). Contains a long interview with Lord Joseph, which includes his considered assessment of his political career

Cosgrave, Patrick, *Margaret Thatcher: A Tory and Her Party* (Hutchinson, 1978)
 Thatcher: The First Term (Bodley Head, 1985)

Fisher, Nigel, *Iain Macleod* (André Deutsch, 1973)

Grimond, Jo, *Memoirs* (Heinemann, 1979)

Harris, Kenneth, *Thatcher* (Weidenfeld & Nicolson, 1988)

Howard, Anthony, *Rab: The Life of R. A. Butler* (Jonathan Cape, 1987)

Jenkins, Peter, *Mrs Thatcher's Revolution* (Jonathan Cape, 1987)

Keegan, William, *Mrs Thatcher's Economic Experiment* (Penguin, 1984)

Klein, Rudolf, *The Politics of the NHS* (Longman, 1983)

Lindsay, T. F. and Harrington, Michael, *The Conservative Party, 1918–79* (Macmillan, 1979)

Maudling, Reginald, *Memoirs* (Sidgwick & Jackson, 1978)

Maynard, Geoffrey, *The Economy under Mrs Thatcher* (Basil Blackwell, 1988)

Oakley, Robin and Rose, Peter, *The Political Year: 1970* (Pitman)
   The Political Year: 1971 (Pitman)

Prior, James, *A Balance of Power* (Hamish Hamilton, 1986)

Pym, Francis, *The Politics of Consent* (Sphere Books, 1984)

Riddell, Peter, *The Thatcher Government* (Robertson, 1983)

Roth, Andrew, *Heath and the Heathmen* (Routledge & Kegan Paul, 1972)

Sampson, Anthony, *The Changing Anatomy of Britain* (Hodder & Stoughton, 1982)

Schoen, Douglas E., *Enoch Powell and the Powellites* (Macmillan, 1977)

Skidelsky, Robert (ed.), *Thatcherism* (Chatto & Windus, 1988)

Stephenson, Hugh, *Mrs Thatcher's First Year* (Norman, 1980)

Walker, Peter, *Trust the People* (Collins, 1987)

Walters, Alan, *Britain's Economic Renaissance* (Oxford University Press, 1986)

Wapshott, Nicholas and Brock, George, *Thatcher* (Macdonald, 1983)

INDEX

PICTURE
ACKNOWLEDGEMENTS

Camera Press: pages 1, 5 above left and below, 6. Private Collections: 2 above and below left. Popperfoto: 2 below right, 4. Topham Picture Library: 3, 5 above right, 7 above, 8. Western Mail and Echo Ltd: 7 below.